NORMATIVE REASO

Reasons matter greatly to us in both ordinary and theoretical contexts, being connected to two fundamental normative concerns:
figuring out what we should do and what attitudes to have, and
understanding the duties and responsibilities that apply to us. This
book introduces and critiques most of the contemporary theories of
normative reasons – considerations that speak in favour of an action,
belief, or emotion – to explore how they work. Artūrs Logins
develops and defends a new theory: the Erotetic view of reasons,
according to which normative reasons are appropriate answers to
normative 'Why?' questions (Why should I do this?). This theory
draws on evidence of how 'Why?' questions work in informal logic,
language, and philosophy of science. The resulting view is able to
avoid the problems of previous accounts, while retaining all their
attractive features, and it also suggests exciting directions for future
research. This title is also available as Open Access on
Cambridge Core.

ARTŪRS LOGINS is Swiss National Science Foundation Ambizione
Fellow at the University of Zurich, Switzerland. He works in epistemology and foundational normative questions, and he has published
papers in *Philosophical Studies, Ethics, Analysis, Erkenntnis, European
Journal of Philosophy, Thought,* and *Inquiry.*

CAMBRIDGE STUDIES IN PHILOSOPHY

General Editors
Nomy Arpaly
Brown University
Sanford Goldberg
Northwestern University

Cambridge Studies in Philosophy is the cornerstone of Cambridge University Press's list in mainstream, high-level analytic philosophy. It serves as a forum for a broad range of monographs on the cutting edge of epistemology, the philosophy of language and mind, ethics, and metaphysics.

Recent Titles

CHRISTOPH KELP AND MONA SIMION *Sharing Knowledge*

RICHARD FUMERTON *Knowledge, Thought, and the Case for Dualism*

JAMIN ASAY *The Primitivist Theory of Truth*

CRAWFORD L. ELDER *Familiar Objects and Their Shadows*

SANFORD GOLDBERG *Anti-Individualism*

MICHAEL J. ZIMMERMANN *Living with Uncertainty*

LYNNE RUDDER BAKER *The Metaphysics of Everyday Life*

DAVID COPP *Morality in a Natural World*

JOSEPH MENDOLA *Goodness and Justice*

FOLKE TERSMAN *Moral Disagreement*

ALEXANDER R. PRUSS *The Principle of Sufficient Reason*

JOSHUA GERT *Brute Rationality*

NOAH LEMOS *Common Sense*

MICHAEL SMITH *Ethics and the A Priori*

KEITH FRANKISH *Mind and Supermind*

D. M. ARMSTRONG *Truth and Truthmakers*

WILLIAM S. ROBINSON *Understanding Phenomenal Consciousness*

ANDREW MELNYK *A Physicalist Manifesto*

JONATHAN KVANVIG *The Value of Knowledge and the Pursuit of Understanding*

JANE HEAL *Mind, Reason and Imagination*

PETER RAILTON *Facts, Values, and Norms*

NORMATIVE REASONS

Between Reasoning and Explanation

ARTŪRS LOGINS

University of Zurich

Shaftesbury Road, Cambridge CB2 8EA, United Kingdom

One Liberty Plaza, 20th Floor, New York, NY 10006, USA

477 Williamstown Road, Port Melbourne, VIC 3207, Australia

314–321, 3rd Floor, Plot 3, Splendor Forum, Jasola District Centre, New Delhi – 110025, India

103 Penang Road, #05–06/07, Visioncrest Commercial, Singapore 238467

Cambridge University Press is part of Cambridge University Press & Assessment, a department of the University of Cambridge.

We share the University's mission to contribute to society through the pursuit of education, learning and research at the highest international levels of excellence.

www.cambridge.org
Information on this title: www.cambridge.org/9781009074742

DOI: 10.1017/9781009076012

First published 2022
First paperback edition 2023

A catalogue record for this publication is available from the British Library

Library of Congress Cataloging-in-Publication data
NAMES: Logins, Arturs, author.
TITLE: Normative reasons : between reasoning and explanation / Arturs Logins, University of Zurich.
DESCRIPTION: Cambridge, United Kingdom ; New York, NY, USA : Cambridge University Press, [2022] | Series: CSP Cambridge studies in philosophy | Includes bibliographical references and index.
IDENTIFIERS: LCCN 2022011790 (print) | LCCN 2022011791 (ebook) | ISBN 9781316513774 (hardback) | ISBN 9781009074742 (paperback) | ISBN 9781009076012 (epub)
SUBJECTS: LCSH: Reasoning. | Question (Logic) | Normativity (Ethics) | BISAC: PHILOSOPHY / General
CLASSIFICATION: LCC BC177 .L65 2022 (print) | LCC BC177 (ebook) | DDC 160–DC23/eng/20220513
LC record available at https://lccn.loc.gov/2022011790
LC ebook record available at https://lccn.loc.gov/2022011791

ISBN   978-1-316-51377-4   Hardback
ISBN   978-1-009-07474-2   Paperback

This book is dedicated to Jānis Logins (1957–2021)

Contents

Preface

My interest in normative reasons grew naturally out of my PhD thesis work on evidence. It is a popular view in epistemology that evidence is best understood in terms of reasons to believe. Thinking about reasons to believe naturally led me to the topic of normative reasons in general. But, while focusing on reasons in general, I quickly realised that it is a complex issue, with many parallel debates and multiple, sometimes overlapping distinctions. In a sense it also felt like reasons are one of those things where, as Saint Augustine notes about time, you know what they are when no one questions you about them but find it difficult to explain when someone asks you what they really are. One thing that I was desperately looking for but had a hard time finding during the initial stages of my interest in reasons was a bird's-eye view of the topic, an overview of all the major theories of reasons, the most important distinctions, arguments, and key implications of thinking about normative reasons. Of course, there are already a number of formidable texts on normative reasons that could serve as an introduction to the topic, but I couldn't find one comprehensive treatment of the subject. Realising that I might not be alone in longing for such an overview, I eventually concluded that I had to create it myself. This in-depth overview of the debates now occupies an important part of the present monograph. Somewhat unsurprisingly, once I had a better understanding of the contours of contemporary discussions, I arrived naturally at my own positive view of what normative reasons are. The core idea of the positive view defended in this monograph then landed almost effortlessly in a dot-connecting moment once I arrived at my own bird's-eye view of reasons.

Section 1.3 of Chapter 1 has previously appeared as a journal article (Artūrs Logins, 'Subjective Unpossessed Reasons', *Thought: A Journal of Philosophy*, 7:262–270, 2018). It has only minor modifications here. (Also, I have retained the original acknowledgements, in which I thank the reviewers for the journal that originally published the article.)

The main argument in Section 2.6 of Chapter 2 has also previously been published as a journal article (Artūrs Logins, 'Normative Reasons without (Good) Reasoning', *Ethics*, 130[2]:208–210, 2020). Again, it has only minor revisions, a new passage where a possible new worry for the argument is considered, and some modifications in order to suit the present format and avoid unnecessary repetition. Apart from the changes to the introductory sentences of the article, the text reproduced here is almost the same as the previously published version.

I have to thank many people for discussions, long and short, during my work on this monograph. I would like to thank Pascal Engel, Sebastian Schmidt, and Aleks Knoks for written comments on (parts of) the manuscript. Many thanks also to people with whom I had the chance to discuss ideas from the book, including Davide Fassio, John Hawthorne, Anne Meylan, Jacques Vollet, Jörg Löschke, Daniel Whiting, Ralph Wedgwood, Mark Schroeder, Steve Finlay, Atay Kozlovski, Benoit Gaultier, Edgar Phillips, Fabrice Teroni, Julien Deonna, Michele Ombrato, and surely others. I would like to thank audiences at the University of Geneva, the University of Zurich, Collège de France (Groupe de Recherche en Épistémologie), and the 2019 Joint Session of the Aristotelian Society in Durham. Special thanks to the editors of the series, in particular to Sandy Goldberg for all his support and patience throughout this project. Thanks also to Hilary Gaskin from Cambridge University Press and to two extremely constructive and helpful anonymous readers! Thanks also to Kathleen McCully for her invaluable help with proofreading the manuscript. I would like to express my gratitude also to my good friend and artist Hadrien Peltier, who conceived and realised the image of the mysterious tree with unknown roots and with leaves of different shapes specifically for the cover of the present book. Most of all, thanks to my family for their continuous support and belief. I am grateful to my wife Alla, my daughters Anastasia and Agate, my mother Ināra, and my sister Agnese. I received the offer of the contract from Cambridge University Press two weeks or so after my father passed away unexpectedly. I never told him about my manuscript, hoping to surprise him with good news. This book is dedicated to his memory.

The manuscript was completed with generous support from the Swiss National Science Foundation (grant nos. 171464, 171466, and 186137). The open-access publication of this book has been published with the support of the Swiss National Science Foundation (grant no. 10BP12_206406).

Introduction

I.1 An Examined Life and Reasons

According to an old and venerable philosophical dictum that Plato attributes to Socrates, 'The unexamined life is not worth living'. Stated as such, this dictum may sound a bit too harsh, especially for those who are incapable of undertaking the method of *examination* as understood by Socrates. Yet something close to its converse looks like a platitude. Figuring out and understanding how one should act; what to think or believe; what to regret; when, if ever, to get angry or feel guilty; when to be afraid; when to indulge in sadness and melancholy; or when to be grateful and happy are some of the fundamental questions that matter for everyone who aims to lead a meaningful life, a life worth living. In other terms, part of a meaningful life is to aim to figure it out and to arrive at a better understanding; and, in particular, to figure out what to do, or which attitudes to hold when, and to understand better the facts about oughts and shoulds that apply to us.

A related observation is that reasons are central to our lives. That is, it matters to us what reasons there are for us and others to act in certain ways or to believe certain things and to hold other attitudes. Reasons here are to be understood roughly as considerations that count in favour of some act or some attitude (in the contemporary philosophical jargon, these are *normative* reasons). When examining whether I should take my work with me on vacation, it matters for me what considerations count in favour of this option and what considerations count against it. That I will be able to make progress with my manuscript certainly counts in favour of taking the work with me. However, that I will miss out on spending fun time with my family counts clearly against taking the work with me. That your friend hates pistachio ice cream counts in favour of not buying one for your friend. That you see your partner's car in the driveway counts in favour of taking it for granted – that is, believing that your partner is at home.

Arguably, reasons thus understood matter for us precisely because they help us to figure out what to do and what attitudes to have, and because they help us to understand better why we should do certain things and why having certain attitudes is fitting in a situation. The consideration that taking my work with me on vacation will make me miss out on fun time with my family can help me to figure out whether to take the work with me or not. That your friend hates pistachio ice cream explains why you should not buy one for her.

The talk about reasons to act and to have attitudes is also popular in contemporary philosophy. Indeed, reasons seem to be the 'new black' in the so-called normative fields of philosophy – that is, in fields that are concerned with exploring aspects of obligations, values, and virtues, be they moral, political, aesthetic, or epistemic. Reasons prove themselves to be particularly useful for discussing meta-normative questions – that is, questions about the very foundations and principles governing oughts, values, and virtues. According to one prominent approach in recent meta-normative debates, the so-called *reasons-first* approach, reasons are indeed essential to understanding *all* other normative statuses and properties (see Scanlon 1998; Schroeder 2007; Skorupski 2010; Parfit 2011). On this view, what one ought to do is, roughly, what one has most reason to do, what is good is what one has sufficient reason to value, what is admirable is what one has sufficient reason to admire, what is justified or rational is what one possesses reasons to do and so on. And crucially, reasons cannot be reduced, on this approach, to any other normative properties (some reasons-first proponents think that this doesn't mean that they cannot be reduced to some natural properties – for example, one's desires, though cf. Schroeder 2007).

One problem with the reasons-first approach thus understood is that it lacks informativeness in characterizing reasons. It doesn't say much about what reasons are. On the standard reasons-first view, reasons just are considerations that count in favour. But considerations that count in favour of an act or attitude just are reasons. No substantive, explanatory definition of reasons is possible, according to the reasons-first approach. However, such a lack of informativeness about reasons is problematic, since the view seems to end up in taking up arbitrary commitments when it has to distinguish among considerations that count in favour of some act or attitude in different ways. An already classical illustration of this is the problem of the 'wrong kind' of reasons (cf. Rabinowicz and Rønnow-Rasmussen 2004; see also Section 1.4 for more and for further references). A threat can certainly count in favour of admiring a despicable person. But is it a reason to admire the threatener? If the reasons-first proposal is taken literally and considerations that count in favour are reasons, then the threat has to be a reason to admire. And yet, it is not properly connected to admirability; the threatener is not admirable. Thus, if one takes this line of thought at face value, it seems one has to conclude that admirability cannot, after all, be reduced to reasons to admire. But then reasons are not fundamental in the normative realm – admirability is not explained in terms of reasons. On the other hand, one might try to avoid this conclusion by introducing different senses in which something might 'count in favour'. On this view, there are genuine normative reasons to admire that are connected to admirability (whatever it amounts to exactly), and then there are the 'wrong kind' of reasons to admire. However, for such a move to be theoretically acceptable, one needs to provide independent grounds for such a distinction. But the reasons-first view's lack of substantial definition of reasons prevents its proponents from providing such an independent motivation. Thus, the reasons-first view seems to face a dilemma. And at the heart of that dilemma is the inability of the view to provide a more substantive, informative account of reasons. Reasons are important, but we should be able to say something more about them than just that they are things that count in favour of acts and attitudes.

In the light of the worries affecting the reasons-first programme, reductive accounts of reasons are proliferating within contemporary literature. Indeed, I think it is not an exaggeration to say that nowadays an (academic) article per week is published on reasons. And some of the existing accounts are illuminating. Indeed, a starting point of the proposal to be developed in what follows is to observe some of the significant insights about reasons that we have received from the most promising existing reductive theories of reasons.

I.2 Reasons in Reasoning or Reasons in Explanation?

Once we agree that reasons are important and that the reasons-first approach should be our last resort in theorizing about reasons, the question that naturally arises is: but how do we go about building a reductive account of normative reasons? Where do we start? A reasonable place to start is to consider the role of reasons. Why do we need reasons? What roles do they play? Investigating central functions of our ordinary concept of *reason to do something or to believe or to fear and so on* might help us advance on this issue. So, what are the central functions of our ordinary, common-sense concept of *reasons*?

One central function of *reasons* seems to be to pick out elements that help us to figure out what we should do, believe, fear or what other attitude to have. In other terms, *reasons* seem to pick out premises in good reasoning/deliberation. As Paul Grice has put it, 'Reasons [. . .] are the stuff of which reasoning is made' (Grice 2001: 67).

Another central function of *reasons* appears to be to pick out elements that help us to better understand what we should or ought to do, believe, fear and so on. In other terms, *reasons* pick out considerations that contribute to explaining why we should or ought to do certain things or to have certain attitudes.

Now, as I see it, most, if not all, existing reductive theories of reasons can be classified as belonging to one of the two following general frameworks. On the one hand, roughly, there are the views that attempt to explain reasons by appeal to the role of reasons in good or fitting reasoning. Views belonging to this approach combine two elements in explaining reasons: reasoning and a normative property (e.g. goodness, fittingness). There is much to be said about this approach, most notably that it does seem to capture the *figuring-it-out* element that we commonly associate with reasons. Reasons are important to us, since in a sense they help us to figure out what we should do, what to believe, and what other attitudes to have. Reasoning-centred views bring to light this important aspect that we standardly associate with reasons.

On the other hand, roughly, there are views that propose to define reasons by an appeal to the role of reasons in explanations of why one ought to do certain things or to have certain attitudes or, alternatively, why it would be good for one to do certain things or have certain attitudes. Views belonging to this approach also combine two elements in explaining reasons: explanation and a normative property – for example, [facts about] oughts, goodness. Again, there is much to be said in favour of this sort of explanation-centred approach; not least that it does seem to bring to light the other fundamental aspect that we typically associate with reasons, an aspect that makes reasons important for us: that reasons help us to *understand better* what to do/which attitude to have or what would be good to do/which attitude to have by providing a [partial] explanation of why we ought to do certain things or have certain attitudes. We value reasons since they help us to understand better normative/evaluative facts that concern others and us.

Unfortunately, however, despite their promising and insightful aspects, both approaches also have serious pitfalls. The exclusive focus on the role of reasons in reasoning leads inevitably to overlooking the explanatory role that we commonly associate with reasons. And conversely, the exclusive focus on the role of reasons in the explanation of normative or evaluative facts (or considerations) leads to overlooking the importance of the role of reasons in good/fitting reasoning (towards appropriate actions and attitudes, or conclusions about what one ought to do/which attitude to have). In short, the main insights from both approaches are also their main weaknesses.

I.3 Our Positive Proposal: The Erotetic View of Reasons

In light of the problems with the two most promising reductive views, we might be tempted to draw a pessimistic conclusion that our concept of *reasons* is incoherent and that it is naïve to expect to find one single, overarching theory of normative reasons (compare to Wedgwood 2015). Such a temptation should be resisted, though. A key objective of the present work is to explain why. In short, according to the positive thesis developed in Chapters 5 and 6, there is an overlooked view of reasons that can integrate the lessons from reasoning- and explanation-centred views and can also explain what is the most fundamental common element that both of these views capture only partially. Thus, contrary to what a pessimist about reasons might think, there seems to be a unificatory and well-motivated account of normative reasons at a more fundamental level, such that the apparent failures of reasoning-only- and explanation-only-centred views of reasons are accounted for while their respective insights are well respected. The unificatory idea, simply put, is that most fundamentally normative reasons are appropriate answers to normative 'Why F?' questions. Normative 'Why F?' questions are of the form 'Why should/ ought one do this or that or have this or that attitude?'. Crucially, answers to normative questions, exactly like answers to any 'Why?' questions, come either as premises in arguments/patterns of reasoning or as elements of explanation. This is the essence of our positive view, the question-centred view of reasons, or, as we will call it, *the Erotetic view of reasons*.

If we need a slogan for the main thesis of the present book, it could be 'no questions, no reasons'. In other words, we suggest that the point of normative reasons is to answer normative questions. That's what reasons do; that's what reasons are for. We need reasons insofar as we deem it important to reply to normative questions, questions like 'Why do this? Why believe that? Why be angry?' and so on. The view builds on insights from Pamela Hieronymi's (2005) view on which reasons bear on questions, as well as on insights from argumentation theory, informal logic, and linguistic observations about questions. Combining these two lines of insights together and reconsidering the role of reasons in good reasoning and explanation, we arrive at the following conclusion. Central functions of our ordinary concept of *reasons to F*, namely, the function of playing a role in good patterns of reasoning towards F-ing and the function of playing a role in a normative explanation (e.g. explanation of why one ought to F) are subsumed under an even more fundamental function, the general function of playing a role in answering the normative questions.

How is the function of playing a role in answering normative questions a more general function? The insight from informal logic, argumentation theory, and language use has it that it is a general feature of 'Why?' questions that they come in two varieties. Or rather, when we ask why such and such is the case, depending on the context of the conversation we may be asking one or the other of the following two things. We might be asking for an explanation of why such and such is the case. Or we might be asking for an argument for the claim that such and such is the case. And *pace* Hempel and the deductive-nomological model of explanation, we know that arguments and explanations are distinct. Why are dolphins mammals? This question may be understood as a request for an argument for the claim that dolphins are mammals, typically when we don't yet know or believe the conclusion (appeal to the fact that they are warm-blooded would reply to the question on this reading). But it can also be understood as a request for an explanation, typically when we know or accept the conclusion but want to understand it better (an appeal to the evolutionary history of dolphins would constitute a reply to that reading of the question). Our main contention is that the same holds with respect to 'Why F?' questions. When we ask why should I do this or that or why should I believe, fear, hope that such and such and so on, we may be asking either for an argument to the conclusion that I should indeed act in these ways or have these attitudes or, alternatively, we may be asking for an explanation of why I should act/have the relevant attitude. Thus, the fundamental normative question may have either a premise in a reasoning reading or an element of an explanation reading. Sometimes our possible answers to these two readings of 'Why F?' questions will coincide, but not always. Insofar as reasons are properly understood as appropriate answers to normative questions, both reasoning and explanation functions of our notion of *reasons* are understood as two facets of the same, more funda-mental phenomenon. Note also that the difference between our view and Hieronymi's is that, at the end of the day, Hieronymi's proposal looks very much like a variant of the Reasoning approach, since bearing on questions for her is roughly the same as figuring in a reasoning. The Erotetic view also does justice to the explanation-requesting reading of normative questions.

Reasons matter to us since they enable us to answer normative questions. But they always enable us to answer the normative questions in one or the other reading of 'Why F?' questions, either by providing a premise in a good argument/pattern of reasoning or by providing elements of an explanation of the relevant ought. The former helps us figure out what we should/ought to do, believe, and so on. The latter helps us better understand the shoulds and oughts that we may already suspect to hold. We cannot do without reasons insofar as we cannot do without arguments for and explanations of the relevant oughts or shoulds as possible appropriate answers to normative questions. We cannot do without reasons insofar as we cannot stop trying to figure things out and understand the normative facts that apply to us. Asking normative questions just is a part of who we are as agents aiming to live meaningful lives.

The dual life of the normative 'Why F?' question explains the duality of normative reasons as the possible appropriate answers to normative questions. Thus, the view to be developed here can both vindicate the insights of the Reasoning approach *and* the Explanation approach to reasons, and also explain in a theoretically motivated way why neither of these can be accepted as such.

I.4 What's in the Book?

Here is a brief summary of the content of the chapters to come. Chapter 1 consists in some ground clearing. Here we consider some of the most prominent distinctions and clarifications about reasons – for example, the difference between motivating reasons and normative reasons. We also look (in a historically informed way) at some much-debated issues within the contemporary reasonology – for example, are reasons causes? are all reasons subjective? what is needed to possess reasons? – only to set these venerable debates aside in what follows. We also present tenets of the reasons-first approach and review the much-debated 'wrong kind' of reasons problem for the reasons-first approach. Chapter 2 begins a proper investigation into reductionist theories of normative reasons. We begin in Chapter 2 by considering the advantages and problems of the reasoning-centred approaches to normative reasons. Chapter 3 then focuses on the explanation-centred approaches. Chapter 4 then examines the so-called Evidence view of reasons, according to which reasons are evidence that one ought to do something/have an attitude. One might think that the Evidence view is a third possible reductionist account of reasons and doesn't fit into our overall classification. The main suggestion in exploring that view is that in the most plausible form of the Evidence view, it reduces to a version of the Reasoning view and as such inherits some of its most problematic aspects. Chapter 5 begins developing our positive proposal, the Erotetic view of reasons. Chapter 6 then develops the view further by showing how it can be applied fruitfully to make progress in one notorious debate in epistemology, the debate concerning the possibility of pragmatic reasons for belief. The Erotetic view can be applied to show that both pragmatists and evidentialists can be right within this debate since there is a clear sense in which there can be pragmatic reasons to believe, and a clear sense in which there cannot. If the proposal is on the right track, then this provides an additional consideration in favour of our new proposal.

Reasons matter for us, in ordinary as well as theoretical contexts. Building a viable theory of reasons helps us to better understand some, and perhaps the most fundamental, of our normative concerns. It may even help in complying with Socrates's dictum about leading an examined life. Advancing this task is what I hope to do in the chapters to come.

Stage Setting
Distinctions and Starting Points

This chapter provides an overview of the main concepts and distinctions about reasons in the literature. It starts with the less contentious distinctions and moves on to the more debated notions and distinctions. Another function of this chapter is to establish the boundaries for the discussion to come. It introduces and sets aside a number of notions and debates that are or have been somewhat important within the general philosophy of reasons but will not fall directly within the scope of working out an informative account of what normative reasons are. Yet, having an idea of these notions and debates will be useful when we turn to (reductive) accounts of normative reasons.

1.1 Normative, Motivating, Explanatory Reasons

The first thing that philosophers typically observe when discussing reasons is that the word 'reason' (as a countable noun) has a multitude of distinct uses in our ordinary language and that our common-sense judgments can vary a lot when considering different cases involving reasons. According to one popular view and following our ordinary language use and common-sense judgments, there are two or perhaps three distinct roles (or kinds) of reasons.[1] We are focusing here on 'reason' as a countable noun only and setting aside 'reason' as a mass noun, which seems to refer most prominently to a faculty or a general disposition, somehow related to rationality. So, according to the distinction in question, 'reason' (a countable noun) can refer to (i) a consideration that speaks somehow in favour of an action or an attitude (e.g. a belief, an emotion). This use is exemplified in constructions having 'a reason to' + a verbal construction in infinitive form – such as 'that the gas tank indicator shows that the car is almost out of gas is a reason for John to stop at the gas station', 'that the weather

---

[1] For paradigmatic examples of this distinction, see Alvarez (2010, 2016) and Engel (2015a).

forecast announces heavy rain for tomorrow is a reason for Mara to postpone the hike', or 'that John's car is parked in front of Mara's house is a reason to think/believe that John is at Mara's place'. Constructions involving verbs in the infinitive are characteristic of expressions that refer to normative aspects, such as oughts, obligations, or permissions (see Hawthorne and Magidor 2018 for more on this) – for example, 'we must go' or 'you are allowed to eat a cake'. Thus, it is not surprising that expressions with the structure 'a reason to' combined with a verb in the infinitive are commonly understood as bringing in a normative aspect too. Thus, the first kind of reasons (or, alternatively, the first role of reasons) is the normative kind/role of reasons. Reasons of this sort are called 'normative reasons' and are the primary object of our investigations in what follows.

In the second place, according to the popular view, 'reason' (a countable noun) can also refer to (ii) a consideration on the basis of which one acts or has an attitude. This use is exemplified in our ordinary talk about *one's reasons for* which one acts or has an attitude, as, for instance, in 'John's reason for parking in front of Mara's place was that he couldn't find a free spot elsewhere,' or 'Mara's reason for thinking that Zoe will come was that she said she will.' Reasons in this sense are the considerations that have actually played (or can potentially play) the role of the foundation of one's actions and attitudes from one's own perspective. It is common to call reasons of this kind 'motivating reasons'. Of course, it is also widely agreed that if we focus on reasons for attitudes and not exclusively on reasons for action, then explaining reasons in this sense by reference to motivation as ordinarily understood might be a bit misleading. For, typically, it is conceded we don't have a motivation for believing this or that, yet our beliefs are based on some considerations – that is, we believe often (if not always) for some reason. Thus, some philosophers prefer to use the label 'operative reasons' to refer to this kind of reasons (see Scanlon 1998: 19). In what follows, we stick with the established use and talk about 'motivating reasons', assuming the relevant technical sense (e.g. the basis for S's F-ing from S's own perspective) and not the ordinary sense of 'motivating'. Yet, note that the technical sense here might not be so alien to a somewhat archaic sense of 'motives'. Consider, for instance, the Scholastic notion of *motiva credibilitatis* (motives of credibility) understood as a basis for rational faith that can be discovered by reason alone (without divine revelation), such as considerations about the origin of the universe as speaking in favour of the existence of God constituting motives of credibility for theism.

Finally, we may also think that 'reason' (a countable noun) can also refer to (iii) considerations that explain or contribute to explaining why an action/attitude occurred. This use seems to be exemplified by our talk of *reasons why*, as, for instance, in 'the reason why I was late was that I was stuck in traffic', 'the reason why she was not selected for the job was that the hiring committee was biased', or 'that you grew up in a religious environment is the reason why you believe in God'. The referents of 'reasons' in this sense are commonly called 'explanatory reasons', since they explain or participate in explaining why one acts in the ways one does or why one has the attitudes one has. Of course, it is also the case that typically considerations that play the role of motivating reasons (considerations on the basis of which one acts/has an attitude from one's own perspective) will also help explain the action or the attitude in question. That John couldn't find a free spot elsewhere explains (partly) why he parked in front of Mara's place. That Zoe told Mara she will come explains at least partly why Mara believes she will come. However, as the aforementioned examples demonstrate, not distinguishing the two, the motivating and the explanatory reasons, would leave a number of cases unexplained. Some considerations seem to be able to play an explanatory role for actions or attitudes without also being considerations on the basis of which one acts or has an attitude from one's own perspective. That I was stuck in traffic can explain why I am late, but it is not a consideration on the basis of which I base my being late. Similarly, one will hardly accept that one's own implicit biases and prejudices are reasons for which one acts in the ways one does, yet they may still be part of an explanation for one's actions and attitudes. Also, as Maria Alvarez (2016) has observed, some cases seem to be best interpreted as cases where one acts for no reason at all, yet there seem to be reasons why one acts in the ways one does. Consider, for instance, the case of one going for a run for no specific reason, or one deciding to grow a beard for no reason, just on a whim. Even if there are no reasons *for* which one does these things, we may still come up with some plausible reasons why one does the things in question.[2] Conversely, one might also think that, at least in some contexts, considerations for which we act don't really contribute to explaining our action. Dramatic cases of implicit bias might instantiate such a possibility. That candidate A has all the skills that are required for the job might be one's motivating reason, the consideration for which one selects candidate A. And yet, arguably, that candidate A has all the necessary skills doesn't

---

[2] See Hawthorne and Magidor (2018) for further examples and discussion.

even partially explain why one selects candidate A, given that candidate B is equally skilful. The choice in this case is explained by one's implicit bias against B. Thus, one might think there are three distinct kinds of or roles for reasons (understood as references to the countable noun 'reason'): normative reasons, motivating reasons, and explanatory reasons.

Note, however, that the case for distinguishing motivating from explanatory reasons gets somewhat complicated if we reject the idea that deliberation (or reasoning) is necessary for acting for reasons (and for having attitudes for reasons). If deliberation and acting (having an attitude) for a reason can come apart, as recently argued by Arpaly and Schroeder (2012), then presumably some of the aforementioned cases might lose their appeal. Think, for instance, about the case of going for a run for no apparent reason or the case of deciding to grow a beard just on a whim. Perhaps these only appear to be cases where one doesn't have a reason for doing what one does, because these are cases where one doesn't undertake prior deliberation that concludes in the relevant action/intention. But once we distinguish prior deliberation from acting for a reason and admit of the possibility of action for a reason without prior deliberation, we may hesitate to conclude that these are genuine cases where one has no reason for doing what one does. At any rate, we don't aim to solve this debate here. The crucial point for what follows is that normative reasons – that is, the object of our investigation here – are commonly distinguished from motivating reasons. The question of whether motivating reasons and explanatory reasons should be further distinguished lies beyond the scope of the present work.

1.2   A (Recent) History of Reasons in Three Acts (and the Reasons–Causes Distinction)

Reasons are central to contemporary philosophy. They play a prominent role in contemporary debates in meta-ethics, epistemology, and philosophy of action, to name but a few. Yet talk of reasons hasn't always been so popular in philosophy. How did the notion of *reasons* become so central? This section proposes one possible reconstruction of the rise to prominence of *reasons* by distinguishing three major episodes that have shaped the understanding of this notion over the twentieth and twenty-first centuries. The story proposed here is a rough one, and as such it certainly misses some important historical details and oversimplifies some complex theoretical debates. Yet the aim here is not to provide an exhaustive genealogy of *reasons* or a complete history of debates in normative philosophy; rather, it is to draw attention to some aspects of past debates that may help us to better situate the object of our inquiry (i.e. the nature of normative reasons). A central theme in our reconstruction of the rise to prominence of *reasons* will be the supposed difference between reasons and causes.[3]

The debate that inspired the contemporary interest in reasons, the first episode in our reconstruction of contemporary reasonology, is exactly the early twentieth-century debate about the distinction between reasons and causes. According to late Wittgenstein (in particular in his Blue Book: Wittgenstein 1958), we can distinguish between two kinds of explanations: on the one hand, there are explanations by causes, and on the other hand, there are explanations by reasons.[4] One way of further developing these thoughts from Wittgenstein is to conclude that only the explanation by reasons is appropriate in explaining action. This conclusion, drawn explicitly by Wittgenstein's followers (see Melden 1961, and Anscombe 2000 in particular), was thought to have far-reaching theoretical consequences. To see the importance of this distinction, we have to revisit the early twentieth-century discussions concerning the unity and methodology of sciences, and, in particular, of the nature of scientific explanation. According to one trend in the philosophy of science, inspired by Carl Hempel, a genuinely scientific explanation is causal, and crucially it must appeal to empirical laws. A notable and controversial consequence of this positivist view is that, if social sciences, psychology, and the humanities (e.g. history) are genuinely scientific disciplines, then they

---

[3] In my working through this, I am much indebted to Pascal Engel, especially with respect to a better understanding of the Davidsonian approach and its discontents (in particular, I am inspired here by 'la Présentation' in Davidson 1993, translated by Engel 1993: V–XXXI). My general overview here is also partly inspired by Livet (2005) and Ogien (1995: 35–51). See also Wiland (2012), especially chapter 1, for some relevant historical references beyond the twentieth century in connection with the faculty of Reason, which is assumed to be connected to reasoning and hence to judging and doing things for reasons (cf. Wiland 2012: 9). The focus of the present section is on contemporary history only.

[4] Arguably, this distinction between reasons and causes has its predecessor in the Fregean distinction between grounds that can justify our judgments and mere causes of our judgments. Frege distinguishes the two in his discussion of psychologism in logic; see, for instance

> With the psychological conception of logic we lose the distinction between grounds that justify a conviction and the causes that actually produce it. This means that a justification in the proper sense is not possible; what we have in its place is an account of how the conviction was arrived at, from which it is to be inferred that everything has been caused by psychological factors. This puts a superstition on the same footing as a scientific discovery. (Frege 1979: 147)

I discovered this passage from Frege in Benmakhlouf (2018), who suggests that Frege distinguishes here between reasons and causes; see Benmakhlouf 2018: 13–14.

must also conform to this model, and they have to provide causal explanations while appealing to empirical laws (or universal generalisations). This, within the positivist framework, amounted to quite problematic behaviourist assumptions in the human sciences. Thus, taking Wittgenstein's remarks about explanation by causes and explanation by reasons at face value in this context leads to a rejection of the positivist model of scientific explanation as inadequate, or at least as inadequate with respect to human and social sciences. For, if the distinction between causes and reasons is on the right track, positivists' assumption about the necessarily causal nature of explanation is radically misguided when considering a (scientific) explanation of action, which is presumed to be connected to reasons and not causes. In this context of the early twentieth century, then, the nature of reasons as opposed to causes becomes a central philosophical battlefield with respect to debates about human action, scientific methodology, and the unity of the sciences more generally.

It is, then, no surprise that Wittgenstein's followers invested so much energy and effort in working out in detail positive arguments in favour of distinguishing reasons from causes. Roughly, according to the Wittgensteinians, one can give at least three distinct lines of argument in favour of the distinction between causes and reasons. (Wittgenstein himself, in fact, does not enter much into argumentative details concerning the distinction, and even seems to accept the possibility of reasons that are causes without explaining how this might be.) The first kind of argument relies on some epistemological assumptions. In short, it begins with an assumption that causal explanations are discoverable by observation. More specifically, causal explanations can be reached by means of repetitions of experiments that confirm or give a basis for rejecting a hypothesis. Typically it happens when we (i) observe an effect E, following an event C; (ii) we repeat the event; and (iii) we observe the effect again. This then provides the basis for inferring a causal correlation between C and E. This is thought to be a standard procedure in discovering a cause and hence uncovering a causal explanation. However, when it comes to explanations by reasons, the procedure for reaching them is nothing like this. We do not discover our reasons for acting by repeated observations that can confirm the hypothesis that such and such is a reason to act. On the contrary, according to the Wittgensteinians, we have non-observational knowledge of our reasons (see Anscombe 2000: 14). This non-observational knowledge is, according to this line of thought, of the same nature as our knowledge of our own body. This epistemological difference between causes and reasons, then, is thought to uncover a substantial difference between the two that should give us pause in lumping the two together. The second consideration that has been proposed by Wittgensteinians in favour of distinguishing reasons from causes is of a conceptual nature. It begins with an assumption that there exists an intrinsic link between reasons and actions. The idea is that the very concept of *action* presupposes or subsumes the concept of *reasons*. In other words, we cannot understand action (i.e. grasp the concept of *action*) without grasping the concept of *reasons*. The intrinsic link between the two is supposed to be of the same order as the conceptual link between the concept of a *premise* and the concept of a *conclusion*. Understanding one involves understanding the other. Yet, crucially, there is no such intrinsic link between *cause* and *effect*. Indeed, according to this line of thought, we can quite easily conceive of a cause without conceiving of its effect. The third line of argument in favour of the reasons–causes distinction relies on an observation about the ontology of causes. The observation here is that causal chains can be, in principle, infinite. That is to say, there is nothing in principle that would prevent the possibility of infinite regress in the search for causes of an event (and, if the past is infinite, then such an infinite regress in causal chains even makes sense). However, this is not the case with respect to reasons. Clearly, reasons do not admit even in principle the possibility of infinite regress. Reasons are always reasons for someone, and they do stop at the level of someone. One way to think about it would be to think of reasons as pointing to someone's responsibility for doing something. Once one's responsibility for doing something is established, it doesn't make sense to look further. So, for instance, if you are going to explain my action of going to the grocery store, you might appeal to the fact that I am out of milk or beer, or whatever, but once you have established the relevant considerations (that I am out of milk and need some more, etc.), there is no sense in going further back in explaining *my* action of going to the grocery store by, say, appealing to considerations about why I am living where I do or why I eat what I do.

Whatever the value of these arguments, the point that I would like to observe here is that the modern interest in reasons seems to have first been initiated in the context of the opposition between Wittgenstein and especially his followers to the logical positivist view of methodology and the unity of the sciences, and in particular about the nature of an appropriate explanation of action. The question of whether the explanation of action has to appeal to reasons, as opposed to causes, was of crucial importance to that debate in the early and mid-twentieth century.

In the heyday of Wittgenstein-inspired philosophy of action (i.e. the mid-twentieth century), it seemed that the validity of the distinction between reasons and causes had been established for good. However, things changed rapidly when Donald Davidson came up with his influential – in a sense, neo-Humean – approach in philosophy of action (see Davidson 1963). He challenged established Wittgensteinian views in philosophy of action, and a key element of his attack was the rejection of their reasons–causes dichotomy as over-simplistic. Davidson's novel take on the relation between reasons and causes in the 1960s and the discussion that unfolded after it, in particular in moral psychology, constitute the second major episode in our rough reconstruction of the recent history of reasons.

A central element in Davidson's rejection of the simple reasons–causes dichotomy was to show that, contrary to what his opponents seemed to take for granted, reasons for which a subject acts are actually causes of the subject's action. Reasons for which a subject acts are the bases of one's action and as such are causes of one's action. Another important element in Davidson's view is his adoption of a sort of neo-Humean approach to action, according to which, roughly, action is explained by appeal to the belief–desire pairs. On this view, then, my desire to drink a beer, combined with my belief that there is a beer in my fridge, is my reason for getting up and heading to the fridge. This combination is a reason and also a cause that explains my action. Crucially, the explanation is causal. The desire–belief pair is the relevant cause. In providing this line of thought, Davidson is also rejecting another common assumption in the earlier debates, namely, that causal explanations have to appeal to some general laws and have to be discoverable by repetitions of experimental observations. Such a view of causal correlations is overly restrictive on Davidson's approach, for there are some singular causes. We do not need multiple observations to know that pouring nail polish on my pants will ruin them instantly. A single experience of this kind is largely sufficient to know this. Thus, general laws and multiple observations are not necessary for establishing a causal correlation. Certain reasons, reasons for which we act (e.g. our psychological states), are causes of our actions in this sense according to the Davidsonian approach.[5]

The debate between Davidson and Wittgenstein's followers focused much on motivation in debating the correct account of action. An interesting point to note is that the parallel debates in meta-ethics at that time

---

[5] For a recent critical discussion of the Davidsonian idea that reasons are causes, see Dietz (2016).

were also largely focused on aspects of moral psychology. A central meta-ethical debate at that time concerned the correct account of motivation (see Scanlon 2014: 1–2 for related historical observations about the centrality of morality and in particular the centrality of the question of moral motivation to the mid-twentieth-century debates in meta-ethics). This focus can be explained in part by the growing interest in non-cognitivism in meta-ethics during the 1970s. A central argument for non-cognitivism – the approach according to which, in a nutshell, moral judgments such as 'this action is/is not morally appropriate' are expressions of non-cognitive states (e.g. desires) – relies on the very idea that moral judgments should motivate us to act and that only desires (given certain background beliefs) can motivate us to act in a certain way. Thus, a Davidsonian (and broadly neo-Humean) mentalistic theory of reasons, where reasons are psychological states (e.g. desires with background beliefs), becomes central to meta-ethical debates, for it provides crucial construction blocks for non-cognitivist arguments in meta-ethics (and moral psychology). In short, these debates, initiated in a sense by the Davidsonian rejection of an oversimplified dichotomy between reasons and causes, have the notion of *reasons* as a key element and in that sense have certainly contributed to placing this notion at the very epicentre of contemporary normative fields of philosophy.

The third major episode in the growth in popularity of *reasons* as I see it corresponds to the increasingly widespread realist objections to mentalist, non-cognitivist, or psychologising approaches in meta-ethics, starting in the 1990s and continuing well into the twenty-first century. Indeed, many of these objections are directly based on a divergent understanding of the very nature of reasons. In short, we can observe a certain anti-Humean movement in meta-ethics towards the end of the 1990s and in the 2000s. It is characterised by turning the focus specifically on reasons understood as facts, facts that speak in favour of an action or an attitude. Authors like Derek Parfit, Thomas Scanlon, and John Skorupski are among some of the most important players in this realistic turn. Instead of focusing on reasons for which we act (with their link to motivation), these philosophers have insisted that we focus on reasons to act (or have an attitude). Reasons to act (and have attitudes) are, in a sense, independent of our motivations and psychological states. According to this approach, the fact that there is a fire in the building is a reason for everyone in the building to get out of it immediately. Crucially, it is a reason regardless of the psychological states of people inside the building. A further thought, then, is that reasons understood in this way are considerations that play a central or even definitional role in determining what one ought to do, what is right or fitting, what is justified or rational, and so on. Those who take this further step often think of reasons as fundamental and prime elements in the normative domain, as things that cannot be further analysed but can be appealed to in order to understand other normative notions and statuses (the next section provides a more detailed explanation of this prominent approach within contemporary philosophy).

We may sometimes hear contemporary philosophers complaining about the omnipresence of reasons in recent debates – the worry being that *reasons* could mean so many different things and that philosophers often use it in ways that don't seem to exhibit any unity. And indeed a healthy scepticism about putting too much emphasis on this notion may be sensible, given the proliferation of distinctions and ways of understanding it. However, to give up on reasons too quickly is also to forget the tremendous importance that this notion has had in past debates, starting at least in the early twentieth century. We have surveyed above what seem to be three major episodes in philosophical debates where the notion of *reasons* has played a crucial role: the debate between logical positivists and Wittgensteinians on explanation of action; the debate between Wittgensteinians and Davidson about the reasons–causes distinction; and the debate between neo-Humeans and realists in meta-ethics. All these debates have relied in one way or another on appeals to reasons and to some extent have been fruitful. It is apparent that the prominence of reasons in contemporary philosophy has not come out of the blue; it is largely due to the role of reasons in these past debates. Insofar as these debates have not all been futile, we can conclude that theorising about reasons is a worthwhile endeavour.

1.3   Objective, Subjective, Possessed, Unpossessed

1.3.1   Introducing the Problem

Contemporary philosophy of reasons is characterised by an increasing number of notions and distinctions. While it is certainly true that some crucial notions are universally accepted (such as the distinction between *normative* and *motivating* reasons), it is also true that recent reasonology debates have become increasingly idiosyncratic. One response to such idiosyncrasy might be to appeal to Ockham's razor by investigating whether and how some notions within the debate can be reduced to others. So, for instance, instead of having both the concept of *motivating* reasons and the concept of *operative* reasons, philosophers are willing to accept that, in fact, people have used two different names for the same concept.

In such a context, the tendency is to assume the same kind of reduction with respect to *subjective* reasons (as opposed to *objective*) and *possessed* reasons (as opposed to *unpossessed*). According to this assumption, there is no distinction between possessed reasons and subjective reasons at all: thus, there are no reasons that are subjective but not possessed, and equally no reasons that are possessed but not subjective. Rather, just as 'motivating' and 'operative' are two names for the same thing – that is, a certain sort of reason – so 'subjective' and 'possessed' are two names for a sort of normative reason.[6] Here are two [explicit] examples attesting to the popularity of the identification of subjective with possessed reasons:

> . . . But in some sense or other, Freddie [i.e. the guy who likes to dance and knows that there is going to be dancing at the party], unlike Ronnie [i.e. the guy who likes to dance but has no clue about the party], *has* this reason [to go to the party], since he knows about it, and Ronnie does not. This second sense of 'has a reason' is the one I will later distinguish as the *subjective* sense of 'reason'. (Schroeder 2008: 59)

> I reject the Factoring Account, so I deny that subjective reasons are a subset of objective reasons. I also deny that the status of something as a subjective reason is independent of its being possessed. (Smithies 2018: 20 fn 29)[7]

Not everyone within the debate accepts that there are any objective/ unpossessed normative reasons. Some think that all normative reasons are *subjective/possessed*. Yet, even in this case, the assumption is often that the distinction makes sense and, in particular, that 'subjective' and 'possessed' are merely two different names for one set of normative reasons, whereas 'unpossessed/objective' (or perhaps simply 'unpossessed')[8] refers to another

---

[6] Hawthorne and Magidor (2018) is one rare place where this identification has been rejected. They rely on this rejection in their objection to Mark Schroeder's arguments against the so-called Factoring Account of reasons. Sylvan (2016) also appears to distance himself from the identity view.

[7] Here is another example: 'One common way of drawing the distinction [between "objective" and "subjective" reasons] is in terms of the reasons there are for some agent S to A (so-called objective reasons) and the reasons S has to A (so-called subjective reasons)' (Fogal and Sylvan 2017: 6, fn 6). Note that Fogal and Sylvan do not endorse such a distinction themselves.

[8] This is to indicate that I do not want to imply that the approach that I criticise in this section has to assume that the sets of subjective and objective reasons are disjoint. My opponents may well hold that subjective reasons constitute a subset of objective reasons and that it makes sense to distinguish between possessed objective reasons (i.e. subjective reasons) and unpossessed objective reasons (i.e. merely objective reasons). Thanks to an anonymous referee for this suggestion.

[possible] set of normative reasons. That is, it makes sense to accept a distinction between two *sorts* of reasons even if, in fact, nothing falls under one term or the other.

The aim of this section is to challenge the identification of *subjective* with *possessed*. I will argue that *subjective* reasons are distinct from *possessed* reasons. More precisely, I will argue that while there are possessed subjective reasons, there are also unpossessed subjective reasons.[9] The distinction between subjective and possessed reasons is not like the [merely apparent] distinction between motivating and operative reasons. In what follows, I will first review the basics of one theoretical framework that appears to imply the distinction between subjective and possessed reasons. Then, I propose intuitive considerations in favour of the distinction, before indicating some of its further theoretical implications.

1.3.2   A Background Theory

To keep things clear, let us focus on the following senses of 'possessed' and 'subjective' reasons:

> **Possessed reasons (PR)**: a reason r for S to F is possessed by S, just in case S is in a position to use r in deliberation.[10]
>
> **Subjective reasons (SR)**: a reason r for S to F is a subjective normative reason for S to F just in case r's being a reason for S to F depends on S's evidence.[11]

---

[9] While I believe that *subjective versus objective* and *possessed versus unpossessed* are orthogonal and not merely different distinctions, in what follows I will focus exclusively on the *subjective (possessed or unpossessed)* reasons.

[10] Compare to: '[T]here is a familiar distinction between the reasons there are for a person to act and the reasons she possesses for acting, where a person possesses a reason for acting only if she is in a position to act for that reason ... A common suggestion is that to possess a reason requires standing in an epistemic relation to the relevant consideration' (Whiting 2018: 3). See also: 'The contrast between possessed and unpossessed reasons we have in mind is fairly intuitive. When a glass contains poison but an agent is unaware of this, there is a reason for the agent to avoid drinking from the glass, but that reason for avoidance is something that the agent is not in a position to use as a consideration when acting' (Hawthorne and Magidor 2018: 2).

[11] See, for instance:

> Roughly our envisaged objective 'ought' ranks actions according to the best outcome, while the subjective 'ought' ranks according to the best expected outcome by the lights of the agent's evidence ... (We think of evidence as what the subject knows, though much of what we say could be adapted to other frameworks for thinking about evidence.) This basic structure covers both reasons to act and reasons to believe. (Hawthorne and Magidor 2018: 2)

Compare to: 'Second, it is fairly common in the literature we are concerned with (and elsewhere) to distinguish between *objective* and *subjective* "should's". On a simple way of drawing this distinction, what you objectively should do is determined by the facts of your situation, whereas

Three clarifications are in order here. First, note that ordinary English possessive constructions such as 'S has a reason to F' or 'S's reason to F' are extremely context-sensitive and do not always capture the sense of 'possession', which is of interest for normative debates.[12] Consider (a) 'The building is on fire. She has a reason to leave.' The reason attribution here may be appropriate in a sense, and, importantly, the two phrases may be true, even if the subject has no clue whatsoever about the ongoing fire.[13] Crucially, the sense of 'having' reasons in (a) is not the one that we intend to capture by (PR) (nor by [SR]). In short, the context sensitivity of possessive constructions calls for extra caution when relying on linguistic data to theorise about the possession of reasons. Our specification of 'possessed reasons' does not pretend to correspond to all possible uses of possessive constructions involving 'reasons'.

Second, 'being in a position to do something' is a context-sensitive expression. Consider, for instance, (i): 'Carl is in a position to prove Gödel's Incompleteness Theorem.' The utterance (i) may well be true in a context where we focus on, say, comparing typical humans to some cognitively less developed species. There is a sense in which a human, named Carl, and not, for instance, a jellyfish, is in a position to prove the Incompleteness Theorem. This is a very weak sense, a sense that attributes the ability to prove the theorem to Carl merely because he is a human with a sophisticated cognitive capacity (and not a jellyfish). In a different context, (i) will not come out as true. For instance, it will be false in a context where we focus on Carl's ignorance of mathematics and logic. The sense of 'is in a position to', which is relevant for our discussion here, is not a weak one. We can follow Whiting, Hawthorne, and Magidor (see footnote 10) and think of 'is in a position to use r in deliberation' as introducing an epistemic constraint. It requires that the subject's epistemic situation does not prevent the subject from using the relevant consideration in deliberation. Crucially, the mere fact that p follows from the subject's evidence does not guarantee that the subject is in a position to use p in her deliberation in the relevant sense. After all, one may believe or

---

what you subjectively should do is determined by your perspective on your situation' (Way 2018: 14).

[12] Thanks to an anonymous referee for reminding me of the importance of this context sensitivity.

[13] See Hawthorne and Magidor (2018) for similar and more sophisticated examples. An anonymous referee also proposes the following example as an illustration of the context sensitivity in question: 'It turns out that we had good reason to proceed with caution, though of course we could not have known it at the time'. See also Fogal and Sylvan (2017) for further observations about the context sensitivity of the possessive constructions.

know that *p* and fail to know or even believe a proposition that follows from *p*.[14]

Third, while 'depends' in (SR) is a bit vague, hopefully it is still clear enough for our purposes here. The crucial point is that 'depends' differs from 'consists of'. More specifically, the point of (SR) is that we do not characterise one's subjective reasons as consisting only of one's evidence. Certain facts that are *determined* by one's evidence will count as subjective reasons on this specification even though they are not themselves part of one's evidence. One might think of a subject's evidence as a set of propositions that the subject knows (e.g. Williamson's E=K thesis).[15] Yet what follows is also compatible with different views about evidence.

One theoretical framework that vindicates the distinction between subjective and possessed reasons is the view that takes seriously the context sensitivity of 'ought' and other modals.[16] According to this linguistically informed approach, 'ought' can have different senses, since it is taken to order actions (and attitudes) according to a standard.[17] There are objective oughts and subjective oughts. The former rank actions (and attitudes) relative to what is best, given all the facts; whereas the latter provides a ranking relative to what is expected to be best in the light of some agent's evidence (cf. Hawthorne and Magidor 2018: 2). The suggestion, then, is to apply a similar line of thought to normative reasons, since the construction 'a reason/reasons to F' is taken to encode the ought modality (cf. Hawthorne and Magidor 2018). A natural conclusion is that 'a reason/reasons to F' is context-sensitive in the same way as 'ought' is. This supports the idea that there are at least two sorts of normative reasons – objective and subjective. Subjective normative reasons are restricted by the subject's evidence, whereas objective normative reasons are not restricted in this way. This approach does not identify subjective normative reasons with possessed normative reasons. For a consideration, *r*, to be a subjective normative reason for S to F, just is for *r* to speak in favour of F-ing for S, given the set of S's evidence. In numerous cases, when *r* is a subjective normative reason for S, S will possess *r*. Yet, the

---

[14] Thanks to an anonymous referee for drawing my attention to the need to clarify this issue.

[15] Cf. Williamson (2000: 184–237). See also Logins (2017), among others, for a recent defence of E=K.

[16] The view sketched here has been proposed recently by Hawthorne and Magidor (2018).

[17] A more precise formulation would appeal to the rankings of states of affairs. The linguistic theory in the background of this view comes from Kratzer (1981) (and elsewhere). This presentation is a very rough and incomplete one. A number of important elements need to be added here (such as a reference to modal bases or domains of states of affairs that are ranked).

familiarity with such common cases need not lead us to the identification of the two. There might be cases where a consideration *r* is a normative subjective reason for S to F (it is determined by S's evidence), yet S does not possess *r*, since S is not in a position to use *r* in her deliberation.

This was a quick summary of a theoretical view that supports the distinction between subjective and possessed reasons. However, we have not yet seen a convincing case that cannot be well understood unless we adopt the view in question. That is, now that we have filled in a conceptual space, we need some motivation for taking this option seriously. Does it actually have a useful application? The next section aims to explore this question.

1.3.3   A Case

Consider an ordinary participant on the famous *Let's Make a Deal* show (also known as the Monty Hall show).[18] Let us call him Ben. He stands in front of three doors. There is a luxury car behind one of these doors and goats behind the two others. Ben has been given a chance to choose one of the three doors. Let us say Ben chooses door number 1. Now, the show's host, Monty Hall, is obliged to open one of the three doors (that is the rule). Yet he is not permitted to open the door that Ben has chosen. Neither can he open the door with the car behind it. Ben knows the rules of the game. Let us say Monty Hall opens door number 2. Of course, there is a goat behind it. Next, Ben is offered the chance to change his initial choice. That is, Ben can change his choice from door 1 to door 3. Given what Ben knows, the thing to do (as long as he wants to win the car) is to switch to door 3. Given Ben's evidence, it is clearly more probable that the car is behind door 3. In fact, by opening door 2, Monty Hall gave Ben a crucial piece of information. Given the 1/3 probability that Ben's first choice was the lucky one, there was a probability of 2/3 that Monty Hall did not have any choice other than door 2. That leaves a 2/3 chance that the car is behind door 3. Now, it makes sense to think that the consideration (*r*) 'it is more likely that the car is behind door 3 than door 1' (alternatively, 'the car is more unlikely to be behind door 1') is a normative reason for Ben to switch to door 3. That is, *r* is a reason for Ben, in a sense.

---

[18] This case is well known (especially within probability theory) as giving rise to the Monty Hall Problem; see vos Savant (1992: 199–209).

It may still be the case that the car is behind door 1. Hence, in another sense (an *objective* sense that is not tied to Ben's evidence), *r* may also be no reason at all to switch. However, as long as we focus on the evidence that Ben possesses, *r* is, intuitively, a normative reason (in a sense) for Ben to switch.

Crucially, Ben has the 'Monty Hall condition' – that is, the condition of being unable to see that it is more probable that the car is behind door 3 than door 1. As a matter of fact, a number of participants on the actual show were unable to see that, given what they knew, it was much more probable that the car was behind door 3 (i.e. the door that was not initially chosen by the participant and was offered as a possible choice for a switch). It may take some time, repeated calculation, reading explanations, and watching tutorials to overcome the 'Monty Hall condition' and finally be able to understand that it is more probable that the car is behind door 3 than door 1. After all, it is common to describe the theoretical choice the participants face on the show (when they have been offered the chance to switch a choice) as a problem or puzzle or even a paradox.

Assuming that Ben has the Monty Hall condition, we do not want to say that he possesses the consideration 'it is more likely that the car is behind door 3 than door 1' as a normative reason. For Ben is not in a position to use it in any kind of deliberation. Crucially, the 'being in a position to', which is relevant here, is an epistemic one, exactly as in (PR) – namely, there is something in Ben's epistemic position that prevents him from using the relevant consideration in his deliberation. After all, Ben does not believe and does not know that it is more likely that the car is behind door 3 than door 1. The distinction between subjective normative reasons and possessed normative reasons seems to be the best way of making sense of the intuitive judgments about this case. The consideration 'it is more likely that the car is behind door 3 than door 1' is a subjective reason for Ben to switch, yet he does not possess it. It is an unpossessed subjective normative reason.

Those who collapse the distinction between the subjective and possessed normative reasons might object to the claim that *r* is a normative reason for Ben to switch. One line of objection to this claim relies on the idea that only facts that determine [evidential] probability and not the probability facts (such as the fact that it is probable that *p*) can be reasons. According to this line of objection, only the relevant pieces of Ben's evidence are reasons for him to switch (for example, that Monty opens door 2, that Monty cannot open door 1, and so on). The fact that, on Ben's evidence, it is more likely that the car is behind door 3 than door 1 is not a reason, according to this line of thought.[19]

However, this line of objection leads to unacceptable conclusions, since it would generalise to a myriad of ordinary considerations that we typically take to be our reasons to act. Giving up the idea that probability facts, such as that p is probable or that p is more likely than q, can be reasons for a subject to F would result in a massive denial of our ordinary intuitions. For example, consider a situation where it is likely, on my evidence, that it will rain in five minutes. Do we really want to say that we are not authorised to hold that the consideration 'it is likely on my evidence that it will rain' is a reason for me to close the windows or to look for my umbrella? To the contrary, the fact that the rain is very probable on my evidence speaks in favour of closing the windows or taking the umbrella. The probability fact here is a normative reason for me to act in certain ways.

The following examples may help to illustrate this point further. Let us say that a mountain expedition has been organised, and the participants are set up at the base camp and planning their ascent to the summit. Given what they know, it is 80 per cent probable that there will be a heavy storm tomorrow. Do we want to say that this probability fact does not speak in favour of not planning the ascent for tomorrow? Given what his doctors know, it is more likely that a patient has the rare, severe, and extremely contagious disease X than a simple flu. That probability fact speaks in favour of the doctors recommending the patient's immediate hospitalisation. It is unlikely, given the available scientifically informed evidence, that a plague epidemic will break out in the city you live in anytime soon. It would seem odd to say that this consideration is not a reason for you to dismiss allegations of a major plague risk in your city. Rejecting the idea that probability facts can be normative reasons leads to an unwarranted scepticism about a large number of ordinary normative reasons.

Hence, I conclude that the Monty Hall example provides at least prima facie support for the possibility of subjective unpossessed reasons.

1.3.4 Theoretical Implications of the Distinction

Taking subjective unpossessed reasons seriously has further theoretical relevance. Here are two places where they might play a significant role.

A major theme in epistemology during the last twenty years or so is our presumed *cognitive homelessness*. Roughly, this view states that our inner

---

[19] Thanks to an anonymous referee for drawing my attention to this possible objection.

life is not always available to us. According to an influential argument by
Williamson (2000: 93–113), there is no non-trivial condition C, such that
when C obtains, one can always know that one is in C. In particular,
Williamson has argued that it is not the case that when we know that p, we
always know that we know that p. His Anti-Luminosity argument for that
conclusion has received sustained interest throughout the early twenty-first
century. While it is far from being universally accepted, the Anti-
Luminosity argument has, nonetheless, moved contemporary mainstream
epistemology towards taking the possibility of our cognitive homelessness
more seriously.

The situation within the contemporary meta-normative debates seems
to be quite different in this respect. The fact that it is common not to
distinguish between subjective and possessed normative reasons seems to
reveal the prevailing tendency within the meta-normative field to assume
that people's inner lives, and in particular their inner normative lives, are
always available to them. However, if what precedes is on the right track,
then this common assumption needs to be revisited. The Monty Hall case
shows that items within our inner (normative) life (such as subjective
reasons) are not always available to us: even people's subjective reasons
to act are not something that they are always in a position to know
they have.

On a somewhat related note, much debate in contemporary epistemology has centred on the so-called internalism/externalism divide about
epistemic justification. Even though the debate does not seem to be over
yet, there are substantial lessons that epistemologists have already learned
from it. One of these seems particularly relevant for our discussion,
namely, that there are two ways of making the general characterisation of
internalism more precise. Internalist *accessibilism* is, roughly, the thesis that
justification is determined by one's internal states that are accessible (to
oneself) upon reflection alone; whereas internalist *mentalism* is the view
that justification is determined by one's (internal) mental states, regardless
of whether they are accessible or not. Now, it makes an important
argumentative difference whether one defends internalist accessibilism or
internalist mentalism, and epistemologists have noticed it. A similar contrast seems to apply to normative reasons as well. However, its importance
has not yet been fully appreciated. More precisely, the distinction proposed above, between possessed and subjective normative reasons, parallels
in a way the accessibilism/mentalism distinction about justification. One
may think that practical rationality is determined either by one's subjective
reasons or by one's possessed reasons. These are two different theses that

the distinction between subjective–possessed reasons enables us to clearly separate. This matters, since one of these theses seems to be more demanding than the other. At least, certainly, the same arguments will not work for or against both of them. Overall, just as epistemologists have made progress by distinguishing accessibilism from mentalism, meta-normative debates could benefit from taking the possessed/subjective reasons distinction more seriously.[20]

1.3.5 Concluding Remarks about Objective–Subjective Reasons

Philosophy of reasons has reached a point of increased terminological complexity. In such a situation, a natural tendency is to simplify the debate and reduce the number of postulated distinctions. One such tendency is to reduce subjective normative reasons to possessed normative reasons. I have argued here that such a tendency has to be resisted or at least not accepted from the outset. A respectable (yet, of course, debatable) and well-understood theoretical framework licenses such a distinction. More importantly, some cases can be best understood with this distinction in place. Hence, simplifying the debate in this way has theoretical costs. A better strategy for advancing philosophy of reasons might be to pursue deeper theoretical issues, as many do, such as assessing the overall merits of contextualist approaches.

More fundamentally, what the Monty Hall case shows is that our cognitive limitations inevitably lead to the disparity between normative reasons that derive from what we know (or, at any rate, what we have as evidence) and normative reasons that we are in a position to use in deliberation. Not all members of the former category belong to the latter. Sadly, even when reasons are properly connected to a specific person, the person may not always be in a position to take advantage of that connection.

---

[20] Note also that internalist accessibilism, as defended recently by Declan Smithies (cf. Smithies 2012), has to focus on possessed reasons to believe and not merely subjective ones (assuming that what justifies one to believe something are normative reasons to believe). Subjective reasons that are not possessed are not accessible and, hence, cannot determine justification according to internalist accessibilism. Therefore, it is unfortunate that Smithies fails to distinguish between possessed and subjective reasons (see the aforementioned quotation). This makes his view problematically ambiguous between a reading that cannot be true, given the very formulation of accessibilism, and a reading that is internally coherent but very demanding. Thanks to an anonymous referee for drawing my attention to the problem that the subjective–possessed distinction applied to reasons to believe might raise for Smithies's accessibilist account.

1.4   Reasons-First and the Wrong Kind of Reasons

According to a prominent, indeed arguably the majority view until recently, reasons cannot be analysed or defined in other terms; they are rather to be taken as fundamental with respect to other normative properties/notions. This view goes under the name of *reasons-first*, or *reasons fundamentalism*. There are thus two elements in this approach – reasons are taken to be prime, in the sense of not being analysable or substantially explainable in other terms. And reasons are explanatorily fundamental in the sense that we have to appeal to reasons in order to explain all other normative notions. Among prominent defences of the reasons-first programme are Scanlon (1998), Parfit (2011: especially 31–42), Schroeder (2007), and Skorupski (2010); a more recent defence is Rowland (2019); see also Engel (2015b) for an overview and exploration of the general aims and prospects of the reasons-first programme.

An important thing to note about reasons-first views is that as presented above they need not be *all-things-considered* reasons-first. The general view is that within the normative domain, reasons are prime and fundamental. The general view, as presented here, is not committed *per se* to the claim that there cannot be a plausible reductionist story of reasons by appeal to non-normative properties. Of course, some (perhaps even most) reasons-first theorists would not endorse such a possibility. But some do accept it. Mark Schroeder is one prominent recent proponent of a reductive reasons-first approach in this sense (Schroeder 2007 is a book-length defence of such an option). According to Schroeder, all normative properties can be analysed in terms of reasons, but reasons can be reduced (in the specific, constitutive, non-symmetric sense) to non-normative properties, which on Schroeder's own preferred Humean account amounts partly to appeal to one's desires, promotion, and explanation.[21] As Schroeder puts it:

> But if attractive views about what is distinctive of the normative so often take this *structural* form, then the result that *good*, and *right* and *just* and *reason* and so on are truly normative properties, is one that it is actually incredibly *easy* for a reductive theorist to get right. Since being normative is a matter of a *structural* relation to some basic normative property like that of being a *reason*, the reductive theorist can accept this characterization of the

---

[21] More specifically on Schroeder's account:

> **Reason** For R to be a reason for X to do A is for there to be some p such that X has a desire whose object is p, and the truth of R is part of what explains why X's doing A promotes p.
> (Schroeder 2007: 59)

normative. Then, she can accept whatever analyses of each *non*-basic normative property in terms of the basic property are accepted by the non-reductive theorists who share this conception of what is distinctive of the normative. And finally, she gives her reductive theory as an analysis of the basic normative property or relation. So it turns out that even the normativity of normative properties is easy for a reductive theory to capture. (Schroeder 2007: 81)

More specifically Schroeder accepts the following fundamentality claim about reasons in the normative domain:

Reason Basicness What it is to be normative, is to be analyzed in terms of reasons. (Schroeder 2007: 81)

In what follows, we will limit our focus only to the question of the possibility of intra-normative analysis/explanation of reasons. That is, we will leave out the discussion about the prospects of a viable reductive account of normative reasons in non-normative terms (though note that Schroeder's account shares some key aspects with 'Explanation' accounts of reasons, ahead, and as such might face some of the same objections that we will present to versions of the Explanation accounts – for example, value-based explanationist accounts). The focus here is on the question of whether reasons are basic/fundamental within the broadly normative domain or whether we can propose a viable view that explains what reasons are by partial appeal to other normative/evaluative properties.

As I see it, there are two main lines of thought that have been presented to support the reasons-first approach. The first line of thought is that there is simply no more informative account available of what normative reasons are. If we try to explain reasons, all we can get at best are circular accounts. Reasons just are, according to this line of defence, unanalysable, since no viable analysis or substantial, informative account is available. I take it that this line of thought is implicit in the now famous passage from Thomas Scanlon that has been taken to be the paradigmatic expression of the reasons-first approach:

I will take the idea of a reason as primitive. Any attempt to explain what it is to be a reason for something seems to me to lead back to the same idea: a consideration that counts in favor of it. 'Counts in favor how?' one might ask. 'By providing a reason for it' seems to be the only answer. (Scanlon 1998: 17)

Also, this line of thought has more to it than mere appeal to linguistic or common-sense observations. For instance, some proponents of the reasons-first programme have explicitly argued against reductive accounts/analysis of reasons. John Brunero, for example, has argued at length and on various occasions against some of the most promising existing reductive accounts of reasons (see, for example, Brunero 2009, 2013, 2018; see also Rowland 2019, in particular chapter 11). The idea here is that if it can be shown that all the existing, most promising, informative, reductive accounts of reasons are mistaken, then this alone gives some ground for taking the reasons-first approach seriously. However, as we will see ahead, even if Brunero and others are partially right in criticising the *existing* reductive accounts, there are still other options that have not yet been explored in the literature. The present proposal will actually amount to putting on the table one such overlooked reductive account that avoids the main objections to the existing reductive accounts.

The second line of thought that can be discerned in the reasons-first proponents' texts consists in an appeal to the fruitfulness of the reasons-first programme. In short, according to this line, given that taking reasons as prime and fundamental leads to theoretically useful results. For example, it helps to better understand such and such other thing, or to solve elegantly such and such previously unsolved problem, we should take the reasons-first view seriously. As I see it, there are two slightly different versions of this line of defence. The first appeals to the fruitfulness of theorising with reasons about other normative notions and statuses. The idea here is that given that by reducing all other normative notions to reasons, the reasons-first account provides a simple, theoretically unified, and hence explanatorily very powerful approach. So, for instance, on this view, what one ought to do is what there is most reason for one to do, what one is rational to do is what one's possessed reasons support overall (or, alternatively, what one's subjective reasons support overall), what is good is what anyone has reasons to prefer/desire/have a pro-attitude towards, and so on. Rowland provides a recent version of a proposal along these lines (limited to practical normativity only, however):

> On the account that I have provided we can analyse all moral, evaluative, deontic, and normative notions in terms of normative reasons. So, facts about moral, evaluative, deontic, and normative properties just consist in various sets of normative reasons. Every part of this unified picture of the practically normative has explanatory advantages. And the unified picture itself tells us what unifies the moral, the evaluative, the deontic, and the normative as all practically and normatively important domains. Namely, these domains are unified because facts about morality, the evaluative, the deontic, and the normative consist in facts about normative reasons. (Rowland 2019: 217)

If borne out, such a proposal would provide an explanation of the whole normative domain. It would have an extremely high degree of generality and explanatory power.

The second variant of the fruitfulness argument appeals to the role of reasons in sorting out prominent debates in normative philosophy. The idea here is that various standard opposing views in, say, moral philosophy or meta-ethics achieve better traction when transposed to the domain neutral topic of normative reasons in general. Here is one popular expression of this idea:

> Most meta-ethical debates have been about morality. But I shall first discuss non-moral practical reasons and reason-implying oughts. Our questions here take simpler and clearer forms. These are also the most important questions if, as I believe, normativity is best understood as involving reasons or apparent reasons. Things matter only if we have reasons to care about them. In the conflict between these various theories, reasons provide the decisive battlefield. If Naturalism and Non-Cognitivism fail as accounts of reasons, these theories will also fail, I believe, when applied to morality. (Parfit 2011: 269)

If this is on the right track, then appeal to normative reasons can be fruitful not only in sorting out what other broadly normative/evaluative notions are but also in helping to overcome some of the most persistent disagreements in meta-ethics and, presumably, other normative fields. This would, of course, constitute another consideration that speaks strongly in favour of the reasons-first approach.

Despite its very enticing promises, however, the reasons-first approach has to be set aside in what follows. For one thing, as we've noted already, all the options for developing a viable reductive view of reasons have not been explored yet. Given the methodologically plausible constraint that we should not postulate (normative) entities beyond what is necessary, any view that doesn't introduce an independent entity of normative reasons but manages to reduce/explain reasons by appeal to already known normative notions/properties has the advantage of theoretical simplicity.

Another reason for putting the reasons-first approach on hold is that, as several philosophers have recently observed, its promise of providing an effective reduction of all the other broadly normative/evaluative properties/notions doesn't bear out. Without this element, however, the reasons-first approach loses any bite. If other normative properties/notions cannot be reduced to reasons, then reasons are not fundamental in the sense of being explanatorily indispensable and the ultimate element within the normative domain. Recent discussion about this has focused in particular on the reasons-first promise to reduce values to reasons. This debate is often referred to as concerning the buck-passing account of values (the idea being that the buck stops at reasons in explaining values; sometimes the term 'buck-passing accounts' is used more broadly to refer to attempts to reduce any normative/evaluative property to reasons; cf. Löschke 2021). Scanlon is a standard source of contemporary reasons-first buck-passing accounts of value:

> Chapter 1 explained and defended my decision to treat the notion of a reason as primitive. In this chapter, I will use the notion of a reason, taken as the most basic and abstract element of normative thought, to provide a general characterization of a slightly more specific normative notion, the idea of value. (Scanlon 1998: 78)

One general way of putting the proposal, a way that abstracts over specifics of concrete proposals from the reasons-first theorists, has been recently helpfully summed up (but not defended!) by McHugh and Way:

> What it is for X to be good is for there to be sufficient reason for anyone to value X. (McHugh and Way 2016: 577)

To value here is understood as having a relevant pro-attitude – for example, desiring, wishing. And good here is understood in the sense of goodness *simpliciter* (not in the sense of good-for, nor in the sense of attributive goodness) (cf. McHugh and Way 2016). Note that this general buck-passing proposal is easily generalised to goodness-for, attributive goodness, as well as to further more specific values – for example, one is admirable when there is sufficient reason to admire one. And indeed it is supposed to be generalised in this way. Moreover, this general aspect of the view might be taken to be a further advantage of the view (see McHugh and Way 2016: 578–579, who make precisely this observation).

The problem with the reasons-centred buck-passing account of value is that to think that values can be reduced to reasons seems to be a mistake given our pre-theoretical judgments about some fairly simple cases. The main objection here appeals to the so-called wrong kind of reasons problem. Formulations of this problem that are already classical appear in Crisp (2000), D'Arms and Jacobson (2000a, 2000b), and Rabinowicz and Rønnow-Rasmussen (2004); see Gertken and Kiesewetter (2017) and Engel (2020a) for recent overviews of the debate. A well-known example that has been used to state the problem (from Rabinowicz and Rønnow-Rasmussen 2004) is, roughly, that of a despicable demon that threatens to punish one severely, say to kill one, unless one admires the demon (and admires the demon for what it is). It is worth noting that, of course, the strength of the argument would be just the same if transposed to an ordinary situation that preserves the same structure. Two natural observations about such a possible situation when taken together clashes with the reasons-centred buck-passing accounts. The first is that one has sufficient reason to admire the demon in this situation. Indeed, if the threat of terrible pain doesn't give one sufficient reasons, what else could give it? And second, clearly the demon is not admirable; it is despicable. On a buck-passing account, however, if we hold to the view that one has sufficient reason to admire the demon, we have to conclude that the demon is admirable. Thus, something has gone wrong, for we know that the demon is not admirable. If we take these considerations at face value, then it seems that we have to conclude that values cannot be analysed in terms of reasons and hence reasons are not the first and most fundamental elements of the normative domain.

Now, one popular line of response to the wrong kind of reasons problem on the part of reasons-first proponents has been to distinguish between *state-given* reasons and *object-given* reasons (cf. Parfit 2011: appendix A; Piller 2006). Roughly, the idea here is that some reasons arise from or are given by some features, including benefits, of being in a given state, such as from being in a state of admiration of someone; while other reasons are given by the objects of attitudes – for example, by someone's magnanimity in the case of admiration. Crucially, state-given reasons can only be reasons to want to be in a state, or for undertaking actions to try to make oneself have/get into the relevant state (cf. Parfit 2011: 432). They are not reasons to F or reasons to have the relevant attitudes/states (e.g. admiring someone). On the other hand, object-given reasons are reasons to F. Applying this distinction to the case of the despicable demon, the proposal is that the demon's threat to kill one unless one admires the demon can only be a state-given reason. It cannot be an object-given reason, since it is not connected to the demon being magnanimous or generous or otherwise admirable, for the demon is not magnanimous or generous or admirable. The threat can only be a state-given reason in this case. Thus, the threat can only be a reason for one to want to admire the demon or to attempt to (try to) make oneself get into the state of admiration of the demon. If so, then the project of analysing values in terms of reasons might still be maintained. Having state-given reasons in the demon's case – that is, reasons to want or to try to admire the demon – even if sufficient, don't entail that the demon is admirable, since these are not reasons to admire. Admirability reduces only to sufficient reasons to admire, not to reasons to want or to try to get into the state of admiration.

Naturally, the story extends to other values as well: on this picture, roughly, X is good just in case there are sufficient reasons for one to value X, which are different from reasons to want to value X or to try to get into the state of valuing X (see the quotation from McHugh and Way 2016: 577 above).

I think there are two key worries with this line of reply to the wrong kind of reasons problem for reasons-firsters.[22] First, such a proposal looks somewhat ad hoc and arbitrary, given the fact that reasons-first proponents are in no position to provide a substantial account or a definition of reasons. To have a theoretically well-motivated distinction between two kinds of the same thing, we need to know well what is the common element that unifies the two kinds. But the only characterisation that we have from reasons-firsters is that reasons are considerations that speak in favour of a response. The threat in the demon example certainly seems like something that speaks in favour of admiring the demon. Do reasons-firsters have sufficient theoretical grounds that are independent from the need to respond to the wrong kind of reasons problem, for maintaining that normative reasons are of two kinds and that only sufficient object-given reasons to value X really entail that X is valuable? It is not clear how proponents of the reasons-first view could provide us with a satisfactory response to this question. If, say, correctness considerations or justification considerations are worked into the account of object-given reasons by suggesting, perhaps, that only object-given reasons can render an attitude correct/justified (and assuming in addition, for example, that one being admirable and it being fitting/justified to admire one are connected, perhaps, by a biconditional), then reasons would not be first after all. For one would then also appeal to correctness/justification in explaining what object-given reasons are and thus the overall explanation of values would not rely exclusively on normative reasons to value.

Pamela Hieronymi seems to propose a similar, if not the same, line of objection; for instance, she writes: 'As long as a reason is simply a consideration that counts in favor of an attitude, we are left without an obvious way either to draw a useful distinction between these very different sorts of reasons or to say why one of them seems to be the "real" sort of reasons' (Hieronymi 2005: 443). Hieronymi also argues convincingly that it is not clear at all that all state-given reasons are reasons to want or to try to be in a state F, rather than reasons to F, as, for instance, in the case of

---

[22] Thanks to an anonymous reader for Cambridge University Press for making me realize the need to develop these further worries in detail.

imagining that there is no heaven (cf. Hieronymi 2005: 442). Thus, by itself the state-given/object-given reasons distinction cannot help with the problem of the wrong kind of reasons. Reasons-firsters have to appeal to a more substantial and independent account of reasons to distinguish in a non ad hoc way between reasons to which values can be reduced and reasons to which values cannot be reduced. But this is precisely what proponents of the reasons-first approach cannot do, for, according to them, there is nothing more substantial we can say about reasons than that they are considerations that speak in favour of some response. In short, the first line of objection to the object-given/state-given distinction based response to the wrong kind of reasons problem for reasons-firsters is that such a move creates a dilemma for reasons-firsters. On the first horn of the dilemma, they need to provide an independent, theoretically motivated account for why there is a significant distinction between object-given and state-given reasons. Such an account would involve telling us something above and beyond the mere characterisation of reasons as considerations that count in favour. And thus, it would undermine the reasons-first project, according to which we have a robust grasp of reasons and we cannot say anything more substantial about them than that they are considerations that speak in favour. On the second horn, refusing to provide a more substantial, theoretically motivated, and independent account of the distinction between object-given and state-given reasons while relying crucially on this distinction in the treatment of the wrong kind of reasons problem is merely ad hoc and arbitrary and should not be accepted in the present context of debate.

Second, and somewhat connectedly, is that at the end of the day this line of response amounts to an attempt to dissolve rather than solve the wrong kind of reasons problem (cf. Engel 2020a). However, it is not clear that the proponents of the reasons-first approach are in a position to justify such an attempt. The initial assumption that triggered the wrong kind of reasons problem was that, for example, threats appear to constitute genuine and arguably sufficient reasons to admire the despicable demon. After all, it is specifically admiring the demon, and not attempting or wanting to admire the demon, that could save one's life in the imagined case. Insisting that only object-given reasons are reasons to, for example, admire the demon would amount to a scepticism about the wrong kind of reasons; that is, to the denial of the very idea that the wrong kind of reasons are genuine normative reasons and bear normative force. Now, of course, scepticism about the wrong kind of reasons is a possible move within the overall debate about these cases. And philosophers have been willing to endorse this option while trying to explain why we have the intuition that the wrong kind of reasons considerations speak in favour of a response F without equating these considerations with reasons to F (cf. Way 2012, see also Skorupski 2010, see also Gertken and Kiesewetter 2017 for further references and discussion). However, the worry in our present context is that scepticism about the wrong kind of reasons is not a viable option for reasons-first proponents (cf. McHugh and Way 2016). The worry is that, contrary to reductive accounts of reasons, which propose to explain reasons in other terms and to explain our intuitions away in the wrong kind of reasons cases, reasons-firsters are ill-placed to provide an error theory of why we are, allegedly, massively mistaken in thinking that threats and similar considerations can speak in favour of admiring and other attitudes. Suggesting that we are all massively mistaken in thinking that threats speak in favour of admiring becomes problematic if one's view entails that we are supposed to have a robust grasp of reasons and of speaking in favour. Reasons-firsters presuppose that we have a robust, intuitive grasp of reasons and of speaking in favour of F-ing. But if they endorse scepticism about the wrong kind of reasons, then they also have to admit that our grasp of reasons is not so robust after all, since we are massively mistaken about an important category of considerations that seem to be reasons and speak in favour of F-ings. There is then an unresolved tension in such a proposal: if reasons are first, then we both have and don't have a robust grasp of what normative reasons are. And this sounds very much like a paradoxical conclusion.

Moreover, even if we bracket the issue with the robust grasp of reasons, it is not clear that reasons-firsters could provide an independent theoretical motivation for taking the scepticism route. Again, they cannot say anything more than that reasons are considerations that speak in favour of F-ing. We don't get a theoretical and independently motivated answer from reasons-firsters of why we are massively mistaken in thinking that some considerations appear to speak in favour but are, contrary to appearances, not reasons at all to F. But without a plausible error theory, scepticism about the wrong kind of reasons is unsatisfactory. It would seem, then, that combining the reasons-first approach with scepticism about the wrong kind of reasons is unpromising. The wrong kind of reasons problem is still an important concern for the reasons-first approach.

Note also that appealing to the idea that somehow the wrong kind of reasons problem is an instance of a more general and pervasive issue that is a problem for everyone, not only for reasons-firsters (cf. Schroeder 2012, 2013), doesn't seem to help either. As Kieswetter and Gertken have persuasively argued, there is not necessarily a problem for alternative accounts (see also Hieronymi 2005, 2013 among others). A fittingness-first approach, for instance, as defended by McHugh and Way (2016), doesn't seem to be vulnerable to such a problem, since they don't endorse the claim that correctness is explained in terms of reasons, but can explain an X being valuable directly as it being fitting to value X. It is not clear then that there is a more general wrong kind of reasons problem that everyone has to face. It would seem to be a genuine problem first and foremost, if not only for those who think that reasons come first in the order of explanation in the normative domain.

Thus, I conclude the wrong kind of reasons problem is still a major problem specifically for reasons-first views, since notable attempts to solve it seem to be unsuccessful. I don't aim here to suggest that the issue has been closed and that the reasons-first approach has been ultimately shown to be mistaken. Indeed, we have not even examined all the possible proposals to deal with the wrong kind of reasons problem. The debate is still on-going. However, the suggestion that I would like to make here is that in the light of the present situation of the debate, it is still worthwhile to explore alternative, non-reasons-first accounts of normative reasons. Again, finding a successful reductive account of reasons would be enough by itself to put the reasons-first approach on hold. We now turn to exploring the prospects for this task.

CHAPTER 2

The Reasoning View

2.1 Varieties of Reasoning Views

According to a popular view about normative reasons, they can be explained in terms of good reasoning. The idea here is, roughly, that if we are going to give a reductionist account of what normative reasons are, we should look into what reasons do. And what they do is, mainly, to figure as premises in reasoning; not any sort of reasoning, though. If they are normative, and hence speak in favour of some F-ing for us, then they have to figure in reasoning that satisfies some standards – in short, reasoning that can, everything else being equal, steer us towards doing the right thing/having the right attitude. In what follows, I propose to explore this view in some detail, look at its most popular versions, rehearse the most popular arguments in its favour, and focus on a number of worries that this view seems to prompt. This section introduces the view in general and some of its more specific versions.

Imagine that the only way for you to enjoy watching the first episode of the new season of your favourite TV show with your friends tonight is for you to arrive at your friend's place by 7:00 p.m. Imagine that your practical deliberation in this situation contains the following steps: you intend to be at your friend's place by 7:00 p.m., you know that the only way for you to be there by 7:00 p.m. is to catch the 6:30 p.m. bus, you intend to catch the 6:30 p.m. bus. Given the background assumptions in place, it seems perfectly natural to describe the consideration that the only way for you to be at your friend's place by 7:00 p.m. is to catch the 6:30 p.m. bus as your reason for intending to catch the 6:30 p.m. bus – that is, to describe it as your reason in the motivating reasons sense. For it is a consideration on the basis of which you intend to catch the 6:30 p.m. bus. You rely on it in your deliberation. Crucially, however, this consideration is not merely your motivating reason in this situation. It is quite natural to see it equally as a normative reason for you to intend to catch the bus. If anything, it is a consideration that, given the relevant background, can make you immune to a reasonable informed criticism for intending to catch the 6:30 p.m. bus. For instance, it would appear inappropriate or unreasonable for a well-informed colleague of yours to criticise you for intending to catch the 6:30 p.m. bus. Insofar as she knows that you intend to be at your friend's place by 7:00 p.m. and that the only way for you to be there on time is to catch the 6:30 p.m. bus, her criticism of your intention to catch the 6:30 p.m. bus would appear groundless. For instance, she cannot reasonably claim that your intention is baseless. Moreover, one might think that there is something more than mere immunity to reasonable criticism. One might think that your intention to catch the 6:30 p.m. bus is perfectly rational and that it is rational in virtue of it being based on the consideration about the 6:30 p.m. bus being the only way to be on time (plus the relevant background details). Furthermore, perhaps, this property of rationality of your intention makes it the case that intending so is also what you ought to do (at least in the so-called deliberative sense of 'ought'). In sum, this consideration about the 6:30 p.m. bus being the only way to arrive on time at your friend's place is not merely a basis for your intention; it has some normative force and import for you, however exactly we may spell it out. Whatever else we can say about the situation, it seems difficult to deny that there is a normative reason for you to intend to catch the 6:30 p.m. bus and that that reason is exactly the same consideration that figures crucially in your practical deliberation, a consideration on the basis of which you intend; in other terms, it is also your motivating reason.

If one accepts the apparently natural idea that in a number of ordinary cases, like the bus case, a normative reason corresponds to one's motivating reason and, in particular, to a consideration that plays a role in one's deliberation, one may be tempted by a very natural, or so it seems, further claim – namely, the view that normative reasons are just a subset of motivating reasons or, at any rate, a subset of considerations that can play a role in deliberation. It is a naturally tempting view given its incredible simplicity (no need for genuinely different sorts of reasons), its naturalistic flavour, and its straightforward explanation of the link that many think of as a crucial constraint on any theory of reasons, namely the link between motivating and normative reasons (more on this ahead).

The Reasoning view of reasons takes this line of thought seriously and attempts to work it out by filling in the details and exploring its implications. We can capture this idea in its most general form with the following schema:

> A consideration r (on many accounts, a fact) is a normative reason for S to F just in case r is a content of a premise-response (along with other possible premise-responses) in S's possible good/sound reasoning towards F-ing

(i.e. conclusion-response). (cf. Williams 1979, 1989, 2001; Velleman 1999; Hieronymi 2005, 2013 (on some interpretations); Setiya 2007, 2014; McHugh and Way 2016; Silverstein 2016; Asarnow 2017; Way 2017)

We can then introduce the Reasoning view as a proposal that takes the apparently intuitive claim that normative reasons have to be available as motivating reasons, and then provides us with a recipe for how exactly to specify which subset of motivating reasons (or possible motivating reasons/ considerations that play a role in one's deliberation) are normative reasons. More specifically, according to the Reasoning view, normative reasons are those potential or actual motivating reasons that correspond to appropriate premises in good patterns of reasoning that S can undertake to F-ing (given the relevant background). In our case, the fact that catching the 6.30 p.m. bus is the only way for you to make it on time to your friend's place corresponds to a premise in a pattern of good/sound reasoning from this premise (and the relevant other premises) to the F-ing (or, intending to F). In sum, there are two elements in the Reasoning view that are appealed to in order to define normative reasons: reasoning and soundness/goodness/ norms of reasoning. The former is a descriptive element, the latter a normative element. Thus the general thought underlying the Reasoning approach can be captured as follows: 'If reasons in general are consider- ations that figure in reasoning, normative reasons are considerations that figure in sound reasoning' (Silverstein 2016: 2).

Now, there are a number of versions of the Reasoning view, some of them more elaborated than others. Typically, the 'first generation' modern versions of the Reasoning view are programmatic and have a number of implicit assumptions and underdeveloped aspects. I suggest classifying Williams (1979, 1989, 2001), Raz (1999), Harman (1986), Velleman (1999), and Grice (2001) as instances of this 'first generation Reasoning view'. Proposals in Hieronymi (2005) and Alvarez (2010: 42) come very close to the general idea of the Reasoning view but may be open to a different interpretation, though. See Section 2.2 for an in-depth overview of the literature and exegetical comments.

The situation is different with respect to more recent variants of the Reasoning approach or what we may call a 'second generation' of Reasoning views. Recently some authors have gone into considerable detail in elaborating the view, considering the problems for some of its versions, and proposing positive arguments in its favour. Among the main recent ('second generation') defences of the Reasoning view are Setiya (2007, 2014), Asarnow (2017), Silverstein (2016), Way (2017), and McHugh and Way (2016). If we assume a relaxed sense of 'reasoning' then, arguably, Gregory (2016), which claims that normative reasons are good bases, would also count as a version of the Reasoning view. Let me conclude this introductory section by merely putting on the table some of their views without going much into the details of their proposals. We will return to some of the relevant details of their proposals throughout this chapter when we examine the pros and cons of the Reasoning view more systematically.

In his 2007 book, Kieran Setiya proposes the following version of the Reasoning view (which he develops further in Setiya 2014):

> Reasons: The fact that p is a reason for A to ϕ just in case A has a collection of psychological states, C, such that the disposition to be moved to ϕ by C-and-the-belief-that-p is a good disposition of practical thought, and C contains no false beliefs. (Setiya 2007: 12)

A central element of his approach is to specify the goodness/soundness aspect of good reasoning in terms of good dispositions of practical thought (the focus is more specifically on reasons for action).

A different way of precisifying the exact nature of the goodness/soundness aspect in the general Reasoning approach has been recently undertaken by Conor McHugh and Jonathan Way (see, in particular, McHugh and Way 2016; see also Way 2017 for relevant details). According to them, the goodness/soundness aspect is explained in terms of fittingness (or correctness, appropriateness, rightness):

> For that p to be a reason for a response is for that p to be a premise of a good pattern of reasoning from fitting responses to that response. (McHugh and Way 2016: 586; compare to Way 2017: 254)

On their view, reasoning is understood quite broadly, to include any passage from some mental attitude (premise-response, in their terminology) to another attitude or action (conclusion-response) where the latter is held on the basis of the former.[1] On their view, good reasoning will be defined, roughly, in terms of fittingness preservation. And the qualification of 'from fitting[/correct] responses' in their account is supposed to appeal to a general requirement covering not only the requirement of having (or potential having) true beliefs but also fitting non-doxastic states (including fitting/appropriate intentions, perceptual states, and others). This

---

[1] 'Here, reasoning is understood broadly, as a certain kind of transition in which a set of responses, which we can call premise responses, leads to some (further) response, which we can call the conclusion response. This transition is such that the conclusion response counts as based on, or held in the light of, the premise responses' (McHugh and Way 2016: 586).

constraint ensures that considerations towards clearly and radically immoral acts are not recognised by the Reasoning view as normative reasons. Consider, say, a villain who strongly desires to terminate human life on Earth. Assume that the only way to terminate any human life on Earth is by initiating a global nuclear war. Now, there is a pattern of reasoning that contains the villain's desire and his true belief about the nuclear war being the only way to terminate human life on Earth as premise-responses and initiation of a global nuclear war as the conclusion-response. This pattern of reasoning is in a sense 'good'; it is valid in the intuitive sense introduced earlier: if premises are appropriate/fitting, so is the conclusion. But that the way to terminate human life on Earth is by initiating a global nuclear war is clearly not a reason for anyone to initiate a global nuclear war. That it is not a normative reason is ensured by the soundness condition (not the validity condition), and this soundness condition is explicated in McHugh and Way's account in terms of having fitting premise-responses (all the actual or potential premise-responses have to be fitting). The particularity of their approach is that they take fittingness to be fundamental and a prime normative property that they don't define in further terms (another defence of the fittingness first approach is Chappell 2012). Silverstein (2016) assumes Way's (2017) version of the Reasoning view and provides a further defence of the view.

Asarnow specifies his version of the Reasoning view by appeal to norms of practical reasoning together with a soundness condition (incorporating an anti-defeat condition) on possible premises of the patterns of reasoning. What exactly are the norms of practical reasoning is left undefined in his account. However, he does point to some uncontroversial examples of such norms – for example, the *modus ponens* rule. His recent statement of the view is as follows:

> REASONING VIEW* A normative reason for A to φ is a set of facts, F, such that the norms of practical reasoning endorse the transition from a set including beliefs with those facts as their contents and (optionally) one or more elements of A's practical standpoint, to A's intention that A φ, and there are no defeaters for that transition. (Asarnow 2017: 626)[2]

It may be useful to note that Asarnow separates the goodness condition of reasoning from what he calls the 'soundness condition'. Roughly, the soundness condition ensures that only true beliefs (or more generally states

---

[2] A version of the Reasoning view that is more specifically attentive to the possibility of non-belief states providing reasons is proposed by Asarnow (2016: 174), in the following terms: 'RV NORMATIVE REASONS. A normative reason for A to φ is a set of facts, F, such that the norms of

corresponding to facts) can be reasons. Asarnow's formulation doesn't include an appeal to the fittingness of [potential] premise-responses, contrary to McHugh and Way's formulation. How then does his view block considerations towards immoral acts from counting as reasons in cases where these considerations can play a premise role in valid reasoning? The trick is accomplished here by the anti-defeat clause and an assumption that strict moral requirements can play the role of defeaters: 'While the norms of reasoning endorse the transition from Caligula's desire to have pleasure and his belief that harming innocents will bring him pleasure to the intention that he perform that violent act, the fact that the violent act is morally forbidden is a defeater for that piece of reasoning' (Asarnow 2016: 628). Note that moral requirements are not the only thing that can play the defeater role in Asarnow's theory. He thinks that another category of potential defeaters comes from 'an agent's especially strong or especially deeply held volitional commitments' (Asarnow 2017: 627).

Let me stress that a common feature of these views is that they consider a pattern of good reasoning/disposition of [practical] thought as a sort of abstract entity (cf. Asarnow 2017: 616). A subject is not required to have *all* the relevant premise-responses (to use McHugh and Way's terminology), let alone actually undergo a concrete piece of reasoning in order for there to be a reason for her. All that is required is only that there is *a* good pattern of reasoning/disposition of [practical] thought and that the agent has some of the relevant states (that constitute premise-responses). It is possible that r is a reason for a subject even if the subject doesn't believe that r. It is only required that there is a possible reasoning from a possible belief that r and some other premise-states to the relevant conclusion-response.

With all these views on the table, let us examine whether we have good arguments for adopting one or another version of the Reasoning approach. Before that, I propose a brief exegetical historical overview of the most influential variants of the 'first generation' of Reasoning views. The section can be skipped without losing anything of substance from the overall argument.

2.2 A Fuller Exegetical Overview of Reasoning Views

The most prominent proponent of the Reasoning view was probably Bernard Williams (cf. Williams 1979, 1989, 2001). His version of the

---

practical reasoning endorse the transition from a set of possible mental states, M, the elements of which are appropriately related to the elements of F, to A's intention to ϕ'.

view is somewhat implicit, and it is not entirely clear how exactly his view is supposed to go, but it is closely tied to his famous internalism about reasons, a version of Humeanism according to which reasons are defined partly by appeal to one's motivational set – that is, 'the set of [one's] desires, evaluations, attitudes, projects, and so on' (Williams 1989: 35). He takes reasons to be fundamentally motives. On his account, when '*A* has a reason to φ' is true '*A* has some motive which will be served or furthered by his φ-ing' (Williams 1979: 101). He maintains that any conception of reasons has to respect the constraint according to which we should be able to act on the basis of our normative reasons in order for them to have any normative force. The closest we get to a definition of reasons in Williams is:

> (1) A has a reason to φ only if there is a sound deliberative route from A's subjective motivational set [. . .] to A's φ-ing. (Williams 2001: 91; compare to Williams 1979, 1989)

He is not clear on how exactly we should understand the soundness element in his view of reasons. Actually, he seems to endorse this vagueness and hints towards the idea that the vagueness of his account is a point in its favour. For example: 'It is sometimes held against the combination of the internalist view with this broad conception of deliberation that it leaves us with a vague concept of what an agent has a reason to do. But this is not a disadvantage of the position. It *is* often vague what one has a reason to do' (Williams 1989: 38, original emphasis). He also doesn't seem to conceive of patterns of reasoning/deliberative routes as always corresponding to well-known patterns of reasoning. He maintains that imagining can constitute a sound route of reasoning (Williams 1989: 38), which raises the question of how even to think about the standards of sound reasoning.

Another prominent proponent of the Reasoning view (at least in its general form) is, arguably, Joseph Raz. For some passages in Joseph Raz's work – in particular, in his earlier work – may be interpreted as expressing a version of the Reasoning view. Consider, for instance, the following passage:

> (2) Statements of facts which are reasons for the performance of a certain action by a certain agent are the premises of an argument the conclusion of which is that there is reason for the agent to perform the action or that he ought to do it. (Raz 1999: 28, second edition of *Practical Reason and Norms*)

Under the assumption that 'argument' here corresponds to patterns of reasoning, this quotation seems to be in the spirit of the Reasoning view. One may, however, be suspicious about this interpretation, given the absence of the 'soundness' element in this quotation. However, it is not clear that there is no such implicit assumption about the soundness or goodness requirement of the argument in Raz's formulation (see also Raz 1978, *Practical Reasoning*, introduction, where he appears to be more explicit about the truth condition of premises). That is, it is not clear that Raz thinks of normative reasons in mere terms of inferences without any references to good or sound inferences. Raz does mention the validity aspect of a practical inference and holds that it is an important aspect. Once this validity aspect of inferences is recognised, it is only a small step from there to recognition that some inferences are sound. Soundness is understood in the usual way as validity plus truth of premises in the case of theoretical inferences and, perhaps, appropriateness/fittingness plus satisfactoriness in the case of practical inferences (see Kenny 1966). Indeed Raz thinks that the appeal to valid inferences is an advantage of his account. For instance, he writes:

> (3) One welcome result of this approach is that practical inferences are defeasible, that is, the addition of further premises can turn a valid argument into an invalid one. (Raz 1999: 29)

And Raz does maintain that he understands practical inferences as inferences that conform to the logic of satisfactoriness as it appears, for instance, in Kenny (1966) (where, roughly, satisfactoriness is to practical reasoning what validity is to theoretical reasoning; cf. Raz 1999: 207, fn 7). Hence, it is not that unreasonable to classify at least early Raz as a proponent of the Reasoning view.

Something like the Reasoning view also seems to be accepted by Gilbert Harman in his *Change in view* (1986). For instance:

> (4) To say that a consideration C is a reason to do D is, I suggest, to say that C is a consideration that has or ought to have some influence on reasoning, leading to a decision to do D unless this is overruled by other considerations. The consideration C might be an end or a belief one has, or it might be some line of thought which one finds or would find attractive or persuasive on reflection, for example, an argument of some sort. (Harman 1986: 129–130)

An appeal to the idea that reasons have to be connected to reasoning is also present in Grice's work. For instance:

> (5) Reasons (justificatory) are the stuff of which reasoning is made, and reasoning may be required to arrive (in some cases) even at the simplest of reasons; so it seemed proper to proceed from a consideration of reasoning to a consideration of reasons. (Grice 2001: 67)

'Justificatory' reasons seem to correspond to what we refer to as 'normative' reasons.

The Reasoning view or something quite close to it is also endorsed by David Velleman (1999). His version of the Reasoning view is to be understood in accordance with his specific account of practical reasoning and within his wider philosophical project, which we are, unfortunately, in no position to fully rehearse here. According to Velleman:

> (6) The reasons for an action are things represented in premises from which intending or performing the action would follow as a conclusion in accordance with practical reasoning. (Velleman 1999: 198)

This following as a conclusion is understood as '[enhancing] the agent's self-knowledge by satisfying some self-conception' (cf. Velleman 1999: 198). This, then, provides the basis for the official definition of reasons on Velleman's account as follows:

> (7) [R]easons for an action are those things belief in which, on the agent's part, would put him in a position to enhance his self-knowledge, in this distinctively practical way, by intending or performing that action. (Velleman 1999: 198, original emphasis removed)

One particularity of Velleman's account is that, contrary to much of the current orthodoxy, he allows for false beliefs to be reasons (cf. Velleman 1999: 200). However, he qualifies this contention by insisting that in the case of false beliefs, their falsity speaks against them and against acting on them: 'their falsity is a reason for abandoning them and hence also a reason against acting on them in their capacity as reasons' (Velleman 1999: 200, fn 9). Presumably this move and the link between reasons and an agent's enhancing her self-knowledge in practical reasoning is enough to satisfy the 'soundness/goodness' aspect within the general form of the Reasoning view according to which reasons are premises in good/sound reasoning. However, a more complete exegesis of Velleman's view would be necessary to establish this classification of his view within the camp of the Reasoning view with any degree of certainty.

It is sometimes claimed that Pamela Hieronymi is another prominent proponent of the Reasoning view (for instance, in Silverstein 2016; Way 2017; Whiting 2018). However, it is not entirely clear that Hieronymi subscribes to the Reasoning view as it has been introduced here. Certainly, some passages may be reasonably interpreted as committing Hieronymi to something close enough to the Reasoning view. For instance: 'To start reflection, we can note that, most generally, a reason is simply an item in a piece of reasoning' (Hieronymi 2005: 443). However, it is also clear that for Hieronymi a reason is a consideration that bears on a question rather than on F-ing itself. For instance: 'So I suggest, for consideration, the following account of a reason: a reason is a consideration that bears on a question' (Hieronymi 2005: 443). And: 'This account differs from the original formulation in taking the fundamental relation in which a consideration becomes a reason to be a relation to a question, rather than to an action or attitude' (Hieronymi 2005: 443). Nevertheless, it is not unreasonable to see Hieronymi as a proponent of a version of the Reasoning view, in particular given her comment on her view, where she doesn't seem to make a difference between bearing on a question and bearing on a conclusion: 'One could say, "a consideration that bears on a conclusion." I do not think there would be any relevant difference, though I find the idea of answering a question more intuitive for capturing the activities of rational agents' (Hieronymi 2005: 443). For now, we can tentatively classify Hieronymi's view as a version of the Reasoning view. But we will come back to Hieronymi's view shortly, when elaborating our positive proposal, since, as we will observe, it contains another crucial insight for our view beyond its focus on reasoning.

One might also think that something close to a version of the Reasoning view is presupposed in Maria Alvarez's argument in favour of propositionality and factivity of all reasons (though she doesn't appeal to validity or soundness):

> (8) A better reason for arguing that the most perspicuous way of expressing reasons is propositionally is that reasons must be capable of being premises, i.e. things we reason, or draw conclusions, from, whether in theoretical or in practical reasoning. Otherwise, the connection between reasons and reasoning would be lost. (Alvarez 2010: 42)[3]

However, we lack sufficient grounds for ascribing a full-blooded endorsement of the Reasoning view to Alvarez.

If it can be reasonably held that (most of) the abovementioned views are versions of the Reasoning view (e.g. the 'first generation Reasoning view'), it can nevertheless also be recognised that they are not really elaborated in detail. They appeal to the general idea of explaining normative reasons in terms of some norms or value of reasoning (e.g. sound/good patterns), but they don't spend much time working out the details of how exactly the view works. Also, they are a bit shy on giving positive arguments in favour of the view. Rather, the impression is that they are happy with putting this view on the table and working out its implications for their further

---

[3] See, for the factivity part: 'My view is that all facts are indeed reasons merely by virtue of being potential premises in (theoretical or practical) reasoning' (Alvarez 2010: 42).

theoretical views, which *can* be taken as a case in favour of the Reasoning view, if successful. Moreover, they don't appear to spend much time considering possible shortcomings of the Reasoning view and how to address them.

2.3 Arguments in Favour of the Reasoning View

Given the state of the debate about the Reasoning view, it is not always obvious how to extract positive arguments in its favour. On some occasions (in particular, in the context of what I have called the 'first generation' of the Reasoning view; see Section 2.2), the Reasoning view appears to be merely endorsed, taken as obvious, and considered to be in no need of further theoretical defence. Nevertheless, a number of more elaborated positive lines of thought can also be found (in particular, within the context of the 'second generation' Reasoning view). As far as I can see, there are five general lines of argument in favour of the Reasoning approach within contemporary debates. (Some of these are so closely related that it would not be unreasonable, however, to lump them together.) Let us look at them briefly.

First, as Jonathan Way (2017) observes, it is a valuable feature of any view of normative reasons if it is general enough to be applicable to normative reasons of *all* varieties. Arguably, there are normative reasons not only to act or intend but also for attitudes – for example, beliefs, emotions. The Reasoning view is perfectly adapted to account for this and hence to have the necessary level of generality. As long as there is a good pattern of reasoning (understood broadly enough to count emotional attitudes – for example, fear, anger, pride, as conclusion-responses) towards the relevant conclusion-response (and the other relevant conditions obtain), there can be normative reasons for the conclusion-response in question. Thus, the fact that the Reasoning view can deal with reasons of various sorts speaks in its favour.

Second, the Reasoning view not only seems to correctly predict and explain what things can have normative reasons but also accurately predicts for what kinds of things there cannot be reasons. In this manner, for instance, the Reasoning view can explain why there are no reasons for values. This point is again observed by Way (2017), who suggests that given the Reasoning view we can easily explain why there are no reasons for, say, having green hair, being tall, being healthy (as distinct from eating healthy food), and perceiving so and so. These are things towards which there cannot be any reasoning. Hence, there cannot be good patterns of reasoning towards having green hair, being healthy, perceiving red, and so on. The Reasoning view has the right degree of discrimination: it excludes precisely the things we intuitively don't want to count as being reasons-sensitive.

Third, as many proponents of the Reasoning view observe, it is also well placed to explain the pre-theoretical thought that reasons to F have to be somehow connected to reasoning and to reasons for F-ing (motivating reasons). Indeed, many think that it is a platitude that reasons are what reasoning is made of (cf. Grice 2001: 67). The Reasoning view has a straightforward explanation for this. Other views arguably struggle to explain it in simple terms (this observation is strongly connected to the next point). Now, if one takes on board a further somewhat natural assumption that all motivating reasons (reasons *for* which we F) are pre-mises in our reasoning (assuming again that reasoning is broadly construed to include all kinds of relevant transitions towards F-ings), the Reasoning view has again a simple and powerful story about how and why normative reasons are connected to motivating reasons. Reasons, normative or moti-vating, just are premises in patterns of reasoning. And in the normative case, they are appropriate premises in good/sound patterns of reasoning.

Fourth, and probably the most popular line of argument in favour of the Reasoning view, is a comparative argument. Strictly speaking, the observed points can be also understood as boiling down to comparison to other views. Hence, the lines between these five points are not really strict; it is more about dialectical accents and framing. Let me give three examples here that illustrate the comparative argument.

Pamela Hieronymi (2005), for instance, thinks that the Reasoning view (or at least something similar to it; see Section 2.2) is clearly better off than the reasons-first approach with respect to the so-called wrong kind of reasons problem (see Section 1.4). In fact, according to Hieronymi, there is not really a problem for the Reasoning view. Roughly put, proponents of the reasons-first approach cannot satisfactorily explain why, say, a demon's threat is not a normative reason for the demon's victim to admire it, despite clearly counting in favour of one admiring it, given the demon's threat to punish one severely for non-compliance with the order to admire. Proponents of the Reasoning view have tools to explain this sort of case: the threat from the demon is not a reason to admire, since it cannot be a premise in a good piece of reasoning to admiration, but we can still account for the counting in favour intuition in such cases, since the threat can figure in a premise of good reasoning not towards admiration but, say, towards attempting or wanting to admire the demon. According to this line of thought, the Reasoning view is to be preferred to the reasons-first approach (which is not, of course, to say that it is winning against all of its possible alternatives). Note also that the objection against the reasons-first approach according to which their distinction between the 'wrong' and 'right kind' of reasons to admire is ad hoc or self-contradictory doesn't apply to the Reasoning view (see Section 1.4). The Reasoning view is not presupposing that reasons are prime or fundamental; it does provide a theory of reasons and hence can legitimately propose substantial distinctions among kinds of reasons, contrary to views that consider reasons as undefinable.

For Kieran Setiya (2014), the best arguments in favour of the Reasoning view rely on its comparison to other views. One line of thought here is that if we assume that reasons are somehow connected to rationality, a theory of reasons has to explain that link. According to Setiya, the Reasoning view does better on this account than its competitors (by connecting rationality to good reasoning dispositions and by defining reasons in terms of good patterns of reasoning). However, notice that similar to the abovementioned point, Setiya also gives at best only the beginning of a full positive argument here. He compares the Reasoning view only to some of its competitors on this topic. He shows that views that connect reasons to the way a rational or virtuous (exemplary) person would be moved to act in a situation have shortcomings in cases of non-virtuous agents who still can have normative reasons to act in certain ways in which virtuous agents would not be moved to act. And Setiya does suggest that a possible improvement on that view – namely, the ideal adviser model, where the focus is on an idealised and fully rational version of oneself as an adviser for the current situation in which one finds oneself (cf. Smith 1994, 1995), is still unsatisfactory compared to the Reasoning view. However, one might worry that these views, which seem to lack the appropriate degree of abstraction from actual agents to capture the nature of normative reasons, are not the only competitors with respect to the explanation of the connection between reasons and rationality. For instance, some reasons-first approaches might claim to be able to account for the reasons–rationality connection by appeal to the possession condition of reasons or the perspective dependence of reasons (for a recent version of this strategy, see Lord 2017 and Kiesewetter 2017, 2018). Arguably these other alternatives will not have the same problems as the abovementioned views (e.g. the 'example' and the 'ideal adviser' models). More work is probably needed in order for this line of thought to gain real traction against all the Reasoning view's competitors.

According to Samuel Asarnow (cf. Asarnow 2016, 2017), we have to accept Rational Internalism, the view that connects normative reasons to motivating reasons (e.g. normative reasons have to be able to be motivating reasons) on the basis of a roughly Davidsonian idea of rationalisation, rather than on the basis of Setiya's (2007, 2014) internal dispositionalism (see also Gibbons 2013). According to Asarnow, Rational Internalism provides an argument against Objectivism about normative reasons (cf. Broome 2013). Now, the consideration that speaks in favour of the Reasoning view, according to Asarnow, is that it provides an attractive alternative to those who are sympathetic to Objectivism, since it allows for objective values (where the existence of objective values was, according to Asarnow, a central motivation in favour of Objectivism about reasons). Whatever the merits of this sophisticated argument, it is, again, a comparative argument that relies on some substantive assumptions but also suggests that accepting the Reasoning view brings in some unexpected advantages over Objectivism about reasons (e.g. reasons as facts about oughts) and over hardcore internalism (e.g. reasons as one's psychological states).

The fifth line of argument explores the idea that the Reasoning view enables a simple reductive story where normative is reduced to descriptive. One version of such an argument appears in Silverstein (2016). A central task of that paper is to elaborate in detail an account of soundness or goodness of reasoning. A central assumption there is that reasoning has to have not only a merely formal aim but also a substantive aim and that such a substantive aim can be put in descriptive terms. If he is right, giving grounds for such a reductionist approach is another advantage of the Reasoning view, compared to other alternatives that sometimes struggle to provide a clear and straightforward story on this account. But again, the argument has a limited scope, since it is not absolutely evident that all the possible alternatives will be ruled out here.

In this section, we have looked at five existing lines of defence of the Reasoning view. The rest of this chapter is concerned with its potential shortcomings.

2.4 First Set of Worries I: Outweighing and Weight

As we have seen earlier, the Reasoning view enjoys some initial plausibility. However, on reflection, it has also some puzzling aspects. Let us start with worries that are already well-known (in Sections 2.4 and 2.5 in particular) before turning to some new problems (in Sections 2.6).

There are, as far as I can see, two general lines of prima facie problems for the Reasoning view within the literature. The first one arises from the observation that not all acts or attitudes that are recommended by reasons always correspond to outputs of a good pattern of reasoning. Some reasons are outweighed and yet remain normative. This is the problem of so-called outweighed reasons. The second worry arises from the observation that good patterns of reasoning can contain among their premises statements of mere enabling conditions for F-ing. And yet it doesn't feel always right to consider mere enabling conditions as genuine normative reasons to F. Let us look at the details of these worries a bit more attentively and review some of the most influential existing responses to these worries. This section is devoted to the former worry (outweighed reasons), while the next one focuses on the latter worry (enabling conditions).

To begin with, let us first clarify certain aspects of the Reasoning view a bit more. The general idea of the Reasoning view, as we saw earlier, is that there are good/sound patterns of reasoning (which presumably mirror patterns of good/sound arguments) and normative reasons are premises of such patterns. Let us start with the general version of the view. Recall:

> **The Reasoning view (general, rough)** A consideration r (on many accounts, a fact) is a normative reason for S to F just in case r is a content of a premise-response (along with other possible premise-responses) in S's possible good/sound reasoning towards F-ing (i.e. conclusion-response).

How should we understand what is meant by 'good reasoning' here? Variations of the view exist in this respect. However, on a very general level of abstraction, everyone agrees that reasoning is, roughly, a transition from some mental states to others, where the arrival state (i.e. the state at which one arrives through such a transition) is held on the basis of the initial state/s. That is, it is not a *mere* transition, where one happens to transit, say, randomly or in a purely mechanical way, from one state to another. There has to be some more substantive link between the arrival state and the initial state. And this required link can be, for the time being, described roughly as 'basing' – holding one state on the basis of or in virtue of the other one.

Reasoning so conceived can be evaluated. Some such transitions are appropriate, while others are clearly not. Jumping to a conclusion via purely fearful or wishful reasoning is not appropriate. Say, jumping to the conclusion that you will be able to meet a short deadline for submitting a new project, when you know that there is a massive past record of your failure to meet deadlines that speaks against you having such an ability, is inappropriate. The fact that you very much want to meet the deadline doesn't make your reasoning any better in such a situation. On the other hand, the reasoning that originates in your intention to have a party at your place together with your belief that the only way to have that party is to invite some friends, and that terminates in your intention to invite/ invitation of some friends, appears to be an appropriate piece of reasoning.

Pieces of reasoning correspond to patterns of reasoning (we can think of them as abstract entity). Some patterns are good/sound, while others are not. Say, a pattern of reasoning that mimics a *modus ponens* argumentative structure and has the appropriate initial states is clearly good. And a pattern of reasoning that mimics the Affirming the Consequent argumentative structure is clearly not good. We will return to this in a moment. For now, let us only focus on the claim to which all proponents of the Reasoning view are committed, namely that normative reasons are premises (or contents of initial mental states/premise-responses) in good patterns of reasoning. So, on the Reasoning view, if r is a normative reason for a subject S to F, then there has to be some good pattern of reasoning for S from some premise-responses (initial mental states), where one of these premise-responses has r as a content towards F-ing/intending to F. S is not required to have all the relevant premise-responses (for instance, S may not even believe that r), but S has to have at least some of the relevant premise-responses. Maybe I only have the intention to have a party but haven't yet realised that the only way to have a party is to invite friends. The Reasoning view predicts, plausibly, that the fact that the only way for me to organise the party is to invite some friends is a reason for me to (intend to) invite some friends. In this case, all that is required is that there is a good pattern of reasoning along the following lines: intention to G, belief that the only way to G is to F, (intention to) F. Even if I do not undergo any concrete piece of reasoning, the mere fact that there is such a pattern of good reasoning from some of my mental states (premise-responses) to the relevant F-ing is enough for r to be a normative reason for me to F in case where r is a content of one of these actual or some merely possible premise-responses of mine.

Now, the problem of outweighed reasons arises from the simple observation that a pattern of reasoning is either good or bad; that is, it either complies or doesn't comply with the standards of reasoning/argument. And a consideration either is or is not a content of the premise-response (possible or actual mental state) of a good pattern of reasoning. However, given standard assumptions, some patterns of reasoning will be classified as bad even though we might have a strong inclination to see one or more of the considerations in the premise-responses as normative reasons. To make the objection a bit more concrete, consider the following version of a classical example (the original example goes back to Ross 1930: 18). You have promised to meet your friend for a coffee today. On your way to the coffee shop, you witness a traffic accident. As it happens, you are the only witness and some of the people involved in the accident are severely injured. Suppose you undergo reasoning (indeed, it may be almost instantaneous) that concludes in (an intention to) call the ambulance and help the injured. Now, you did the right thing, no doubt about that. Everyone agrees that there is no all-things-considered ought for you to leave the injured and go to see your friend instead. There is no *sufficient* reason for you to go on to your meeting with your friend. However, it is nevertheless natural to think that there is still *a* reason for you to go to see your friend. That you promised to meet your friend over a coffee is still something that counts in an intuitive sense in favour of going to meet your friend. This promise still exercises some normative force upon you. Of course, everyone agrees that it is a massively outweighed reason in the circumstances of the accident, but it seems to be a reason nonetheless. One popular way to further motivate this observation is to appeal to the fact that if it were not a reason for you to go to meet your friend, it would be difficult to explain the fact that it is appropriate for your friend to be somewhat annoyed with you for not showing up. It seems that the sensible thing for you to do would be to excuse yourself later or at least to explain him why you didn't show up (we are assuming here that helping the injured in the accident necessarily entails that your will miss your coffee break). Moreover, if your promise (and additional considerations, such as the desire to meet your friend) is not a reason to go on, then we have a hard time explaining why it appears OK for you to feel slight regret at missing the coffee break.

The problem of outweighed reasons is that the Reasoning view, in its simple form (given some further standard background assumptions), entails that there is no normative reason for you to go to meet your friend in the circumstances of the accident. That is, there is not the *slightest* reason, according to the general Reasoning view, not even a tiny one. This is so because there is no good pattern of reasoning for you in this case (given your beliefs, desires, intentions, and other states) towards going to meet your friend. More precisely, there is no good pattern of reasoning given some standard assumptions about good patterns of reasoning. The pattern that corresponds to our accident case is, roughly, the following: intention to respect a promise to meet a friend for a coffee, belief that the only way of respecting the promise is to go to the coffee shop (the meeting place), intention to help the heavily injured persons in an accident, belief that the only way to help them is to stay and call the ambulance (which entails not going to the coffee shop), intention to go to the coffee shop. The presence of the intention to help and the belief that the only way to help is to stay and call the ambulance is what 'makes' the pattern of reasoning bad, according to this line of objection. These elements undermine, so to speak, the reasoning from the initial premise-responses of intention to respect the promise and belief that the only way to respect the promise is to go to the coffee shop, to the conclusion-response of going to the coffee shop. These additional elements (intention to help the injured and the belief that the only way to help is to stay and call the ambulance) function as defeaters of the goodness of reasoning. We can represent the pattern of reasoning in this case more schematically as a transition from initial states (premise-responses) intention to F, belief that P-ing is the only way to F, intention to G, belief that Z-ing (entailing not-P-ing) is the only way to G, to the conclusion-response of P-ing. The fact that the agent has the intention to G and the belief that Z-ing is the only way to G *in addition* to the intention to F and belief that P-ing is the only way to F is what makes arriving at the conclusion-response of P-ing because of the given premise-responses inappropriate (given the assumption that good patterns of reasoning cannot be undermined by additional defeating elements). Hence, the Reasoning view in its general form (plus standard assumptions) appears to predict that the consideration that the only way for you to respect your promise is to go to the coffee shop cannot be a normative reason for you to go to the coffee shop. There seems to be no good pattern of reasoning for you that has this consideration as a content of one of your premise-responses to the conclusion-response of going to the coffee shop. Being a premise of a good pattern of reasoning is categorical. There are no degrees of being a premise of a good pattern of reasoning. Thus, the Reasoning view appears to predict a counterintuitive conclusion. For, as we observed above, that the only way for you to respect your promise is to go to the coffee shop is a normative reason for you to go to the coffee shop. It is a reason, even if it is clearly not a sufficient reason. And this presents a problem that cannot be easily dismissed, since our ordinary lives are over-packed with all sorts of outweighed reasons. Arguably, every situation where one faces a non-trivial choice (and that is not a situation of a genuine dilemma) is a situation with at least one outweighed reason. A view that predicts that there cannot be outweighed reasons is problematic.

I follow Way (2017) in classifying the possible replies from the proponents of the Reasoning view to this problem in two camps. On one side, there are those who revise the view (the definition in the Reasoning View) in ways that are supposed to allow for outweighed reasons. On the other side, there are those who revise some of the background assumptions concerning patterns of good reasoning. Let us look briefly at both of these lines of reply.

The first line of reply proposes to specify the general version of the Reasoning view by qualifying its domain of application. Several specific ways of doing this exist. According to one influential approach (cf. Williams 2001; see also Williams 1979, 1989), in order for one to have a normative reason to F, one has to have some motivational set S (e.g. desires, emotions, and so on) such that there is for one a sound deliberative route from S together with a true belief that p to F-ing. According to one interpretation of Williams's view (see Way 2017), what Williams really meant is that the sound deliberative route ends in one being motivated to F, rather than F-ing *tout court*, where F stands for some action. Such an interpretation is indeed supported by textual evidence. Consider the following:

> This does not mean that when an agent has a thought of the form 'that is a reason for me to ϕ', he really has, or should really have, the thought 'that is a reason for me to ϕ *in virtue of my S*'. The disposition that forms part of his S just is the disposition to have thoughts of the form 'that is a reason for me to ϕ', and to act on them. (Williams 2001: 93)

Assuming that disposition to act on a consideration amounts to being motivated to act by it, Way's interpretation of Williams may indeed bear out. An even clearer case for attributing this interpretation of the Reasoning view to Williams can be found in the following passage:

> There is indeed a vagueness about '*A* has reason to ϕ', in the internal sense, insofar as the deliberative processes which could lead from *A*'s present S to his being motivated to ϕ may be more or less ambitiously conceived. But this is no embarrassment to those who take as basic the internal conception of reasons for action. (Williams 1981: 110)

Now, even if Williams is not explicitly committed to it, one might think that this would be a natural way for a proponent of Williams's account to develop such a view in further detail. It makes sense to go in this direction in particular given the context of the debate in which Williams's account takes part. His opponents are, of course, externalists about reasons, like Scanlon (1998), who do not want to postulate a necessary or essential link between one's motivation set and normative reasons. But Williams also opposes some other views within the broad family of Humean approaches (of which Williams's proposal is a part). For instance, Williams rejects the ideal reasoner models. He doesn't endorse Smith's account, which is committed to classifying desires to F as outputs of the relevant pieces of practical reasoning by one's idealised counterpart. Thus, we may think that on a charitable interpretation of Williams's view reasons are considerations that play a role in a sound deliberative route – good reasoning, broadly understood from one's desires and other states to being motivated to F rather than to F-ing. If so, the objection from outweighed reasons might be blocked as long as we think of being motivated as coming in degrees.

A more detailed version of this line of reply to the objection has been recently developed by Kieran Setiya (2007, 2014). Recall Setiya's account of reasons for action:

> *Reasons*: The fact that p is a reason for A to ϕ just in case A has a collection of psychological states, C, such that the disposition to be moved to ϕ by C-and-the-belief-that-p is a good disposition of practical thought, and C contains no false beliefs. (Setiya 2007: 12, 2014: 222)

On Setiya's view, the relevant element is not a desire (of, say, an idealised and fully informed self), but being moved to F. Arguably, being moved to F and being motivated to F is the same kind of thing. And according to Setiya, this mere fact is enough for his preferred version of the Reasoning view to account for outweighed reasons:

> [T]his principle [that is, 'Reasons' above] is concerned with *pro tanto* reasons, reasons that can be outweighed; accordingly, it speaks of being moved, not of acting or intending. (Setiya 2014: 222)

On the face of it, revising the Reasoning view in such a way allows us to avoid the objection from outweighed reasons. Insofar as motivation, desire, or similar items to which a proponent of the Reasoning view can appeal, come in degrees, there is a possible story to tell about the outweighed reasons. One can claim, following Setiya, for instance, that you have (or there is) both a disposition to be moved to stay and help the injured in the accident (by some of the relevant premise-responses/psychological states) and a disposition to be moved to go and meet your friend (by the relevant premise-responses/states). Both dispositions are good dispositions of practical thought. Hence, the view predicts that the relevant considerations are both normative reasons. The crucial move is to claim that the relative weights of reasons correspond to 'the relative strength of motivation' (Setiya 2014: 229). More specifically:

> Reasons correspond to collections of psychological states that fuel good practical thought. One reason is *stronger* than another just in case it is a

good disposition of practical thought to be *more strongly moved* by the collection of states that corresponds to it, than by the collection that corresponds to the other. (Setiya 2007: 13)

A similar move is also available to theorists who appeal to the desires of an ideal and well-informed self (cf. Smith 1994). On such a view, one (e.g. the ideal self) has a stronger desire to help the injured than to go to the coffee shop. Hence, the relevant considerations (about the accident) outweigh the considerations about respecting the promise to the friend and correspond to a stronger or 'weightier' reason. Yet both remain reasons. On the motivation view: insofar as there is a good disposition to be somewhat moved by the promise consideration, the promise consideration still remains a reason for you to go to meet your friend, even if it is outweighed by the accident consideration, which is stronger since you are more strongly moved to help the injured.

This line of reply, attractive as it may appear, actually raises more problems than it promises to solve. Here are two of the most urgent ones. For one thing, it has trouble in explaining reasons for responses other than action. Take, for instance, reasons to believe. Motivation and belief don't seem to go well together. Normally, we don't have motivation for believing that such and such is the case. Typically, we are not moved to believe, while we are moved to act in some ways. Belief is a state at which we may arrive through reasoning or other belief-producing processes. Normally we don't arrive at a belief that *p* by being moved to believe that *p*. Action and belief appear to be quite different in this respect. Note also that when we do have a motivation to believe something, such a motivation is of a pragmatic sort and hence arguably can be linked only to the 'wrong kind' of reasons. Blaise may well be motivated to believe in God, since he thinks that such a belief will make him better off. But this sort of practical consideration is traditionally not seen as a normative reason for Blaise to believe in God (but see Chapter 6 for more on this). Without varying degrees of motivation to believe, we are thus back to square one. It is not clear how proponents of the Reasoning view who appeal to varying degrees of motivation (or of desire) to explain outweighed reasons to act could account for outweighed reasons to believe, as well as outweighed reasons to have other attitudes (i.e. it doesn't seem clear that we can have motivation to fear, to be angry, and so on, but we have reasons to fear, to be angry, and so on).

Now, one may try to provide even more sophisticated manoeuvres to account for reasons for beliefs and other attitudes. Elaborating on Setiya's account (cf. Setiya 2014), one might think that as we replaced acting by being moved we may also replace believing by having an increased degree of confidence within a more sophisticated Reasoning view. And, according to this line of thought, we might reconcile the Reasoning view with there being outweighed reasons for belief. Alternatively, one might focus on inclinations to believe instead of being moved to believe.

However, critics of such a move remain unconvinced. Consider the case where one is already certain that p (and believes that p). In such cases, no increase in the degree of confidence is possible (and there is no more inclination to believe, for one already believes that p). And yet we might still discover previously unnoticed/new reasons for one to believe that p. That DNA analysis confirms the suspect's presence at the crime scene, that we have witnesses confirming her presence and we know that the suspect had a motive for the crime may convince us, indeed make us certain, that the suspect did it. We believe that she did it. And yet that we find out later that her fingerprints were on the temporarily lost murder weapon can nevertheless constitute another reason for us to believe that she did it, even if it does not incline us to believe that she did it (for we already believe that), nor does it increase our confidence (for we are already certain). It seems that the Reasoning view that appeals to inclinations to believe or degrees of confidence predicts that that there are fingerprints on the weapon cannot be reason for us to believe that the suspect did it.

One could try to get out of trouble by appeal to counterfactual considerations and claim that the relevant consideration only need to incline one to believe or increase one's confidence in some other possible circumstances. This move, however, is a tricky one. As Way notes (cf. Way 2016: 261), it requires, for one, that these other possible circumstances can be specified without appeal to reasons (otherwise, a vicious circularity looms), and it is not clear whether it can be done. For another thing, appeal to counterfactual inclinations to believe and counterfactual increases in degrees of confidence in this dialectical situation presents a risk of committing the conditional fallacy: the relevant changes in circumstances might be such that all other things are not equal and thus the appeal to possible other circumstances in which one is inclined to believe cannot constitute theoretically satisfactory grounds for drawing lessons about what reasons there are for one to believe in the actual circumstances (see Way 2016 for further details and references on these worries). In sum, it is unclear whether proponents of this version of the Reasoning view have any easy and fully satisfactory way of accounting for outweighed reasons to believe and to have other attitudes.

The second problem with this general line of reply is that it is not straightforward that we may be moved to act (or desire to act) in ways recommended by outweighed reasons in situations where the outweighing reason massively outweighs the outweighed reason. Crucially it is not clear that in such cases there is a good disposition of practical thought to be moved to act in ways recommended by the outweighed reason. An objection similar to this one appears in Silverstein (2016).[4] Consider again our example of a promise for a coffee break versus a street accident. Arguably, when you witness the accident and have the relevant premise-responses (e.g. the intention to help, and so on), you are strongly moved to stay and help and not at all moved to go to the coffee shop. Crucially, it is not straightforward that there is a good disposition (or pattern, for that matter) of practical thought in this case from your intention to keep your promise to your friend and the belief that the only way to keep your promise is to walk away to being even the slightest bit moved to walk away. Given this and the abovementioned problem with outweighed reasons for belief, we can tentatively conclude that the move to revise the Reasoning view by focusing on patterns of good reasoning/good dispositions of practical thought that have as their conclusion being moved (or having the desire) to F rather than F-ing (intending to F) are unsuccessful in the light of outweighed reasons.

Given the problems of the revisionary versions of the Reasoning approach, some theorists have turned to an alternative line of reply to the problem of outweighed reasons. Namely, instead of revising the Reasoning view, they propose to rethink some of the background assumptions about patterns of good reasoning (cf. McHugh and Way 2016; Silverstein 2016; Way 2016; Asarnow 2017). The central move here is to reject the idea that good reasoning cannot be defeated; or, put more positively, they suggest that there can be patterns of good reasoning that may be defeasible. According to this line of thought, that reasoning from some premise-responses to a conclusion-response is good doesn't mean that its goodness cannot be undone if other elements were 'added' – namely, if other premise-responses were present. On this view, good

---

[4] I worry there is a more basic problem here, though. Once I realize I can save lives by breaking my promise and leaving you to find your own way home from the airport, I am not moved or motivated to pick you up at all. I recognize that my promise counts in favor of picking you up, but this just does not motivate me in the face of the countervailing considerations. Of course, I may regret that I will not be there to meet you, but I need not feel any motivational tug (or nudge) in the direction of the airport. If that is correct, then it is a mistake to identify the normative force of a reason with the motivation produced by sound deliberation from that reason. (Silverstein 2016: 12)

reasoning is always good reasoning *ceteris paribus*. If other things are not equal, then the reasoning is not good. The core idea is not new. It is a well-known topic in logic and theory of argumentation/reasoning (see Pollock 1986 and Horty 2012 for classical statements). To take a standard example from defeasible logic: one may draw the conclusion (c) that Tweety can fly from the premise (p1) that Tweety is a bird (and some background assumptions, perhaps, that most birds fly). It is an instance of a good inference (even if not classically valid). But it can certainly be defeated; for instance, when another premise is added, say, (p2) that Tweety is a penguin. The idea is often captured by reference to the formal property of consequence relation, known as *monotonicity*. An inference satisfies monotonicity where, roughly, in the case of a valid inference (e.g. where a conclusion follows from the set of premises), adding any other premise to the existing set of premises will not alter the validity of the inference. *Modus ponens*, for instance, is often presented as an inference that satisfies monotonicity: whatever you can add to the set of p, and if p then q, will not undermine the validity of inferring the conclusion q. Proponents of non-monotonicity insist that there can be good or cogent inferences even without such a strong constraint (the term of *cogency* is sometimes used as the equivalent of deductive *validity* in the context of non-deductive inferences).[5] For instance, the Tweety inference (i.e. the inference from p1 to *c*) is good/cogent within the defeasible logic that gives up on the monotonicity requirement for good/cogent inferences. Applying this to the case of outweighed reasons, proponents of the Reasoning view insist that an outweighed consideration, such as the promise consideration in our promise versus accident case, may still count as a reason to leave for the coffee shop. For there is a pattern of good reasoning from your intention to keep your promise to your friend to meet at the coffee shop and your belief that the only way to keep your promise is to leave, to leaving. It is a good pattern, albeit a defeasible one. And in this specific scenario, the reasoning is indeed defeated, since your other premise-responses – namely, your intention to help the injured and your true belief that the only way to help them is to stay – makes the situation such that all other things are not equal. These additional premise-responses undermine the *ceteris paribus* condition. If you were to reason from the promise considerations to an intention to go to the coffee shop, your reasoning in this accident situation would be a bad one – but not because there is no corresponding good

---

[5] Thanks to Aleks Knoks for a helpful discussion on defeasible inferences, and for drawing my attention to the notion of *cogency*.

pattern of reasoning. There is. It's just that moving to the intention to go to the coffee shop, given your promise *and* given further premise-responses in this situation (e.g. your true belief that there is an accident and so on), is not good reasoning.

Now, a question remains: what makes it the case that it is the promise-reasoning that is defeated, rather than the helping-the-injured reasoning? On this view, it has to do with the comparison of the relevant patterns of reasoning. See Way on this:

> [S]uppose R_1 is a good pattern of reasoning which concludes in φ-ing and R_2 is a good pattern of reasoning which concludes in a conflicting conclusion ψ. For R_1 to defeat R_2 is for it to be good reasoning to move from the premise-responses of R_1 to the conclusion-response of R_1, given the premise-responses of R_2, but not good reasoning to move from the premise-responses of R_2 to the conclusion-response of R_2, given the premise-responses of R_1. (Way 2017: 264)

So, the idea here is that two patterns of reasoning can be compared with respect to resilience: whether and which of the two defeats the other one. This measure then is what explains why one of the two reasonings in the cases of outweighed reasons is defeated and the other one is not. The promise-reasoning in our case is the defeated one, because it is less resilient. It is still good reasoning to move from the premise-responses of the accident-reasoning to the conclusion-response of the accident-reasoning, given the premise-responses of the promise-reasoning, while it is not good reasoning to move from the premise-responses of the promise-reasoning to the conclusion-response of the promise-reasoning, given the premise-responses of the accident-reasoning. The promise-reasoning is defeated in this case. Thus, the promise is the outweighed reason in our case. It is still a reason, though, for it still corresponds to a good pattern of defeasible reasoning (that happens to be defeated in the present instance). (For more details of this move, see Asarnow 2016; McHugh and Way 2016; Silverstein 2016; Way 2016.)

This second line of reply appears to deal better with some of the problematic points that the revisionary reply couldn't deal with satisfactorily. For one thing, it applies equally well to the case of reasons to act as well to reasons to believe and other attitudes. For the defeat condition seems to apply equally well to practical as well as to theoretical reasoning. Moving from a belief that Tweety is a bird to the belief that Tweety can fly is *ceteris paribus* good. Also, this line of reply doesn't commit the proponents of the Reasoning view to the questionable claim that one has to be motivated (or desire) to some degree to leave the injured in order to have a reason to go to see one's friend. Given that this second line of reply can account for the existence of the outweighed reasons without being committed to some of the problematic claims to which the first line of reply was committed, it does seem to enjoy better argumentative support.

We can, thus, conclude that the proponents of the Reasoning view may be able to account for the problem of outweighed reasons by appeal to the defeasibility of patterns of good reasoning. However, before moving on, let us note quickly two further worries that one might have about this response and how a proponent of the Reasoning view may reply to these. First, one might worry that this view doesn't really explain why one reasoning is defeated by another by resilience and how exactly this defeat gives rise to the weight of reasons. One might think that there is something mysterious in this element of resilience. Are we supposed to assume, without argument, that some reasonings just are defeated and that this constitutes an ultimate element of explanation of the weight of reasons? Being able to explain the gradability aspect of reasons is a constraint on any viable theory of reasons. Many think of gradability here in terms of the weight of reasons. Where does the relative weight of reasons come from exactly in this picture? This may be understood as a question about what makes it the case that one reasoning defeats another (rather than, say, the other way round).

One may respond to this worry by pointing out that the talk of the 'weight' of reasons shouldn't be taken literally. The analogy has its limits (the next chapter expands on this a bit more). Perhaps an expectation of some deeper explanation of the weight of reasons comes merely from taking the 'weight' of reasons too literally. But there is no mystery here after all. Reasons surely appear to have a gradable aspect. And there are perfectly sensible comparisons of reasons. But there is nothing more substantial to it than that. Appeal to good reasoning and the possibility of one reasoning defeating another good reasoning is all there is as far as the gradability aspect of good reasoning and hence of reasons goes. Asking for a more substantial explanation of the weight of reasons is merely entertaining the illusion that the weight analogy should be taken to be somewhat more substantial. Good reasoning and defeat is where the explanation stops on this view.

A second, related worry here is about how the appeal to defeated reasonings can explain the fact that there can be different reasons for one and the same act, F, that can be compared among them. Both that the injured urgently need my help and the fact that helping the injured will make me feel good about myself might be reasons for me to help the injured. But the former is certainly 'weightier' than the latter. How can the appeal to defeated reasoning account for this difference?[6]

One might reply to this worry that the explanation here is similar to the case of outweighed reasons. Roughly, in situations where r is a reason for S to F and q is a reason for S to F, but r is a more important ('weightier', 'stronger') reason to F than q, the r-reasoning is more resilient than the q-reasoning in the face of further considerations. That is, you can add more considerations to S's premise states without defeating the reasoning from r-premise-response to F than you can add to S's premise states without defeating the reasoning from q-premise-response to F. Concretely, there are further potential considerations that you could add as my premise-responses without defeating the goodness of reasoning from the premise-response of my belief that the injured urgently need my help to the conclusion-response of me helping the injured than there are potential considerations that you could add as my premise-responses without defeating the goodness of reasoning from the premise-response of my belief that helping the injured will make me feel better about myself. Typically, the mere fact that I gave a promise to be at the coffee shop will already defeat the goodness of that latter reasoning (note that to keep comparisons valid, we have to assume that in the case where my reason to help is that it will make me feel better about myself is not a case where the injured urgently need specifically my help to survive). Thus, the Reasoning view also seems to have the resources to account for the apparently different 'weight' of non-competing reasons. Ultimately, the explanation is provided by appeal to reasoning and degrees of resilience of a good pattern of reasoning in the face of further considerations. We can conclude that by revising the standard assumptions about good reasoning, one can save a version of the Reasoning view in the face of the prima facie worry of outweighed reasons (and related considerations about the comparative weight of reasons).

2.5 First Set of Worries II: Enablers

We are now at the following dialectical juncture: we have introduced the Reasoning view and some considerations in its favour, and then observed that there are two main prima facie worries in the current literature about

---

[6] For a somewhat similar line of objection see Star (2018: 255–256), who labels the problem as the problem of 'capturing ranges of weight'.

the Reasoning view. The previous section explored what is arguably the most discussed one of these, the objection from outweighed reasons. The focus of this section is on the remaining one.

The second prima facie problem for the Reasoning view is the problem of enabling conditions. In a nutshell, the problem is that the Reasoning view in its simple form is unable to distinguish normative reasons to F from mere enabling conditions for F-ing. For, according to this line of objection, both of these can figure as premises in patterns of good reasoning. The original point goes back (at least) to Dancy and his defence of holism about reasons according to which, roughly, what is a reason to F varies from case to case (see Dancy 2004). Dancy merely observes that not all premises in practical reasoning are [favouring] reasons for the F-ing that figures in the conclusion of the reasoning. Dancy doesn't focus specifically on the Reasoning view of reasons as we have presented it. However, his point does constitute a serious prima facie worry for anyone who wants to define or explain normative reasons in terms of patterns of good reasoning. Another way to put the worry is that the Reasoning view seems to predict that considerations that we are naturally inclined to treat as mere background conditions are themselves genuine reasons to F. Setiya (2014: 226) extrapolates:

> Dancy's more contentious claim is that even some of these considerations, which are premises of sound reasoning, are mere enabling conditions, not reasons to act. In his example, the fact that I have promised to do something is a reason to do it, while the absence of duress, possession of ability, and lack of competing reasons, though relevant to practical reasoning, are said to be mere conditions (Dancy 2004, pp. 38–41). Here *Reasons* [i.e. 'Reasons', from above] disagrees. It counts every premise of sound reasoning as a reason to act.

It does seem reasonable to take Dancy's observation at face value. Indeed, it is pre-theoretically plausible to see some considerations as mere conditions that make it possible that some other conditions are normative reasons to F without themselves being normative reasons to F. Dancy proposes to:

> [c]onsider the following piece of practical 'reasoning':
>
> 1. I promised to do it.
> 2. My promise was not given under duress.
> 3. I am able to do it.
> 4. There is no greater reason not to do it.
> 5. So: I do it.
>
> (Dancy 2004: 38)

The suggestion here is that not all elements in 1–5 are normative reasons. Indeed, Dancy claims that only 1 corresponds to a normative reason (in his terminology, to a 'favouring' reason). Premises 2, 3, and 4 correspond, according to Dancy, to enabling conditions. Very roughly, not all enabling conditions are alike on Dancy's view. On his account, 2 and 3 enable 1 to favour 5 (we are skipping the details about the differences between these two); whereas 4 enables 'the move from 1 to 5' (cf. Dancy 2004: 40).

Now, it would be unpromising for a proponent of the Reasoning view to dispute the fact that it does seem pre-theoretically very plausible to assume that at least considerations 2 and 3 are not reasons to do the thing referred to in 5. Premise 4 is arguably a slightly less clear case (cf. Setiya 2014).

But then what can a proponent of the Reasoning view propose that could block the argument from these intuitions against the Reasoning view? Unfortunately, there haven't been a lot of replies to this worry in the literature. However, there are still some proposals. Notably, Kieran Setiya has considered the issue and provided what one might think is a promising reply to the worry. Basically, he proposes to defend the thesis that 1–4 are, contrary to appearances, all normative reasons. He gives some theoretical explanation why it is so. And crucially, he sketches elements of an error theory of why it may appear to us that 2–4 are not reasons.

Here are some more details of Setiya's proposal (cf. Setiya 2014: 226–228). His strategy is twofold. First, he proposes an explanation that appeals to pragmatic aspects of communication. He claims that typically it is not sensible to cite 2, 3, and the like as reasons to F. But this, according to Setiya, is not because these are not really reasons, but rather that citing considerations about the absence of duress, one's ability, and so on are not informative enough, given the rarity of duress and so on. The idea here is that 'we assume' the absence of duress and that '[a]bility is arguably a condition of every practical reason' (cf. Setiya 2014: 226). Thus, presumably because something like the Gricean maxim of relation (be relevant or contribute all and only information that is relevant) is in place, we tend to focus on 1 (i.e. the promise) rather than 2, 3, or 4 when citing reasons for F-ing, which is represented in 5. According to Setiya (2014: 226): 'Citing the promise is thus a more informative and more natural way to bring out the pattern of practical reasoning under which the relevant motivation falls'. Compare this line of thought to a recent proposal by Fogal (2016), according to which, roughly, the fact that 'S likes dancing' and 'there is dancing tonight' cannot both express at the same time a reason for S to go to the dancing place, and hence, we should not rely on our language use of 'reasons' too heavily. According to Fogal, reasons might just be proxies or representatives of 'normative clusters' or reason (the referent of mass noun 'reason'). According to Setiya, given the appropriate context, it would be perfectly acceptable to cite 2 and 3 as reasons.[7]

The second element of Setiya's explanation is to deny the additivity principle for reasons according to which, roughly, if $r1$ is a reason of 'weight' x for S to F and $r2$ is a reason of 'weight' y for S to F, then there is a conjunctive reason $r1\&r2$ (alternatively: two reasons) for S to F of a total 'weight' of $x + y$. This enables him to respond, in particular, to the line of thought according to which 4 ('There is no greater reason not to do it') cannot be a reason to F. According to Setiya, we arrive at some absurd consequences by allowing 4 to be a reason to F only if we also accept additivity (note, however, that Setiya doesn't use the label 'additivity', nor 'weight', but talks of 'strength' of reasons instead). If additivity doesn't hold, we don't arrive at the problematic conclusion that 4 adds some more 'weight' to the total 'weight' of reasons that one has to do the thing one promised to do (i.e. 5) and hence there is nothing really absurd about counting 4 and the like among one's reasons.

It may well be that the additivity of 'weight' of reasons fails. That the thing on the menu is a pizza is a reason for me to order it; that the thing on the menu has chocolate cream on it is a reason for me to order it; however, that the thing on the menu is a chocolate cream pizza is in no way a reason for me to order it and hence has no 'weight'. The failure of additivity, sometimes also labelled 'accrual of reasons', is a lively topic in recent debates on reasons (Horty 2012: 61; Brown 2014; Bader 2016; Nair

---

[7] 'In the right context, however, any fact that is a premise of sound reasoning can be given as a reason. If I have been pressured into making various promises, so that duress is salient, the fact that a particular promise was made without duress will be a sensible thing to cite as a reason for keeping it' (Setiya 2014: 226). Note that this latter thought, that there are situations where it is perfectly fine to appeal to abilities or absence of duress as reasons, constitutes a positive argument in favour of the view that there is no significant distinction among enablers (and modifiers, and other conditions) and reasons, given the assumption that this fact about language and common sense is to be taken on board. A similar argument can also be found in Fogal (2016: 101), who endorses a different view on reasons (he is not a proponent of the Reasoning view, but in this aspect his view is similar to the Reasoning view):

> For example, a lot of philosophers want to deny that the ability to φ is itself a reason – or part of a reason – to φ but there are many contexts in which it seems perfectly acceptable to cite one's ability to φ as a reason to φ. [. . .] One option is to bite the bullet and say that they're strictly speaking false, offering some pragmatic story to explain (or explain away) their acceptability. Another – which I favor – is to accept them as perfectly good reasons claims, since the facts cited are good representatives in the imagined contexts and that's all that being – i.e., counting as – a reason really amounts to. Nothing would then follow about the specific metaphysical role the facts play within the cluster they represent – that would be a further, substantive issue, to be settled on broadly theoretical grounds Fogal (2016: 101).

2016; Hawthorne and Magidor 2018; and Sher 2019 contain considerations against additivity), and we will return to it in later chapters (see
Chapter 3, for instance).

However, even if additivity indeed fails and Setiya's second point is well
taken, one may still have some reasonable doubts about the first element of
Setiya's proposal. Presumably, when Setiya appeals to pragmatic explanations in dealing with 2 and 3, the idea is that the fact that in a given situation
it is not felicitous to assert that that one didn't make the promise to F under
duress is a reason to F can be explained by an appeal to implicatures and
conversational maxims. But can the oddity of citing 2 and 3 as reasons to
F really be explained by an appeal to implicatures and conversational
maxims? Consider what such an explanation would amount to exactly.
We referred to the appeal to the Gricean maxim of relation (or relevance)
and an implicature that would be generated by flouting the maxim of
relation in the relevant context (cf. Grice 1975) as a possible explanation
of the oddity. The idea seems to be that we expect people to communicate
the most significant and specific bits of their information. However, according to this line of thought, when one offers 2 or 3 as a reply to the question,
say, 'what reasons are there to F?' (i.e. do the promised thing), one is flouting
the maxim of relation. That is, one is breaking it, by not communicating the
most significant or specific information in the context (namely, 1, the
promise itself) and one is breaking the maxim (i.e. not complying with it)
in a flagrant manner. This flouting, then, should itself generate an
implicature (given the assumption that people are cooperative): others
should be entitled to imply something further from such flouting, from
the fact that one is not providing the most significant bit of information.
A natural thought here, then, would be that according to this line of reply,
one should infer from the fact that a subject offers 2 or 3 rather than 1 that
the subject doesn't actually have any further information other than 2 or 3
(as reasons to F), which then, presumably, according to this thought,
generates the oddity. For we know that there is also 1 and perhaps find it
puzzling that one could have 2 or 3 as reasons to F without also having 1.
Thus, one might develop Setiya's idea here more specifically, as a case where
offering 2 or 3 as reasons to do the promised thing is odd because one is
offering some information that is known not to be the most specific
information but the resulting implicature (there is no reason other than
2 and 3 to F) clashes with that fact (i.e. that there is a more specific bit of
information – namely, that 1 is a reason to F). And, presumably, that 1 is a
reason to F is more specific, because ability to F is always present where one
has a reason to F, and duress is normally absent in typical cases of promises.

This line of reply appears problematic for the following reason.[8] This pragmatic story doesn't survive the cancelability test. It is assumed that implicatures, typically, can be cancelled. So, for instance, if you ask me 'Where are my keys?' and I reply 'Somewhere in the apartment', you are entitled to infer that, assuming that I am in the business of cooperative communication, I am implying that I don't have any more specific information about your keys. For the maxim of relation requires that I give you the most informative reply, and if I know something more specific than that your keys are in the apartment, then I am not giving you the most specific bit of information that I have. Now, it is observed that implicatures can be cancelled. To see how, consider the following modified version of our communication where, upon you asking me where your keys are, I reply not merely that they are somewhere in the apartment, but that 'they are somewhere in the apartment, but I don't mean to imply that I don't have any more specific information about the location of your keys'. If I say this, you are not entitled to infer that I don't have any more specific information. You will probably conclude that I am in a playful mood or that I am trying to give you a paternalistic lesson about the importance of remembering where you put your stuff. Crucially, there is nothing odd from the linguistic point of view in my communication (even though it might not be a very friendly piece of communication on my part). Cancellability is a common, typical feature of implicatures. But does it hold in the abovementioned case of promise and 1–5 reasoning? If Setiya (or rather our reconstruction of his argument) is right, then by offering 2 or 3, one is implying that one doesn't have anything more specific as reason to F (say, 1). Hence, it should be the case that one could cancel the implicature, by asserting something like 'that I am able to do the promised thing is a reason for me to do it, but I don't mean to imply that I don't have any more specific reason to do the promised thing'. However, this assertion and, in particular, its first conjunct still appear odd. Consider a variation on this: 'That I promised to meet you at 2:00 p.m. is a reason for

---

[8] My strategy here is inspired by a parallel argument from Jessica Brown (see Brown 2013), against the view according to which a piece of evidence *e* can be evidence for itself. Brown observes the oddity of such a proposal and considers in detail putative explanations that have been proposed to explain (away) the pre-theoretical oddity of that claim. The strategies that Brown examines (from Williamson 2000) strongly resemble Setiya's proposal here to appeal to pragmatics of conversation in order to explain why it is odd to cite ability and absence of duress as reasons to do the promised thing. Brown rejects in particular the proposal that the claim that evidence can be evidence for itself is explained by the fact that it generates an implicature given the maxim of relation. Brown rejects that proposal on the grounds that, roughly, the oddity remains even if one attempts to cancel the putative implicature.

me to meet you at 2:00 p.m. but so is the fact that I am able to meet you at 2 p.m.'. This seems odd. If Setiya's line of reasoning was correct and the only problem with offering 2 or 3 as reasons to F was that they generate implicatures along the lines that we drew above, then it shouldn't be odd at all to assert this and thereby cancel the alleged source of oddity, the implicature. But it is still odd. And this raises a serious suspicion about Setiya's pragmatic proposal. It doesn't seem that the problems for the Reasoning view from reasoning like 1–5 can be solved by appeal to some pragmatic aspects of communication. This is not to say that there cannot be another more theoretical motivation to reject the idea of enabling conditions not being reasons (see Fogal 2016 for one line of thought; for another, see Kearns and Star 2013: 84–86). However, it doesn't look like there is a forthcoming solution from the Reasoning approach.

2.6   Still More Worries: No Good Reasoning Available

In the two preceding sections, we have been exploring a couple of well-known worries for the Reasoning view. We saw the challenge that the existence of outweighed reasons (and 'weight' of reasons in general) raises for the view, and we also discussed the problem from enabling conditions as distinct from reasons. We also saw that proponents of the Reasoning view have provided some possible replies to these objections and that at least one of these might be on the right track – for example, the appeal to defeasible reasoning as a reply to the objection from outweighed reasons.

This section introduces a new challenge for the Reasoning view. It is a challenge from observations about cases where, roughly, no pattern of good reasoning is available from a given consideration, and yet we have an inclination to count the relevant consideration as a genuine normative reason.

The challenge discussed in the present section, I believe, is more radical and more worrisome than the worries discussed earlier. If the considerations ahead are on the right track, then there is a robust category of normative reasons that cannot even possibly comply with the Reasoning view's definition of reasons.

Let us focus on McHugh and Way's version of the Reasoning view, (RV), according to which 'for that p to be a reason for a response is for that p to be a premise of a good pattern of reasoning from fitting responses to that response' (McHugh and Way 2016: 586). This focus is principally motivated by considerations of simplicity and brevity. I believe that the same sort of worry, *modulo* adapting it to individual specificities, can be advanced against other versions of the Reasoning view.

The worry I put forward here relies on two as-yet-unnoticed but fundamental counterexamples. These two arise given two of McHugh and Way's (independently plausible) commitments in particular. The first commitment is the claim that reasoning is a transition from premise-responses to conclusion-responses of a certain sort. According to them, 'This transition is such that the conclusion response counts as based on, or held in the light of, the premise responses' (McHugh and Way 2016: 586). The second commitment is the claim that all normative reasons are contents of possible true beliefs or of other fitting premise-responses. According to McHugh and Way, a fitting belief is a true belief. They don't require that all the relevant premise-responses are actually held by the subject for the content of the relevant premise-responses to be normative reasons for the subject in question. (RV) focuses on patterns of reasoning. (RV) requires that all the relevant premise-responses are fitting and are part of a good pattern of reasoning – that is, that there is a possible reasoning (for a given subject) from the relevant (not necessarily actually held) fitting premise-responses to the relevant conclusion-responses that respects the criteria for a good pattern of reasoning. How exactly the good patterns of reasoning are defined is not crucial for our purposes here.

2.6.1 Moore-Paradoxical Beliefs

The first of our counterexamples appeals to possible considerations of the Moore-paradoxical form. Consider the following example. The fact that (r) 'the building is on fire, but John doesn't believe that the building is on fire' is, intuitively, a reason for John to check/consider/reconsider/investigate the hypothesis (h) 'the building is on fire.' Yet there is no possible good pattern of reasoning for John from a fitting belief in (r) to reconsidering/ investigation/and so forth of (h). This is so simply because it is not possible for John to have a fitting belief that the building is on fire and that he doesn't believe that the building is on fire. John cannot have a fitting belief that (r) because it is impossible for such a belief to be true. One cannot truly believe that the building is on fire and that one doesn't believe that the building is on fire. The belief in the first conjunct contradicts the belief in the second. On the (RV) account, given that John cannot (in any sense) have a true belief in (r), (r) cannot possibly be a reason for any response from him. However, it appears pre-theoretically plausible to think that (r) speaks in favour of some response for John. Given that the fittingness requirement is central for (RV), Moore-paradoxical beliefs constitute a non-negligible challenge for the Reasoning view.

2.6.2   Self-Undermining Beliefs

The second sort of counterexample appeals to the possibility of other self-undermining beliefs. The fact that (p) 'I just took a drug that erased all of my memories about the past five minutes' is, intuitively, a reason for me to suspend judgment about what I did in these past five minutes (assuming that I haven't yet learned anything new after that). However, to suspend judgment about what I did in these past five minutes entails suspending judgment about whether I took the memory-erasing drug. But there is no good pattern of reasoning from a belief that p towards a suspension of judgment about p. Such a transition (if possible) doesn't satisfy the basic criteria for reasoning. In fact, McHugh and Way define reasoning as a transition where the conclusion-response is held in the light, or on the basis, of the premise-response. In this case, however, I cannot base my suspension about p on my belief that p. To suspend judgment about whether I took the memory-erasing drug cannot be based on the belief that I took the memory-erasing drug. At the very moment when I would suspend judgment, I would lose the basis for the suspension, and it would not count as being held in the light of the relevant premise-response. It is not possible to believe that p and, at the same time, to suspend judgment about p (on the basis of the belief that p). If the fact that I just took a drug that erased all my memories about the past five minutes is a reason for me to suspend judgment about what I did during these past five minutes, then (RV) must be false, since it entails that it cannot be a reason for me to suspend judgment.

Now, a proponent of the Reasoning view might reply to this line of argument from the cases of Moore-paradoxical and self-undermining beliefs by suggesting that in all such cases there are actually facts in the vicinity of the problematic considerations that are both normative reasons for the same F-ing and, at the same time, considerations that can play the relevant premise role in good patterns of reasoning towards F-ing.[9] According to this suggestion – for example, in the Moore-paradoxical belief case – there is a non-paradoxical fact in the vicinity of the Moore-paradoxical consideration, that is a reason for one to check/investigate the

[9] Thanks to an anonymous reader for Cambridge University Press for drawing my attention to the need to address this potential reply to my argument.

hypothesis that the building is on fire. One might, for example, think that the fact that the building is on fire is one such fact, and that the building may well be on fire might be another such fact. A similar line of response has been recently put forward by Hille Paakkunainen in a discussion concerning a similar worry for what she calls the Deliberative Constraint on normative reasons (see Paakkunainen 2017, 2018). Roughly, according to the Deliberative Constraint, a consideration r is a reason for S to F only if r can be a premise in a good pattern of reasoning/deliberation to F (see Paakkunainen 2018: 156 and Paakkunainen 2017: 65 for the more precise and detailed formulation of the constraint, which may be considered as the left-to-right conditional of the Reasoning view, if we spell it out in a biconditional form). Paakkunainen responds in these publications to objections from cases where the relevant considerations seem to be unable to play a premise role in [good] deliberation. We will return to these cases more attentively in the next section within our more general discussion of what other authors have called the Response constraint (cf. Way and Whiting 2016), which is also connected to the more general and theory-driven discussion about the supposed guidance role of normative reasons. But with respect to our present discussion, a proponent of the Reasoning view might well appeal to the same point that Paakkunainen makes in response to these further cases and claim that there are facts in the vicinity of the Moore-paradoxical and self-undermining considerations that can be reasons to check and reasons to suspend and can also still be premises of good patterns of reasoning.[10]

To this worry I would like to reply two things. First, such a response from the proponents of the Reasoning view would amount either to the claim that we don't have the intuition that – Moore-paradoxical considerations are reasons for checking or to the claim that our intuitions are massively mistaken. Neither of these options is promising, though. We may well accept that there are other reasons in the vicinity of Moore-

---

[10] Another point that Paakkunainen makes against these cases where it doesn't seem that the relevant considerations can play a role in (good) deliberation is that there might be alternative evaluative and normative phenomena that constitute the real focus of these cases. In particular, she suggests that the relevant considerations might be explanatory reasons that explain why the relevant F-ing 'would be a favorable outcome from the perspective of [one's] preference-satisfaction; or why [one's F-ing] would be good, or good for [one]' (Paakkunainen 2017: 68). Such a suggestion comes very close to our own positive proposal below (see Chapter 5). Yet, on our proposal, the considerations that don't play a role in a good deliberation can still be reasons. But let us not precipitate that discussion yet. See also Rossi (2021) for a response to Paakkunainen in which a new kind of elusive reasons are introduced. Rossi also provides further considerations for the claim that such reasons are genuinely normative and authoritative.

paradoxical and self-undermining considerations. Yet the argument from Moore-paradoxical and self-undermining considerations still goes through even if there are these additional reasons. Now, one might, of course, claim that it is somewhat indeterminate or not obvious what exactly our judgments track in the relevant cases (cf. Paakkunainen 2017: 67–68). But why should we doubt the reliability of our self-reported judgments specifically in these cases? Why should we think that we are massively in error when we consider Moore-paradoxical and self-undermining belief cases? In order for this response to be successful, we need an independent, theoretically well-motivated error theory that would explain either why exactly our judgments specifically in Moore-paradoxical and self-undermining cases are not about normative reasons to check and alike but are indeterminate or not obvious, or why we are so massively mistaken in having these judgments. As far as I can tell, no independent error theory that could explain this is forthcoming. But without such an error theory, we can take our judgments about these cases at face value.

The second point that I would like to make in reply to this line of response is that it is not clear that the appeal to the facts in the vicinity of Moore-paradoxical and self-undermining considerations would help the proponents of the Reasoning view at all. Our suggestion is that, for example, the Moore-paradoxical consideration is a reason specifically to check or investigate (or similar). But it is not clear why the invoked alternatives in the vicinity of Moore-paradoxical considerations – for example, that the building is/may be on fire – would count as reasons *specifically* to check or investigate, rather than to run away or to call the emergency number. The proposed alternative considerations don't seem to speak specifically in favour of checking. It is specifically the conjunction of the fact that there is a fire, and that one doesn't know about it, that speaks in favour of checking. The ignorance factor that is part of the Moore-paradoxical consideration has normative importance, it would seem. Thus, it is not clear that appealing to these further facts in the vicinity of Moore-paradoxical and self-undermining considerations could help proponents of the Reasoning view to alleviate the problems that our challenge raises. I suggest that the challenge from Moore-paradoxical and self-undermining considerations for the Reasoning view is still germane and cannot be easily dealt with.

2.7   Are Moore-Paradoxical and Self-Undermining Beliefs Really Worse Than Ice Creams and Surprise Parties?

One thing that proponents of the Reasoning view could do in the light of the objection from the preceding section is to appeal to existing moves that have been made within the closely related debate on so-called guidance by normative reasons. A central assumption there is that reasons should be able to guide. And this can be understood in terms of there being a response constraint on reasons. That is, the constraint according to which only if you are able to act/have an attitude on the basis of r, can r be a reason for you to act in the relevant way/have the relevant attitude (cf. Way and Whiting 2016; see below for more details).

Thus, a proponent of the Reasoning view may claim that an independent theoretical motivation for not counting our aforementioned examples of Moore-paradoxical and self-undermining beliefs as genuine cases of normative reasons is that it leads to the rejection not only of the Reasoning view but also of the very plausible response constraint on reasons and consequently to the difficulty of explaining how normative reasons are supposed to guide us. Yet the guidance aspect of normative reasons, they may maintain, is a non-negotiable aspect of normative reasons.[11] That reasons are centrally supposed to guide us is indeed a widely held claim. For some, it is even a platitude that any viable theory of reasons has to integrate. Insofar as the aforementioned examples not only undermine the Reasoning view, but they also entail that not all reasons are such that we can act upon them, they make it difficult to understand how normative reasons could guide us. If they don't guide us, it is not clear in what sense normative reasons are still normative, according to this line of thought. If they cannot guide us, they cannot exert any force on us; hence, they lose their normativity, or so it seems.

However, as soon as someone declares a thesis beyond any doubt, philosophers at once come up with endless counterexamples and try to dispute it at considerable length. This is also what happens with respect to the response constraint on normative reasons. Let us explore this debate briefly and see what can it add to our discussion about the Reasoning view. (In what follows, I borrow some elements of Way and Whiting's (2016) terminology and their way of introducing the debate.)

According to Way and Whiting (2016: 214), it is a common assumption that reasons are supposed to guide us and '[c]onsiderations that cannot guide cannot do what reasons are supposed to do'. In other terms, 'it is the job of a reason to recommend that a person perform a certain act or hold some attitude. If it is [to] do that job, the relevant person must be able to heed and respond to its recommendation' (Way and Whiting 2016:

---

[11] Thanks to Daniel Whiting for making me aware of the importance of this possible line of reply on behalf of proponents of the Reasoning view.

214). Here is their formulation of the response constraint, which they seem to present as a natural way to develop the thought that reasons must be able to recommend actions and attitudes and hence guide us:

> **Response Constraint**: That p is a reason for you to φ only if you are able to φ for the reason that p. (Way and Whiting 2016: 214)

Thus, a central argument in favour of the Response Constraint is that it provides a clear and simple way to account for the guidance aspect of normative reasons. Combined with Humeanism, it also avoids a kind of mysticism that other views on reasons and guidance may have. According to Humeanism (e.g. Williams 1979), reasons are necessarily connected to one's motivational set that contain pro-attitudes (note also that strictly speaking Humeanism is not entailed by the Reasoning view of reasons which doesn't specify on its own the sort of premise-responses that one may have – for example, the Reasoning view is compatible with an interpretation on which only beliefs can constitute premise-responses).[12] Think, for a comparison, of the reasons-first approach that only tells us that reasons exist and presumably that at least some people might respond to them. In the case of the Reasoning view that endorses the response constraint, or a Humeanism with a response constraint, we have a straightforward account of guidance. There is no mystery of how exactly the guidance goes with such a combination. Moreover, the account has a naturalistic flavour, for it seems in principle to be open to a further reductionist account that explores an appeal to some evolutionary story.

Another line of argument in favour of the Response Constraint is that it enables us to explain a number of distinctions within the normative domain. For instance, it allows us to explain why there are no normative reasons for instantiations of value. For example, while there can be a reason for one to want to be a bit taller, there is no reason for one to *be* a bit taller (cf. Parfit 2011: 51). Having certain evaluative properties is not the kind of thing that we are able to *do*, let alone to do for a reason. Hence, it is not something that can have reasons in its favour. More generally, as Way and Whiting observe, the Response Constraint enables one to have the first steps towards an explanation of differences between deontic and axiological properties. Another intuitive distinction that one may be able to explain by

---

[12] Contrary to what can often be seen in the literature, I prefer to avoid using the term 'internalism' for the sort of Humeanism about reasons to act that people associate with Bernard Williams in order to avoid confusions when it comes to the discussion of reasons for belief, where 'internalism' refers to a different sort of view. I am not alone in this. Way and Whiting also avoid using the 'internalism' label.

an appeal to the Response Constraint is the distinction between genuine reasons to believe and pragmatic reasons to believe. One might think that nothing but truth related, evidential considerations can play the role of reasons to believe. Yet sometimes pragmatic considerations are cited as if they were reasons to believe (e.g. that being cheerful is good for one's health is a reason to believe that everything is fine). This gets explained away by appeal to the Response Constraint insofar as we are unable to believe that p for reasons that are not related to p (cf. Kelly 2002; Shah 2006; among others). Again, this is not to say that pragmatic reasons cannot be reasons to want to believe that p (see, again, Chapter 6 for a discussion of this point).

Despite these considerations in favour of the Response Constraint, it is not universally accepted. In fact, there is a battery of counterexamples against the Response Constraint (or at any rate to constraints close enough to it). Julia Markovits (2011a), for instance, elaborates a number of well-known and new cases. Note that at the end of the day, Markovits endorses a version of the Humean (her label is 'internalist') view that still links reasons to one's cares and other states but refuses to accept that reasons have to be able to motivate one. She provides three kinds of cases. First, there are situations where one's being not perfectly rational prevents one from being able to act upon one's reason in a situation (e.g. cases where a sore loser has a reason to leave without greeting their opponent, cases where a delusional subject has a reason to consult a doctor). Second, there are situations where one is not particularly irrational, but the structure of the case is such that one cannot act upon one's reason to F (e.g. cases of deterrent actions, like intending to respond to a nuclear attack, Kavka's toxin case, and soldiers fighting in a just war). Third, there are cases where one ought not to be moved by the reason one has (e.g. an emergency plane landing, complex medical operations, or automatic responses in cases of road accidents, where acting on the basis of the reason one has, say, to save an innocent life, presents a very high risk of screwing the relevant act up). Way and Whiting (2016) centre their discussion specifically on two further cases, and we follow suit in what follows.

First is the case of 'massively outweighed reasons' (cf. Way and Whiting 2016: 215), which comes from Mark Schroeder:

> [Ice Cream] Joel's career, his wife and her career, his friends, his Lakers' season tickets, his family, and his loves of surfing and of mountain climbing all tie him to Los Angeles. But Joel also loves chocolate-cayenne-cinnamon flavored ice cream, which he can only get in Madison, Wisconsin. (Schroeder 2007: 166)

The common diagnosis here is that it appears that the fancy ice cream is a (tiny) reason to move to Madison. See Way and Whiting (2016: 216) on this: '[t]he fact that he can only get chocolate-cayenne-cinnamon flavored ice cream (hereafter, ice cream) in Madison is a reason for Joel to move there'. The problem here is that 'Joel is not capable of moving to Madison for that reason, given how much he cares about all of the things tying him to LA' (Way and Whiting 2016: 216).

The second example that Way and Whiting discuss is the case of 'self-effacing reasons' (cf. Way and Whiting 2016: 216):

> [Surprise Party] There is a surprise party for Beth at her house that starts at 5pm. Beth loves surprise parties and it would make her very happy to arrive home at 5pm. However, were Beth to find out that there is a surprise party for her at 5pm, the surprise would be ruined, and the party would be a disaster. (Way and Whiting 2016: 216)

This second example is attributed to Markovits (2011b) and Schroeder (2007: 165–166) (Way and Whiting also observe that similar examples can be found in Millgram 1996; Sobel 2001; Shafer-Landau 2003: ch. 7; Markovits 2011a; Smith 2009). The problem here is that, first, it appears that that there is a surprise party is a reason for Beth to go home, but, second, it is not possible for Beth to act upon that reason, since it would require, at minimum, that Beth is aware or believes that there is a surprise party, which would entail, paradoxically, that the party is not a surprise party for Beth anymore.

Now, one can always deny that the aforementioned cases, in particular cases of 'self-effacing reasons', are cases of genuine reasons, because one might think that reasons must satisfy the Response Constraint and must guide us. Way and Whiting suggest that it is the most popular line of reply to these cases and identify, for instance, Setiya (2009: 538), Sinclair (2012), and Kiesewetter (2016) as versions of this line of reply.

However, such a denial is problematic. For denying that contrary to our robust judgments about all these various and numerous situations, the relevant considerations are not really normative reasons is a substantial cost for a theory of normative reasons. We have to realise how massive and pervasive cases like these are (see Markovits 2011a for more on this point). One might think that an outright refusal to count these considerations as reasons has an ad hocness flavour. Moreover, one cannot merely deny that the relevant considerations genuinely count in favour of the relevant F-ings in a sense in these cases since our pre-theoretical judgments indicate otherwise. But then if these considerations are not reasons, but still count in favour of the relevant F-ing, one is forced to introduce a new normative category to account for them. Recognising them as reasons appears to be a more parsimonious and theoretically fruitful strategy.

Another option that one can take in the face of these counterexamples to the Response Constraint is to modify the Response Constraint in order to try to avoid them. Way and Whiting themselves take this other option (they also discuss some alternative options of this sort; for matters of simplicity of exposition, I will not review them here; my suspicion is that they will face the same problems as Way and Whiting's proposal). Way and Whiting acknowledge that there are two possible interpretations of the Response Constraint depending on how one understands ability. They follow Mele (2002) in distinguishing two sorts of abilities: general abilities (understood 'as a kind of *power* or *competence*'; Way and Whiting 2016: 219) and specific abilities. To take their example, Andy Murray has general ability to serve (in tennis). He has it even when he is on a plane or drunk or when something is interfering with these abilities, or otherwise he happens to be in unfavourable circumstances (say, there is no tennis court around). Murray has the specific ability to serve when he is playing a concrete tennis game.

According to Way and Whiting, interpreting the Response Constraint in terms of specific ability is unpromising. But when interpreted in terms of general ability, the Response Constraint leaves enough room to respond to the problematic cases. The treatment of cases that they provide is twofold. With respect to ice-cream cases, where reasons are massively outweighed, an interference blocks a subject from exercising her general ability to F for the relevant reasons. For instance, one is, in general, able to move to Madison, but one's actual psychology interferes with this ability – one's other cares and desires block one from exercising the ability to move to Madison. In the case of self-effacing reasons, their explanation is that the subject has some sort of general ability that is relevant for the Response Constraint. So, for instance: 'Beth might well have the general ability to reason "there's a surprise F at location L, so I'll go to L", when surprise F is something that she enjoys or is interested in' (Way and Whiting 2016: 224). This response raises some tricky issues with respect to the level of grain of content of reasons. Yet, without going into details of these, one might wonder whether the suggested strategy can succeed. In particular, one may wonder why the suggested general ability of reasoning from some abstract considerations 'there's a surprise F at location L' should be taken as capturing the specifics of the case, the case where the reason is 'there is a surprise party for her at 5:00 p.m.' and not 'there is some surprise, somewhere'. In what sense is the general, abstract ability of acting upon the consideration that there is some surprise, an ability to act upon the specific consideration that there is a surprise party for me? But even if this line of reply can be worked out for cases like Surprise Party, I think there is another problem that proponents of the Response Constraint face. Let's see this now.

Going back to our initial cases against the Reasoning view, one can claim that there is not even a general coarse-grained ability there. In no sense, neither in a general nor in a specific sense, can one act on the basis of Moore-paradoxical considerations ('p and I don't know that p'). In a way, our case is even more radical than the self-effacing reasons cases. The claim that one might have a general coarse-grained ability to check the building/ investigate the situation on the basis of the fact that there is a fire *and* one doesn't know that there is a fire appears even more problematic than the parallel claim about self-effacing reasons cases – for example, the ice-cream case. One doesn't have the general coarse-grained ability to reason 'there is a fire in the building but I don't know about it, so let's check whether there is a fire in the building'. I don't see how one could have an ability to undergo this kind of absurd reasoning.

At this point, I suppose, Way and Whiting's conciliatory strategy provides no further help. It cannot accommodate the pre-theoretical assumption that our Moore-paradoxical case is a case of a genuine normative reasons. But denying that these considerations are genuine reasons seems to be an ad hoc move, especially after admitting that a number of structurally close, albeit a bit less radical cases (e.g. surprise party) are cases of normative reasons. And again, even if one is ready to deny that Moore-paradoxical considerations are reasons, one cannot, I would like to suggest, plausibly deny that they do count in favour of the relevant F-ings. Now, if one denies that they are reasons but recognises that they still are considerations that count in favour, one is, thereby, introducing a new normative category. But multiplying normative entities and categories should require some caution. A theoretically more parsimonious approach would not classify them as a normative category of its own kind, but rather associate them with the already existing category of normative reasons. That they bear some similarity to the other apparently problematic reasons above introduced (e.g. ice-creams, surprise parties, and Markovits's cases) may be taken as a fact speaking in favour of counting them as reasons as well.

Now, what about the positive arguments in favour of the Response Constraint? Here is a tentative line of thought. I would like to express some doubts about the supposed centrality of guidance for reasons.

According to one prominent argument in contemporary epistemology, the Anti-Luminosity argument (cf. Williamson 2000: 93–113), there is no condition *c* such that one can always know that one is in *c* when one is in *c*. Application of the Anti-Luminosity argument to normativity is not new (cf. Srinivasan 2015; Hughes 2018; Lasonen-Aarnio 2019; see also Section 1.3). Adapting it to the case of guidance by reasons amounts to the claim that, roughly, no reason is such that it can always guide us in F-ing when it is a reason to F, assuming that awareness or knowledge is necessary for being able to act upon a reason. In other terms, Anti-Luminosity appears to put some pressure on the very motivation of the guidance constraint on reasons.

Another line of thought here is a tentative suggestion that part of what people find attractive in the guidance requirement is the underlying thought that one cannot be held responsible for things one cannot possibly have done. And if normative reasons are normative, they are in one way or another connected to criticism and praise. Say, if we think that one ought to do what there is the most reason to do and we think that one can be reasonably criticised for not doing what one ought to do (and acknowledged or praised for doing what one ought to do), then having a reason to F is potentially something that contributes towards one being blamed or praised. And only if one can be held responsible/accountable for F-ing can one be reasonably criticisable or praised for F-ing. Thus, one might wonder: if there is no way for one to F upon a reason to F, how could one be held responsible for F-ing? But there are other possible ways one could deal with this underlying thought than endorsing the Response Constraint. One might, for instance, think that being held responsible and ought are not as tightly connected as one might have initially thought. Or one may think that one might be held responsible for F-ing even if one is in no position to F for a reason *r* to F (see, however, Streumer 2007 against impossible reasons; see also Heuer 2010 for discussion). Finally, one might also attempt to distinguish more clearly responsibility from criticism/praising. Perhaps we have good reasons to keep these categories separate (as some recent work on addictions, for instance, appear to suggest; cf. Pickard 2017). At any rate, this is not to say that there is nothing odd to account for if we accept that Moore-paradoxical and self-undermining considerations can be genuine reasons. It is to say that there might be other ways of accounting for the apparent oddity, ways that don't commit one to the thesis that for a consideration to count as a reason to F, it has to respect the Response constraint (see Chapter 5 for a positive proposal). On the other hand, there doesn't seem to be an utterly convincing way of dealing with Moore-paradoxical and self-undermining reasons without giving up the Reasoning view of reasons.

2.8 Concluding Remarks

A natural move for those who are dissatisfied with the reasons-first approach is to turn towards reductive accounts of normative reasons. A natural first move for those attracted by an attempt to define normative reasons in other more fundamental terms is to look into what reasons are supposed to do and what are the central functions of our common-sense notion of *a reason to act/hold an attitude*. A natural thought here is that normative reasons are those sorts of things that constitute good reasoning, for undeniably there has to be a connection between reasons and reasoning. This chapter has looked at one popular attempt to work out these natural thoughts into a fully elaborated account of normative reasons; namely, the Reasoning view of normative reasons, according to which a normative reasons r for S to F just is for r to be such that it is a content of a premise-response in a pattern of good reasoning from appropriate premise-responses to an appropriate conclusion-response F. In this chapter, we first explored in more detail what such a view amounts to. We reviewed positive considerations in its favour and then examined what appear to be the most troublesome objections to this view; namely, objections from outweighing reasons, enabling conditions, and reasons to F upon which one is not able to F. We saw that responses exist to these worries. But it is far from obvious whether all these are successful. To the contrary, it appears that the cumulative case of these problems favours looking into potential alternatives to the Reasoning view. Before doing just this and exploring other existing prominent reductive views of reasons, let me note that rejecting the Reasoning view doesn't mean giving up the positive insights it provides. Indeed, our positive view that will be developed in Chapter 5 vindicates exactly this. But before we are able to put our cards fully on the table, we need to go through other, also fundamental, insights about reasons that have not been brought to light by the Reasoning view. Namely, we have to look into the very natural thought that reasons are also crucially linked to explanations. Let us now turn to views that explore precisely this other apparently central aspect of reasons.

The Explanation View

3.1 Varieties of the Explanation View

A reductionist approach to normative reasons can be characterised as a proposal to reduce to and explain normative reasons in terms of some other, presumably more robustly graspable, properties. Of course, not all sorts of reduction will be deemed plausible. So how are we to pick out plausible candidates for such a reduction? One common, if often only implicit, strategy among reductionist views in general is to reduce/explain an x by focusing on what appear to be central functions of the ordinary concept of x, the idea being to work out individually necessary and jointly sufficient conditions (within a substantive analysis) for something to be an x in terms of what appears to refer to the central functions of the ordinary concept of x.

This seemed to be the strategy to which proponents of the Reasoning view were attracted. One way of interpreting the Reasoning view is to start with a plausible idea that being able to play a role in good/correct reasoning is an important aspect of our concept of *reasons to act/hold an attitude*. Thus, it appears only natural to try to work out a full theory of normative reasons by an appeal to this aspect of our concept of *reasons to act/hold an attitude*. However, we also observed that a full-blown theory that attempts to define normative reasons only in terms of a role they can play in good reasoning faced some serious problems and is not fully satisfactory. But does it mean that all reductionist proposals about normative reasons are deemed to fail? Not necessarily, of course. But if not good/fitting reasoning, what else could plausibly be appealed to in order to explain normative reasons? Where do we even start looking for alternative reductionist accounts? How are we supposed to proceed?

One natural thing to do at this stage is to look once more into functions of our concept of *reasons to act/hold an attitude* (e.g. the concept that

corresponds to normative reasons). Surely, in our common-sense understanding, reasons should play a role in reasoning; in a sense, reasoning is
made of reasons (see Grice 2001 and Chapter 2). But there is something
else, it seems. Remember our initial normative versus motivating/explan-
atory reasons distinction. The reason why I ate chips was that I was
hungry. It is part of an explanation of why I ate chips. It provides a
descriptive explanation of why I did what I did. One thought is that it is
natural to think that explaining is also what normative reasons do, except
that the explanation here is not about descriptive but normative facts. Of
course, the business of normative reasons is not descriptive explanation,
but it might nevertheless be part of another sort of explanation. Indeed,
considerations that we identify as normative reasons seem to be part of
normative explanation in a sense to be seen. Think, for instance, of facts
about oughts. It is natural to think that in many cases, if not in all of them
(depending on whether you think that the principle of sufficient reason is
true, for instance), when it is the case that S ought to F, it is meaningful to
ask why S ought to F. A natural understanding of such a question is to see
it as a question about what makes it right that S F-s. Think, for instance, of
Karl who ought to call his grandmother. We can meaningfully ask: why is
it the case that Karl ought to call his grandmother? A meaningful answer to
this sort of question will typically consist in our locutor pointing to the
relevant considerations, or a list of considerations that, taken together,
make it the case that Karl ought to call his grandmother. Perhaps it will
contain something like, that she is really sick, that he hasn't called her for a
while, that it would really make his grandmother happy that he calls, and
so on. The same kind of reasoning also seems to apply if you replace
'ought' in Karl's case with 'good in some respect'. It would be good that
Karl calls his grandma, and the relevant considerations will be used to
explain that. But what are these considerations? Well, it appears only
natural to think of them as normative reasons. Indeed, when asked what
makes it right or good and so on that Karl calls his grandma, the balance of
normative reasons comes naturally to mind. It is because there are all these
normative reasons that it is right/good that Karl calls his grandma, indeed,
that Karl ought to call her. If this sort of reasoning is intuitive, and it seems
it is, a theorist of reasons can start building an alternative reductionist
account of normative reasons from here. That is, one may take seriously
this natural role of normative reasons in normative explanations and
define normative reasons in terms of it. And this is exactly what various
recently increasingly popular Explanation views of normative reasons
propose to do.

There is a variety of explanationist accounts of normative reasons[1] and this chapter will consider the most prominent ones in some detail. The common element of these views is, as we just saw, an appeal to a sort of explanation. Unsurprisingly then, the differences among these views will consist in how exactly the details of 'a sort of' are worked out. Most of the existing versions of the explanation views can be classified as being either about explanations of (aspects) of why someone ought to F (which is, arguably, equivalent to why some F-ing is (in some respect) right/correct/ fitting) or about explanation of (aspects of) why some F-ing is good. We can call the first group the 'Deontic Explanation views', given their focus on the deontic facts (oughts), and the second the 'Axiological Explanation' views, given their focus on values. In what follows, we first explore the Deontic Explanation views (first arguments in favour and then objections), and then we turn to the Axiological Explanation views (again, starting with positive arguments before exploring the most serious objections).

3.2 The Deontic Explanation View: Ought, Explanation, and Weighing Explanation

The general approach. According to one prominent version of the Explanation approach, roughly understood, normative reasons can be defined by appeal to explanation and ought. This section focuses on variants of this approach.

Reasons as (parts of) explanation of oughts. Probably the best-known proponent of this sort of approach within contemporary debates is John Broome (2004, 2013, 2015, 2018). According to Broome, while 'ought' in the relevant (central) sense cannot be defined, normative reasons can be defined (Broome only specifies the sense of 'ought' that he is interested in as 'normative, owned, unqualified and prospective'; cf. Broome 2013: 45). He undertakes to provide a functional definition of normative reasons – that is, a definition that is supposed to appeal to the central role of reasons (cf. Broome 2013: 53–54). The role in question is to figure in an

---

[1] I will use the terms 'such and such Explanation view (of reasons)' and 'such and such explanationism' interchangeably in what follows. Of course, the views we discuss here should be clearly distinguished from more specific accounts about the nature of evidential (or indeed justificatory) support in contemporary epistemology (see, for example, McCain 2013, 2018, and further references therein). The term 'explanationism' in these debates is often reserved for a view that opposes probabilistic accounts of evidential support and insists instead on the role of evidence/justifiers in inferences to best explanation. While there might be, and arguably are, connections between the views we discuss here and explanationism in contemporary debates about the nature of evidential support, the focus here is more general, so to say, on normative reasons in general.

explanation of deontic facts, where a deontic fact just is a fact about an ought. More specifically, a deontic fact is a fact that, for example, S ought to F. For instance, the fact that Agnes ought to feed her cats is a deontic fact involving Agnes and her cats.

Now, Broome provides two specific ways in which something can figure in an explanation of a deontic fact: something can explain why one ought to F, and something can be part of a 'weighing explanation' of why one ought to F. To see the difference between the two, we need to look into the details of what Broome means by 'weighing explanation' (and, in particular, why it is not a (mere) explanation of why S ought to F). Before that, note first that Broome doesn't commit himself to the view that these are the only two ways of how something can figure in an explanation of a deontic fact, and second, that Broome doesn't commit himself to the idea that all normative reasons have to correspond to one or another of these ways of playing a role in an explanation of a deontic fact. According to Broome, there are other possible ways in which something can figure in an explanation of a deontic fact, and it is in principle possible that some sort of normative reasons are associated with other ways in which something can figure in an explanation of a deontic fact (see Broome 2013: 61–62). That being said, however, Broome doesn't really provide any other example of a potential way in which a normative reason could figure in an explanation of a deontic fact. In a more recent article, Broome (2018: 12) does mention the conception of reasons that is present in John Horty's *Reasons as Defaults* book (Horty 2012) as another sort of subsidiary reasons, where subsidiary reasons can be seen as one general class of normative reasons, including reasons that play a role in weighing explanations and potentially other reasons, but he doesn't really elaborate on details of why Horty's 'reasons' are distinct from weighing-explanation reasons. He does provide an example of a plausible candidate for another way in which something could figure in an explanation of a deontic fact without being itself a normative reason. Namely, he mentions the cancelling role of some considerations. An example of this is when the fact that one releases a friend from an obligation cancels what would have otherwise been a reason for the friend to keep the promise (see Broome 2013: 62). Thus, strictly speaking, what we find in Broome's work is a theory of two sorts of normative reasons that are associated with two sorts of explanations of deontic facts, but not a full-blown theory of all possible sorts of normative reasons or explanations of deontic facts. Let us examine both of these in due order.

First, Broome observes that there are cases where a fact, r, explains why S ought to F. Broome assumes a simple and somewhat plausible view about explanation according to which the explanation relation just is the reverse of the because relation. When *a* explains *b*, we assume that *b* is the case because *a* and vice versa. Broome also endorses the view that both *explanans* and *explanandum* in any genuine explanation are factive. That is, if *r* explains *q*, then both *r* is the case and *q* is the case. Roughly put, only facts can explain and be explained. Finally, without providing us with a full-blown theory of explanation, Broome notices that many alternative explanations may hold of the same thing, and that this is not really problematic. For example, it may well be the case that the room is dark because it's night and also be the case that the room is dark because the light bulb has burned out, and finally it may also be the case that the room is dark because I forgot to change the light bulb. There are in this case three alternatives and individually satisfying explanations of why the room is dark. But these three are not really in conflict. Which of these three explanations will get to be called 'the' explanation of why the room is dark may depend on purely contextual aspects. Note, nevertheless, that Broome does think that there is one complete explanation that takes all these relevant facts into account.

Now turning back to reasons, the first sort of normative reasons that Broome proposes to define is *pro toto* reasons, the normative reasons that gain their normative aspect because they are *explanations* of why one ought to F. The reason relation in itself is not normative, according to Broome; it is merely a relation of explanation, and there is nothing normative in the relation of explanation. The normative aspect comes from it being an explanation of a deontic fact. He writes: '[I]n "*X* is the reason why you ought to *F*", the "reason why" is so closely attached to the normative "ought" that the two tend to slide into each other. [...] The "reason why" (meaning explanation) bumps into the normative "ought", yielding a normative sense of "a reason" that combines the meaning of both' (Broome 2013: 50). Thus, one sort of normative reasons are merely explanations of some deontic facts. Their normative aspect is directly inherited from the normativity of deontic facts (e.g. oughts). (Note also that because *pro toto* reasons are mere explanations, they also inherit, in Broome's view, the relevant aspects of explanations *tout court*. For instance, there might be two *pro toto* reasons for the same deontic fact without there being any conflict between those two.) Here is Broome's definition of *pro toto* reasons:

> (*Pro toto* **normative reasons**): 'A pro toto *reason* for *N* to *F* is an explanation of why *N* ought to *F*.' (Broome 2013: 50)

Of course, Broome is well aware that accounting for *pro toto* reasons only is not satisfactory for a theory of reasons (even for a non-exhaustive theory). For there are normative reasons for one to F when it is not the case that one ought to F. We saw earlier that Broome assumes the factivity of explanation. If all normative reasons were always explanations of deontic facts, there wouldn't be any outweighed reasons. The looming deadline is a reason for me to stay at home and continue to work; the fact that my kids are waiting for me to pick them up in a few minutes is a reason for me to run out; the second consideration clearly outweighs the first, but the first still continues to count as a reason to stay and work – it is not thereby cancelled. If reasons were always mere explanations of oughts, then such reasons would not be possible (assuming the factivity of explanation). However, ignoring outweighed reasons would be a serious cost for any theory of reasons. Thus, Broome introduces a second and somewhat more sophisticated sort of normative reasons.

The second sort of normative reasons, according to Broome, are what he calls *pro tanto* normative reasons. In Broome's view, (some) deontic facts have 'normative weighing explanation'. Note that Broome considers the question of whether all deontic facts have a corresponding weighing explanation, and leaves open the possibility that some deontic facts may not have a weighing explanation – for example, the fact that one ought not to have contradictory beliefs, conditional on evidentialism about belief (the view that only evidence determines what one should believe) being correct (cf. Broome 2013: 58–60). A normative weighing explanation is analogue, according to Broome, to a mechanical weighing explanation, in which that a balance tips to one side or another is explained by the total weight that there is on both the right-hand pan and the left-hand pan (we are imagining a two-pan traditional balance here). More specifically, in a case where the balance tips right, we explain it by the fact that the total combination of weight on the right-hand pan exceeds the total weight on the left-hand pan. Broome applies this analogy to normative explanation. Normative weighing explanations then, according to Broome, are explanations where in a case where S ought to F, this deontic fact is explained by the fact that the total 'weight' of in-favour-of-F considerations exceeds the total 'weight' of against-F considerations. A *pro tanto* reason, according to Broome, then just is whatever plays the relevant in-favour or against F role in a normative weighing explanation of this general sort. In Broome's terms: 'A reason for you to *F* is analogous to an object in the left-hand pan, and a reason for you not to *F* is analogous to an object in the right-hand pan' (Broome 2013: 52). Somewhat more formally, Broome proposes the following definition of *pro tanto* reasons:

(***Pro tanto* reasons**): 'A *pro tanto* reason for N to F is something that plays the for-F role in a weighing explanation of why N ought to F, or in a weighing explanation of why N ought not to F, or in a weighing explanation of why it is not the case that N ought to F and not the case that N ought not to F.' (Broome 2013: 53)

Consider an example where I ought to return to the school after having picked up my kids from school. There is a weighing explanation of this ought – namely, the fact that we took another kid's scarf inadvertently and it is winter outside outweighs the fact that we will be late for dinner and that we will have lost some time. The fact that the scarf we took is not ours and it is cold outside speaks in favour of returning to the school. The fact that we will be late for the dinner and lose some time (and energy) speaks against returning. On balance, the combination of things speaking in favour of returning have more 'weight' than the total combination of things counting against it. This is one example of Broome's weighing explanation of why I ought to return to the school. The fact that the scarf is not ours and it is cold outside, which brings in the risk that the kid whose scarf we took may get cold, plays a for-returning role. These considerations are on this account *pro tanto* reasons for returning. Other considerations about losing time and energy and being late for dinner play the against-returning role and hence are *pro tanto* reasons not to return (compare this to a case from Broome 2013: 55–56).

Arguments in favour. There are several considerations that seem to speak in favour of Broome's Deontic Explanation view. Let us consider briefly what appear to be the eight most important among them.

First, contrary to what some critics seem to think (cf. Wodak 2020: 2), this approach is in a position to provide a theoretically well-motivated account of why mere enabling conditions are not normative reasons. See Section 2.5 on how a major competitor of the Explanation view, the Reasoning view, doesn't have an easy and well-motivated way to distinguish mere enablers from normative reasons. The account here relies on the well-known distinction with respect to explanations in general: it is common to distinguish *explanans* – that is, things that explain – from mere background conditions. This general distinction can be applied to normative reasons, given that normative reasons are, according to the Deontic Explanation view, entities that play a role in explanations of deontic facts (are either *explanans* or elements of weighing explanation). To take Dancy's examples once more, the fact that a promise was not made under duress and the fact that I am able to keep my promise are, presumably, not normative reasons for me to do the promised thing (cf. Dancy 2004: 38).

Yet they seem to matter normatively nevertheless. A proponent of Broome's Deontic Explanation view is perfectly suited to explain why and how this is so. Ability and absence of duress are, on this view, mere background (enabling) conditions, and not [parts of] an explanation of the relevant deontic facts. If one accepts the general and common distinction between explanation and background conditions, one is in a position to apply it in the normative case as well.

Second, and relatedly to the previous point, some considerations are not strictly speaking reasons to F, they are not [parts of] an explanation of why S ought to F, but nevertheless entail that S ought to F. Presumably, cases of entailing evidence that S ought to F are of this sort. Again, proponents of the Reasoning view have some trouble explaining why this is so, given that considerations that entail p can function perfectly in good arguments/patterns of reasoning towards p (given some assumptions). The Deontic Explanation view explains how this is possible. In general, considerations that entail p are not [typically] parts of a good explanation of why p. This aspect of explanations in general presumably also applies to deontic explanations. Thus, given this general aspect of explanations, the Deontic Explanation view seems to have an important advantage over some of its main rivals at least. Broome himself appears to hint towards this line of argument in favour of the Deontic Explanation view in his brief remarks on what is missing in Raz's view (and on Dancy's objection to Raz's view). He writes:

> Dancy points out that, by Raz's criterion [i.e. a version of the Reasoning view], conclusive evidence that you ought to perform an action would be itself a reason to perform the action. That is not necessarily so. Facts that merely entail that an agent ought to perform the action are not necessarily reasons for her to perform it; to be reasons they must explain why she ought to perform it.[. . .] If a newspaper publishes an article saying that a minister ought to resign, that is evidence that she ought to resign. If the newspaper is extremely reliable it may be conclusive evidence. But it is not a reason for the minister to resign. (Broome 2013: 51)

The Deontic Explanation view can easily explain why considerations that entail that one ought to F are not normative reasons to F, in cases where these considerations are not normative reasons to F.

Third, the Deontic Explanation view can also easily deal with the Moore-paradoxical (and self-undermining) cases that we introduced in the preceding chapter. Remember that in Moore-paradoxical cases, we have considerations like 'the building is on fire but I don't know that the building is on fire'. Intuitively, in situations where these considerations are true, they can be normative reasons in favour of, say, checking, considering, reconsidering whether the building is on fire, and perhaps for running away. Some views – for example, the Reasoning view, that tie normative reasons too closely to one being able to reason from them towards the relevant (intention to) F-ing in a valid/good or fitting way – predict that such considerations cannot be normative reasons, even though they appear naturally to *speak in favour* of some or other reaction. The Deontic Explanation view seems to be able to account for these cases while respecting the pre-theoretical intuition that these considerations are some sort of normative reasons. Suppose that I really ought to check out whether the building where I am now is not on fire. Presumably, in such a case, there is a weighing explanation of such an ought. The weighing explanation of such an ought will appeal to elements from the relevant Moore-paradoxical considerations. To take the example from the Chapter 2, the fact that there is a fire of which I am not aware counts strongly in favour of checking/investigating whether the house is not on fire. It is also a part of the weighing explanation of why I ought to check/investigate/run away from the house on fire. If this is right, then proponents of the Deontic Explanation view are in a position to explain why the Moore-paradoxical considerations appear to be normative reasons. I ought to check the house because there is a fire of which I am not aware. Presumably, a similar account also applies to self-undermining considerations and, in general, about cases where it appears that a subject is not able to F on the basis of the relevant reason to F. Being in a position to explain these cases puts the Deontic Explanation view at an advantage compared to some of its main rivals.

Fourth, the Deontic Explanation view is designed to account for graded normativity. It is often recognised that a theory that has only 'strict' (or categorical) normative notions as opposed to a theory that can account for strict and for graded notions will be somewhat lacking (see Lord and Maguire 2016). It seems that we need both strict notions like 'ought' and 'obligation' and graded or weighed notions that can be appealed to in order to account for apparent normative conflicts (considerations pulling in different directions). This theoretic need for two sorts of normative notions is well known at least since W. D. Ross, who introduced the notion of prima facie oughts. As we observed earlier (cf. Chapter 1), normative reasons are supposed to fit the bill. They are supposed to come in different degrees. By its very design – for example, its appeal to 'weights' of reasons and the weighing explanation of deontic facts – the Deontic Explanation view is poised to account for the graded, non-categorical/non-binary aspect of normative reasons.

Fifth, the Deontic Explanation view is general enough to be easily applicable to action (intention) as well as to the case of belief and other attitudes. Having this level of generality certainly speaks in its favour as long as we expect that a serious contender to the status of the correct theory of normative reasons is able to explain all pre-theoretically plausible cases of normative reasons (and not only to be applicable to some cherry-picked cases). As long as there are oughts that apply to attitudes and as long as there are weighing explanations of (some) such oughts, the Deontic Explanation view predicts that there will be normative reasons for and against attitudes to which such oughts apply.

Sixth, the view also preserves a good level of theoretical generality with respect to some vexed questions in contemporary meta-ethics. For instance, it is, in its simple form, neither committed to nor incompatible with so-called buck-passing accounts of value, where buck-passing accounts suggest that values can be reduced to reasons (see Scanlon 1998, for instance; cf. Chapter 1). Given that buck-passing (in this general form) is not a claim about the relation between oughts and reasons, a proponent of the Deontic Explanation view can accept that values reduce to reasons even though, ultimately, reasons reduce to oughts and explanations. On the other hand, the Deontic Explanation view is also compatible with values ultimately not being reducible to normative reasons; the only thing that the Deontic Explanation view is committed to is that normative reasons do reduce to a combination of oughts and explanations. Thus, it is uncommitted to this much-debated issue in meta-ethics and is compatible with both sides of the debate.

Seventh, and somewhat connectedly but also distinctly, the view can also easily explain why there are no normative reasons for values (instantiations of values). Suppose that there is a value in you being physically fit. It is a valuable state of you being fit and healthy. But as we have already seen in Chapter 2, there are no normative reasons for you to be healthy. That is, there are no reasons for you to be healthy as opposed to there being reasons for you to undertake some training or adopt a good diet, as actions that could lead to you being healthy. Of course, there are reasons for you to go to the gym and eat healthily, but it is not the same thing as being healthy. The Deontic Explanation view is, again, perfectly able to explain why this is so. There are no oughts for states of value instantiation, there is no ought for you to *be* healthy, as opposed to undertaking sport and adopting a good diet. Given that there are no oughts, there are no weighing explanations, and hence the view predicts that there are no normative reasons for you to be healthy. There are, on the other hand, reasons for you to go to the gym, given that you ought to go to the gym and there are weighing explanations of such an ought. Thus, the Deontic Explanation view seems to be able to predict correctly the difference between values and deontic properties and is able to explain in a theoretically well-motivated manner why there are no reasons for values (instantiations of values).

Eight, and finally, the view is in a good position to explain our pretheoretical judgment that there is some kind of connection between normative reasons and explanation. Requests for explanations of some apparent ought to F and requests for reasons for F-ing can often be interchanged without any loss of information. Suppose that I ought to go to the grocery shop and I tell you just that – that is, that I ought to go to the grocery shop. It seems that in such a case, your request for me to give you reasons that I take there to be for me to go to the grocery shop amounts to exactly the same as your request for me to explain why I ought to go to the grocery shop. That is, in such a situation, your reply 'What reasons are there for you to go to the shop?' can be replaced without any loss of information with 'Why ought you to go to the shop?'. Now, it would be somewhat odd if this were a mere accident. The Deontic Explanation view explains this intuitive connection without any need to postulate such an accidental connection. There is an intuitive link between reasons and explanations of oughts, because reasons just are explanations or play a role in a weighing explanation of oughts, according to the Deontic Explanation view.

We have enumerated some positive arguments in favour of the Deontic Explanation view of normative reasons. We have briefly reviewed eight of them. Unfortunately, the view also faces some pretty serious objections. Let us now turn to some of the main worries about the view.

Worries. The first worry appears with respect to Broome's account of *pro toto* reasons. Roughly, the worry is that not all genuine explanations of why one ought to F appear naturally to be reasons for one to F. This worry, or at any rate a worry similar enough to this one, is due to John Brunero; see Brunero (2018) and also Brunero (2013) for a related worry for earlier (and presumably more problematic) versions of Broome's account. Consider the fact that I ought to save a drowning toddler. Is there an explanation of why I ought to save the toddler? If there is an or the explanation of why I ought to save the toddler, then, according to Broome's account, that explanation (*explanans*) is a *pro toto* reason for me to save the toddler. Let's assume that there is an/the explanation why I ought to save the toddler. Given this assumption, Broome's view predicts that this explanation is a *pro toto* reason to save the toddler. But what could possibly be an explanation of why I ought to save the toddler? Presumably, it has to have as part of it the consideration that the toddler will die if I don't save her. But, presumably, it is not only that. It is also that I am not risking anything of a comparative value to the toddler's death by saving her. For instance, I am not risking certain death myself, or the death of my loved ones, or the death of a hundred other innocent babies, and so on (see Singer 1972 for the original example and a theory of altruism based on it; see Timmerman 2015 and Logins 2016a for a recent further discussion). But, crucially, the fact that I am risking neither my life nor the lives of my loved ones or numerous innocent babies are not (parts of) reasons why I ought to save the drowning toddler. These are considerations that correspond to the absence of 'undercutting defeaters' (see Brunero 2018), but are hardly seen as parts of reasons to save the toddler. These are certainly parts of an explanation of why I ought to save the toddler, but they don't appear to be themselves reasons to save the toddler. That the toddler is drowning is a reason to save her and not that that I am not risking my life by jumping into the water to save her. Broome's view seems to predict otherwise.

One possible reply to this worry is to insist on the distinction that the Deontic Explanation view postulates – namely, the distinction among genuine explanation and background conditions, as well as contextual and pragmatic considerations. As in the case of non-normative explanations, what will count as a/the explanation in given circumstances depends partially on background conditions and contextual/pragmatic considerations (e.g. what is of interest for the subject; see Broome 2013: 49). Thus, one might reply that the absence of undercutting defeaters may well be part of the bigger, complete explanation of why one ought to F, but will not be part of some *pars pro toto* explanations of why one ought to F (where a pars pro toto explanation is a partial explanation that stands in for the one big explanation, and in calling a pro toto explanation the explanation we are using a synecdoche, namely the so-called pars pro toto figure of speech, see Broome 2013: 49). But such a reply is unsatisfying, for it presupposes that the complete, big explanation *is* the explanation of why one ought to F, even though there are some *pars pro toto* explanations that don't include the mention of all the background conditions, the absence of undercutting defeaters, and interests. But a complete, big explanation of why one ought to F still counts as an explanation of why one ought to F and hence, on Broome's account, has to be a/the reason why one ought to F. (If this complete explanation is not a reason, it is then difficult to see why partial explanations would be allowed on Broome's view to be *pro toto* reasons.)² But this is precisely what we dispute. The complete explanation is not the/a reason why one ought to F. For parts of the complete, bigger explanation are not parts of a/the reason why one ought to F. The toddler example is just about this. Certainly, the absence of undercutting defeaters has to be part of the complete, bigger explanation of why I ought to save the toddler. But the absence of such undercutting defeaters doesn't appear to be part of the/a reason why I ought to save the toddler.³

The second worry concerns the relation between *pro toto* and *pro tanto* reasons on the Deontic Explanation view. Let us take Broome's own example of a *pro toto* reason, the case where you ought to visit Mr. Reed (cf. Broome 2013: 50–51). Broome (2013: 50) suggests that

> The explanation [of why you ought to visit Mr. Reed] might be that he is the best dentist around. [...] In a different context, the explanation might be that you ought to visit the best dentist around. [...] A fuller explanation would be the conjunctive fact that you ought to visit the best dentist around and Mr. Reed is the best dentist around.

Now, it is quite plausible that in this case, there is also a weighing explanation of why you ought to visit Mr. Reed: the total 'weight' of all for-Mr.-Reed-visiting considerations 'outweigh' the total 'weight' of

---

² That the complete, bigger explanation counts as an explanation of why S ought to F seems to be implied by Broome himself: 'So long as something explains why you ought to *F*, it is a *pro toto* reason for you to *F*' (Broome 2013: 50). The complete explanation does explain why one ought to F. Hence, on a natural reading of these remarks, it is a/the reason why one ought to F. He also writes: 'A *pro toto* reason therefore need not be a unique canonical reason' (Broome 2013: 50). It is natural to take 'x need not be Q' to imply that x nevertheless may be Q. Thus, it is natural to take it that a pro toto reason may be the canonical, complete reason.

³ This worry may be further developed as a problem for the very idea of there being any *pars pro toto* or perfect explanations of why one ought to F. Broome himself struggles in providing an obvious example of a perfect (*pars pro toto*) rather than a weighing explanation of why one ought to F. Strict deontic rules and beliefs in contradictions are two tentative examples. But they do depend on other, debatable assumptions. See Kearns and Star (2008: 36) for a line of worry based on this sort of observation:

> Given Broome's own doubts about these examples [e.g. the examples of rigid deontic rules and there being reasons to never believe contradictions], it is unclear that this third feature of his account [e.g. that the view accommodates the possibility of reasons that are not weighed against each other, cf. Kearns and Star 2008: 36] is really a positive feature. Perhaps it should be discounted.

Without clear cases of *pars pro toto* explanations of why one ought to F, we are left only with the category of alleged weighing explanations of why one ought to F. However, in what sense 'weighing explanation' is an explanation and provides ground for a reductive analysis of reasons remains to be seen. More objections against the account of *pro tanto* reasons in terms of weighing explanation are discussed ahead.

against-Mr.-Reed-visiting considerations. The same line of reasoning that Broome proposes in the cases of typical weighing explanation cases seem to apply here too. There definitely are costs for you in visiting the best dentist around. If anything, this will certainly cost you some money, energy, or time. It will certainly cost you more than visiting some less good but, say, more nearby cheaper dentist. But if we assume that in this case there are both the explanation of why you ought to visit Mr. Reed and a weighing explanation of why you ought to visit Mr. Reed, then the Deontic Explanation account predicts that there are both a *pro toto* reason for you to visit and some *pro tanto* reasons for you to visit. Crucially, it seems that the same considerations will count as *pro toto* and *pro tanto* reasons. Presumably, the fact that Mr. Reed is the best dentist around will come out on this account as both a *pro toto* and a *pro tanto* reason for you to visit Mr. Reed. But if so, aren't we then double-counting a given consideration as a reason to visit Mr. Reed? Aren't we over-generating normative reasons? Does it mean that you have two reasons, two independent elements that count in favour of visiting Mr. Reed on this account? If so, then it certainly counts against the view (see Brunero 2013 for an objection against the Deontic Explanation view along similar lines).

It seems that whether there is a genuine problem here will depend on how exactly proponents of deontic explanationism conceive of the relation between the explanation of a deontic fact and a weighing explanation of a deontic fact. Yet it is not really clear how this relation is conceived. The mere fact that it is not clear how the relation between the two is conceived is in itself somewhat problematic, since it is incumbent on the proponents of the Deontic Explanation view to explain why their view, contrary to what one not completely far-fetched interpretation of their view might imply, is not committed to the problematic consequences of double-counting reasons.

Finally, one might also think that the very fact that Broome's view entails the existence of two radically different sorts of reasons counts somewhat against the view. As Kearns and Star observe:

> [On Broome's view] [s]omething is a normative reason if it is an explana-
> tion of a normative fact or it weighs in favor of a certain action. These
> properties are so different that it is tempting to interpret Broome as
> claiming that 'normative reason' is ambiguous between them. Whether
> we understand Broome to be claiming that 'normative reason' is ambiguous
> or simply that there are two very different ways of being a normative reason,
> this is an unattractive feature of his account. (Kearns and Star 2008: 45)

The unattractiveness according to Kearns and Star comes from the consequence that such a disjunctive view is less simple and elegant than its non-disjunctive competitors. It doesn't seem to fit well with our ordinary way of talking about reasons. If so, it would imply that the concept of reasons doesn't pick out a non-artificial property (see Kearns and Star 2008).

The third concern is more specifically about *pro tanto* reasons. Broome has made it clear that he thinks of the explanation relation as the inverse of the because relation. According to Broome, that X explains Y just means that Y 'is so because' X 'is so' (cf. Broome 2008: 100, 2013). In other terms, X explains Y just when X makes Y the case (cf. Broome 2008: 100). But if this is so, this should also apply to weighing explanations. This, however, may appear implausible in the case of outweighed reasons (see Brunero 2013, 2018, for this line of objection). Take the case where you ought not go on vacation to the seaside. Let's assume that the proponents of the Deontic Explanation view accept that there is a weighing explanation of why you ought not to go on vacation to the seaside. Part of this weighing explanation will be that you broke your leg three weeks ago and it is still not advisable for you to travel far, and the seaside is a long way away. But if this is really a weighing explanation, then according to the Deontic Explanation view, against-not-going-to-the-sea considerations also play a role in explaining why you ought not to go to the seaside. Let us say that a friend of yours has proposed that you stay at their parents' house just next to the sea during the vacation for free, and that the weather is really nice at this time of the year; these are considerations that play the against-not-going role in the relevant weighing explanation. The free-of-charge accommodation and the good weather are considerations speaking in favour of going. According to the Deontic Explanation view then, the free accommodation next to the sea and the good weather then partly makes it the case that you ought not to go on the seaside vacation. But this result appears counterintuitive. If anything, these considerations could make it the case that you ought to go. How can these considerations make it (partially) the case that you ought not to go? Is it really the case that you ought not to go partially because you can have free accommodation next to the sea and the weather is especially clement there at this time of the year? To make the oddness even more vivid, imagine a discussion with a friend. 'You: I ought not to go to the seaside on vacation. Friend: Why? You: for one thing the weather there is really nice now. For another, I have this free house just for us for a whole week.' To my ear, such a conversation sounds really like a joke. However, on the Deontic Explanation view, of course, this conversation shouldn't come out as a joke, but only as a partial explanation of why you ought not to go to the seaside. This seems to be a strongly counterintuitive implication of the view and hence it speaks against the Deontic Explanation view's account of *pro tanto* reasons (see Brunero 2013, 2018, for more details on this objection).

This verdict seems to point to an even more substantial issue with Broome's account of *pro tanto* reasons in terms of weighing explanation. The issue is that it is simply unclear what weighing explanations really are and, in particular, how to understand the idea that some considerations play a 'for-F' (or 'against-F') role in the alleged weighing explanation of an ought fact. For Broome (2013: 54), '[t]he for-*F* role can be identified from the structure of the explanation itself'. How exactly? 'In a weighing explanation of why you ought to *F*, the for-*F* role is the winning one, and that is how it can be identified' (Broome 2013: 55). So, fundamentally we are supposed to grasp which considerations play the for-F role in a weighing explanation and thus be able to grasp which considerations are reasons by grasping considerations that are *the winning ones* in a weighing explanation. However, as Kearns and Star have rightly observed, this suggestion is problematic. In particular, they rightly wonder 'how the winning considerations are meant to be identified *as* winning, if not by weighing up different considerations in order to see which considerations together most strongly *count in favor* of particular actions' (Kearns and Star 2008: 43, original emphasis). The problem is that Broome doesn't actually seem to provide a substantive analysis of (*pro tanto*) normative reasons, since at the end of the day and contrary to what he suggests, we do need to grasp what counting in favour amounts to in order to understand reasons. To grasp what winning in a weighing explanation amounts to just is to be able to grasp various degrees of weight/strength of counting in favour. Following Kearns and Star (2008: 43), we may ask: 'Why should we think we could grasp what it is for certain considerations to be *winning* without a prior understanding that facts can *count in favor* of actions?' Thus, it is not even clear that Broome is offering a substantial or, to use Kearns and Star's terminology, full-blooded, account of *pro tanto* reasons in terms of explanation (of a deontic fact). At the end of the day, the account of *pro tanto* reasons as considerations that play a for-F role in a weighing explanation seems to be parasitic on our prior grasp of reasons counting in favour of F-ing. Perhaps even the very construct of weighing explanation of deontic facts appears intelligible only insofar as we have a prior grasp of reasons speaking/counting in favour of or against F-ing and being comparable in this respect, and not the other way round.[4]

Fourth, and perhaps even more fundamentally, one may worry whether the whole analogy of weight is an appropriate way to capture what normative reasons are. Yet the weight analogy and the very idea of there being 'weighing explanations' is central to Broome's account. Thus, it is not clear whether the Deontic Explanation view tells us anything substantial about reasons once we take away considerations about weight of reasons and weighing explanation (see Hawthorne and Magidor 2018 for this line of objection).[5] It is really dubious that the relative importance of normative reasons can be correctly captured by appeal to 'weights' of reasons. For one thing, weight respects additivity; that is, roughly, the principle according to which adding an object with the weight x to an object with the weight y results in there being something with the total weight of $x + y$ (leaving it open whether it is a new object or a sum of two objects). So, for instance, if you add 2 kg of oranges to 1 kg of kiwis (and nothing more), you have a total of 3 kg of fruit. This simple principle applies universally to anything that has a weight. However, it is violated in the case of normative reasons. Adding a normative reason of the degree of importance x to F to a normative reason of the degree of importance y to F doesn't always add up to there being two/combinatory normative reasons with the total degree of importance of $x + y$. Some reasons just don't add up. To take an example inspired by Hawthorne and Magidor (2018): that this piece of jewellery contains a red diamond is a reason of, say, degree x for you to buy it and that this piece of jewellery contains a ruby diamond is a reason of degree y for you to buy it. But it may still be the case that there are not two reasons/a new combinatory reason with the total degree of $x + y$ for you to buy the jewellery. That the piece of jewellery contains a specifically ruby diamond doesn't add anything to the total degree of reasons that there are for you to buy the jewellery. Or,

---

[4] See also Brunero (2013: 812–816) for a similar objection. Brunero concludes that depending on how we interpret Broome's definition of *pro tanto* reasons as playing the for-F role in a weighing explanation, we get either a false or an uninformative (not a substantial) account of reasons. He writes: '[I]t seems as though Broome's account of reasons, depending on how it is interpreted, is either uninformative or false' (Brunero 2013: 816).

[5] See also Kearns and Star (2008: 44) for a related worry:

A related worry is that Broome's purported analysis of reasons does not give us an analysis of the strength of reasons. He seems to believe it is a brute fact that reasons simply have certain weights of some kind. What these weights are seems to be a mystery. [...] [T]his is another respect in which Broome fails to provide a substantive analysis of reasons.

to take a somewhat different but equally relevant case, discussed more by Schroeder (2007) and Fogal (2016), that you like dancing is a reason for you to go to the party and that there will be dancing at the party is a reason for you to go to the party. But it doesn't follow from these two facts that you have two reasons of some sum of total weight to go to the party. It seems that you cannot generate more reasons or a higher degree of the importance of reasons just by putting these two considerations together.

Moreover, adding two reasons to F sometimes results in having less reason to F than having only one of these (see also our discussion in Section 2.5, which contains further references relevant for this issue). So, for instance, suppose that you like pizza and you like Nutella. That the item on the menu is a pizza seems to be a reason for you to order it. Similarly, that the item on the menu contains Nutella is also a reason for you to order it. However, that the item in question is a Nutella pizza is not a weightier reason for you to order it. Actually, it is not a reason at all for you to order it (say, you hate Nutella pizza). It seems that adding two reasons to F doesn't always add up to having a 'weightier' total of reasons to F. Sometimes adding different reasons to F cancels them all mutually out. See Nair (2016) for similar cases that are adapted from Horty (2012: 61), involving running in wet heat versus running in wet weather and running in heat.

Another aspect of reasons that is incompatible with the simple principles that apply to weighing is that whereas subtracting an element with the weight x from a total (stuff with the) weight of $x + y$ will result in there remaining an object with the weight y. Nothing similar can be universally applicable to normative reasons. It is not always the case that subtracting one normative reason to F from the total of considerations that speak in favour of F-ing will leave you with a smaller amount of considerations speaking in favour of F-ing. Let's take the Nutella pizza example again, but let's modify it a bit. Suppose that that the item on the menu is a Nutella pizza is a tiny reason for ordering it. Say, you are really hungry and you have a reason to eat anything minimally edible. However, that the item on the menu is a Nutella pizza is not a more important reason for you to order it than that the thing is pizza alone, or that the thing is made of Nutella alone. Indeed, any of these two has a much higher degree reason-wise for you than the two of them together. Thus, it seems that normative reasons don't respect the simplest of the principles that apply to weight and weighing. Without these, however, it is not clear in what sense the analogy with weight is still theoretically useful. Broome recognises that the analogy is not to be taken to be perfect, but as Hawthorne and Magidor (2018) note, it is not just about the analogy being perfect; it seems that the analogy breaks down completely, and hence it is not clear in what sense the talk of 'weighing' may still be insightful at all. Without the analogy with weight, it doesn't seem that there is much of substance left in Broome's version of the Deontic Explanation view, given how crucial weighing explanation is for this account.

The fifth consideration that speaks against the Deontic Explanation view, and also points towards what's wrong with it more fundamentally, is that it focuses on one central aspect of reasons as we commonly understand them at the expense of another central aspect that we commonly attribute to reasons. This will be also relevant later, when we discuss our positive account. Remember that a fundamental worry with the Reasoning view mentioned earlier was that it focused exclusively on reasoning (and motivating reasons) and acting/having an attitude on the basis of normative reasons at the expense of other important aspects of reasons. It was not well suited to account for all normative reasons. Some considerations seem to count in favour of F-ing without being premises of good patterns of reasoning (cf. Moore-paradoxical considerations). Of course, the explanation views of reasons can easily account for these cases, as we saw earlier. In Moore-paradoxical cases, for instance, the relevant considerations may still count as parts of an [weighing] explanation of why one ought to F in the relevant ways. However, now we have the reverse problem, it seems. For the Deontic Explanation view is going to the other extreme, so to say. It is neglecting the reasoning aspect in accounting for normative reasons. As Kearns and Star (among others) have rightly observed, being practically relevant is a central feature that we commonly attribute to reasons: '[i]ndeed, the philosophical importance of reasons is due in large part to their importance in everyday life' (Kearns and Star 2008: 39). They suggest that this importance comes from reasons being the kind of thing that can help us work out what we ought to do. They write: 'That is, reasons are our guide to what we should do' (Kearns and Star 2008: 39). And they are so, '*in virtue of being reasons*' (Kearns and Star 2008: 39), not just because the facts that happen to be reasons are also facts that can guide us towards finding out what our deliberative oughts are. In short, we are back to the importance of reasons in deliberation.

One problem here is that even if Broome's account somehow manages to be compatible with the view that facts that are reasons for S to F are effectively facts that S can use in working out what S ought to do/what attitude to hold, this result would come out at best as an accidental by-product of the view, not as a central feature of reasons, which one might think is already odd, given the centrality of guidance for one common way of understanding reasons.

More worrisome still is another problem – namely, on Broome's account of reasons, there will be plenty of cases where one figures out what one ought to do on the basis of some other considerations and not on the basis of her reasons to F. That is, one might come to know that one ought to F, on Broome's view, on the basis of some considerations without even knowing what her reasons to F are. The now famous cabbage example from Kearns and Star (2008: 40) is a case that illustrates the point: 'the fact that a clearly reliable book says that you ought to eat cabbage may reasonably convince you that you ought to eat cabbage, even though this fact doesn't explain why you ought to eat cabbage.' Clearly one can come to know that one ought to eat cabbage on the basis of the reliable book saying so. However, that the mere fact that the book says it is not an explanation (nor part of a weighing explanation) of why one ought to eat cabbage. Thus, a consideration that guides one towards knowledge of one's deliberative ought – that is, the testimony from the book – cannot be, on Broome's view, a *pro toto* or *pro tanto* reason to eat cabbage. This seems excessive. Fundamentally, the problem is that in such cases Broome's reasons play no practical role at all, no role in a deliberation of what one ought to do. Thus, we can agree with Kearns and Star (2008: 41) that 'even if we think that such an action-guiding role is not essential to reasons, it is clear that reasons are generally practically important. However, if agents are able to work out what they ought to do without knowing what explains what they ought to do, then reasons, as Broome conceives of them, are not a vital part of practical life.' Kearns and Star also provide an insightful analogy that sheds light on what might be the root of the problem here. They suggest that deontic explanationism is 'backward looking', whereas their own (and I think we can also say the Reasoning accounts) are 'forward looking'.[6] That is, whereas the Explanation view

---

[6] Consider:

> Broome's view is backward looking. Typically, reasoning that concerns explanation proceeds as follows: A person knows a fact and wishes to explain it. She then infers some other fact by inference to the best explanation. By applying this to the case of normative facts, we get the following picture. We know certain normative facts which we wish to explain. We then infer other facts by inference to the best explanation. These facts are, according to Broome, the reasons we have to act. (Kearns and Star 2008: 41)

This is contrasted with an alternative account: '[o]ur view is a forward-looking view of reasons. That is, reasons are those things that are used to figure out what ought to be done. One is first in possession of reasons to act in certain ways and then uses these to determine how one should act' (Kearns and Star 2008: 41).

starts with an ought, the Evidence and Reasoning views start with considerations that help us to find out what we ought to do. And the Explanation
view gets the phenomenology of deliberation wrong. The idea is that in
deliberating about what to do, what we *should do*, we don't start with
the ought fact, but, typically, we engage in deliberation and reasoning to
find out the relevant ought fact. Given that we don't know what we
ought to do in such contexts, we are not looking for explanations of the
ought facts. Yet reasons are the things we are looking for in deliberation.
Thus, normative reasons cannot all be just explanations (or parts of
weighing explanations) of some ought facts (cf. Kearns and Star 2008:
41). Exploring differences and similarities between reasoning and explanation will be the key and, indeed, the fundamental element of our own
positive account to be developed later. Let us not anticipate that
discussion yet.

Now, someone sympathetic to the Deontic Explanation view may want
to try to amend it in ways that would fix the aforementioned problems.
We conclude this section by considering briefly an alternative view that
also combines an appeal to both oughts and something close to an
explanation, in order to characterise reasons.

Reasons as right makers. The aforementioned five worries appear
rather problematic for the Deontic Explanation view. Yet, as we observed
earlier, there was also a prima facie case in favour of it. What should we
think, then, if it's mistaken? What about the eight arguments that we have
listed in its favour? Were we merely confused? Later, I will argue that such
apparent confusion – a situation where some considerations draw us
towards something like the Explanation view, but other considerations
draw us towards a different understanding of reasons – is only to be
expected, given what reasons are. However, let us now consider another
option for those who are sympathetic to a broad deontic explanationism.
It is based on a line of thought that would keep the spirit of the Deontic
Explanation view and focus on reasons as constitutive with respect to
oughts, while relaxing the theoretically ambitious aims of the approach.
The approach proposed by Laura and Francois Schroeter about [practical]
reasons as right makers seems to be one way of doing just this (Schroeter
and Schroeter 2009). On their view, we should not aim to provide a
reductionist account of normative reasons. According to them, some
substantial constraints on what are normative reasons will always depend
on common-sense intuitions that cannot be captured by purely formal
accounts. Their approach is a way of characterising normative reasons,
which are to be understood in functional terms, by appeal to their role in

constituting rightness (more on this in a moment) rather than to define or reduce reasons to a given role in explaining deontic facts.

The approach might appear to be closer to the reasons-first approach than to an explanationist approach since they refuse to reduce reasons to something else. However, their characterisation of reasons is very much in the spirit of the Deontic Explanation approach. For the positive things that the approach does say about reasons appeal to making conditions and rightness, which can be understood as corresponding to oughts. Despite being of the same broad family of views (i.e. the focus here is on the reverse of 'because' and ought), the right-making approach differs importantly from the Deontic Explanation approach. As we saw already, they don't aim to provide a reductive analysis of reasons in other terms. But there is yet another difference, namely it focuses on the constitution of rightness rather than on mere explanation of deontic facts. The relevant difference between constitution and explanation appears to amount to a difference between two species of the same genus. Contrary to what some passages from Broome might seem to suggest, not everything that can count as (part of) an explanation will count as (part of) the constitution of the relevant thing, which seems to give the constitution approach some advantage over Broome's deontic explanationism. For one thing, the right-maker view doesn't entail that any explanation of why one ought to F has to be a reason to F (cf. the first worry for Broome's explanationism). That I don't risk my life by jumping into the pond can be part of an explanation of why I ought to jump, without being itself a reason for me to jump (that a toddler is drowning is a reason). One might think that such a consideration points only towards the absence of undercutting defeaters for the claim that I ought to jump, and that the mere absence of such a possible undercutting defeater is not, strictly speaking, part of what makes it right for me to jump into the pond.[7] Similarly, the correct meta-ethical theory will provide an explanation of why something is a reason to F while not being itself a normative reason to F. The focus on constitution rather than explanation explains how this can be the case. The correct meta-ethical view doesn't constitute the rightness of F-ing.

---

[7] Yet note that whether this line of thought is well grounded will depend on how we think about constitution. If one thinks that constitution, like explanation, can be of a more or less complete sort, then, arguably, one might also insist that a more complete story of what makes my jump into the pond right – that is, what constitutes its rightness in a more complete sense – has to take the absence of possible undercutting defeaters into account. If so, then the right-maker view doesn't have an advantage over Broome's deontic explanationism here after all.

Another advantage that Schroeter and Schroeter are claiming to have over the Deontic Explanation approach is that, given their relaxed theoretical ambitions – that is, not aiming to provide a reduction of normative reasons to something else – they can also easily deal with cases where some reasons-wise irrelevant facts may play a role in an explanation of why S ought to F, without being counted as genuine reasons to F for S. The job of picking out the relevant facts as reasons is done not by any formal constraints according to this view but by concrete common-sense considerations on a case-by-case basis (cf. Schroeter and Schroeter 2009). Perhaps this line of thought might equally constitute first steps for dealing with the worry of double-counting reasons (cf. the second worry mentioned earlier).

Even though the right-making account might avoid some of the problems of Broome's deontic explanationism, it still has important and similar pitfalls. For one thing, it is not clear how the constitution of rightness works in the outweighed reasons case. Schroeter and Schroeter propose to think of constitution here using an analogy to how bricks constitute a house. It is bricks arranged in some way that constitutes a house. Reasons are supposed to constitute rightness in a somewhat similar manner. Yet in the case of outweighed reasons, it is not clear at all how the fact that a friend proposes that I stay in a house by the seaside can constitute (even if only partially) the rightness of me staying home for my holidays or how is it possible on this view that my promise to meet my friend for a coffee is a reason for me to go to the meeting place in a situation where I witness a traffic accident and am the only one able to help. It doesn't seem that my promise constitutes the rightness of me leaving the injured and going to the place where I promised to meet my friend instead. It is clearly wrong to leave the injured and meet my friend in such a situation. So, my promise cannot constitute the rightness of going to meet my friend here. But it doesn't seem to play any role in constituting the rightness of staying and helping the injured either. The promise to meet my friend is irrelevant with respect to the rightness of helping the injured. Also, it is not clear that the right-maker approach captures the gradable aspect of reasons. In particular, one might think that exactly as in the case of weighing explanation, the right-maker view fails to do justice to the failure of additivity of reasons. For constitution seems to satisfy additivity. If a set A of bricks constitutes a house and a set B of bricks constitutes a house, then, taken together (and without destroying either A or B), bricks A and B constitute either a larger house or two distinct houses that taken together are larger than the A house or the B house taken individually. More fundamentally, and exactly as in the case of deontic explanationism, the right-maker

approach appears to minimise too radically the role of reasons in deliberation. Yet, in a sense, our common-sense understanding of reasons is also
as of things that help us to figure out what we ought to do or which
attitudes to hold. Hence, it is not clear that the right-makers approach is
really an improvement on the Deontic Explanation account, at least on
these problematic points.[8]

3.3 Axiological Explanation View

Another possible way of capturing the pre-theoretical insight that normative reasons have to be tied to explanation of something normative, broadly
understood, is to focus on explanation of values. It is common to see values
as distinct from obligations, and more generally axiological properties (e.g.
values, good, bad) from deontic properties (including, oughts, permissions,
requirements, and so on). We have referred quite vaguely to the common
category of these as broad normativity. At that level of abstraction, the
Explanation approach of reasons is characterised as the view that a normative reason to F is an (partial) explanation (of an aspect) of a normative
feature/fact with respect to F-ing. The preceding section focused on one
prominent way of making this abstract idea more precise, namely defining
reasons as explanations of aspects of deontic facts. The present section
looks at the axiological alternative, an alternative that can be endorsed with
or without endorsing a more ambitious project of defining/analysing other
normative properties/notions, including oughts/obligations and fittingness
in terms of values and thus vindicating the idea of value being the most
fundamental and explanatorily prime normative property/notion (e.g. the
value-first approach). Very roughly then, according to Axiological
Explanation views (be they value-first accounts or not), a normative reason
to F is (a part of) an explanation of why F-ing would be good (has value).
More specifically, we will focus on two recent and arguably the most
promising versions of the Axiological Explanation approach. The first is

---

[8] Another option within the broad deontic explanationism family that has recently been suggested by
Nebel (2019) is to deny the factivity of reason-why constructions but maintain that normative
reasons are reasons why one ought to F. We will not go into details of this suggestion here, in order
to keep our discussion manageable. But note, as Wodak (2020) has recently observed, that while,
strictly speaking, normative reasons – that is, reasons-why one ought to F – on Nebel's account are
not (parts of) explanations of why one ought to F, it is not really clear what exactly they are. If
reasons-why are not explanations, then what are they? Nebel doesn't provide many positive details
about these, and it is not clear that we have a clear pre-theoretic grasp of 'reasons-why' that are not
understood as explanations.

defended by Stephen Finlay, the second by Barry Maguire. After present-ing each of these, we will also look at what appear to be their pitfalls.

The central idea of Stephen Finlay's comprehensive treatment of the explanation-plus-value-based view of reasons, elaborated in a number of recent publications (Finlay 2006, 2012, 2014: 85–115, 2020), is that a consideration is a normative reason for one to F just in case the consider-ation explains why it would be somewhat good for one to F (cf. Finlay 2020: 1). On this view, for relevant F-ings, there is a degree of goodness of a kind in a subject's F-ing. Normative reasons are considerations that explain why this is so. Again, as is common, the approach has to be understood in functionalist terms. Reasons are considerations or, more specifically, facts that play some specific function (or stand in a specific relation, the reasons relation). That function, in this case, is the function of explaining why some F-ing would be good in a sense and to a degree (see Finlay 2014: 85). Thus, on this view, to say that the consideration that my kids are hungry is a reason for me to prepare them some food is to say that that my kids are hungry explains why it would be good that I prepare them some food. It would be good to prepare them some food because they are hungry. Note also that strictly speaking Finlay's account is about 'reasons' statements – that is, a theory of meaning of 'reasons' statements. In what follows, however, for reasons of manageability of discussion, we avoid the repetition of this aspect of his view and will talk about it directly as a theory of reasons.

The approach has a number of considerations in its favour. Before rehearsing some of them, let us, however, unpack slightly the specifics of Finlay's view. Let's see what his view entails beyond its central idea. Exploring these further aspects of Finlay's view will also enable us to sketch later how Finlay's version of axiological explanationism can respond to standard objections to value-based accounts of reasons. The fact that in its more elaborated form Finlay's explanationism has the resources to counter (at least some of) the objections that other, more rudimentary value-based views of reasons cannot respond to successfully will count as another point in its favour.

Presumably, the first and foremost clarification that we have to make about Finlay's account is that he endorses an end-relational view of *goodness*. Again, for the sake of brevity, we will sometimes talk as if Finlay directly provides a view about goodness, while bearing in mind that strictly speaking he is providing a theory of the meaning of 'goodness' and is interested in the related concept of *goodness*. According to Finlay, there is no such thing as goodness *simpliciter*. Things (features, actions, attitudes, states, what have you) are always good with respect to some end, on this view. So, to take Finlay's own example, the sentence 'Umbrellas are good' can be analysed as having the following underlying syntactic form: 'It is good for S_1's doing A_1, for S_2 to do A_2' (Finlay 2020: 6), as, for example, in '*It is* good for people's staying dry in the rain, for them to use *umbrellas*' (Finlay 2020: 6). The idea here is that '"good" fundamentally expresses a relation between two propositional arguments' (Finlay 2020: 7). To take the same example, then, 'people use umbrellas' expresses, according to Finlay (2020: 7), 'the *object* proposition, p' and 'they stay dry in the rain' expresses 'the *end* proposition, e'.

It should be also noted that ultimately something x being good for some end e is understood here in probabilistic terms. Namely, x's obtaining promotes or, more specifically, raises the probability of the end e obtaining (cf. Finlay 2020). So, on this view, to say that it is good for people's staying dry in the rain for them to use umbrellas just is to say that that people use umbrellas increases the probability of them staying dry in the rain (i.e. that they stay dry in the rain).

Another aspect of Finlay's end-relational account of goodness that is important for our purposes is that ends are context-sensitive on this account. So whether something is good will also depend on which ends are salient in a given context. Or as Finlay (2020: 7) puts it, '[o]n this contextualist view, something is correctly said to be "good" (sans phrase) in a particular context only if it is good relative to an end that is in some way salient or privileged in that context'. So, according to this approach, what exactly 'umbrellas are good' means in a context (if meaningful at all) depends on which end or outcome connected to someone using umbrellas is salient or privileged in the context. If the relevant end in a context is that of people staying dry in the rain, then to say that umbrellas are good amounts to saying that people using umbrellas is good for (i.e. it increases the probability of) people staying dry in the rain, in that context.

Finlay's approach is highly flexible, given its many moving parts. Before we reproduce the whole official complete account, let us precis one last aspect of his account. Goodness-for-an-end on this account is understood in probabilistic terms, namely as an increase in probability of the relevant end given the relevant 'goodness' considerations (that the end is more probable given the relevant consideration than it is without it). But to make sense of an increase in probability (of a hypothesis h, given some consideration e), we need to know what probability we are talking about and, in particular, what is the relevant background information b, or in Finlay's terms 'information-base' (cf. Finlay 2020: 10). The relevant background, or information-base, is also highly flexible on this account. It can be constituted by shared knowledge in a given context, but it can also be relativised to what one or another subject believes in a context (interpreted in intensional terms; cf. Finlay 2020: 10); it can also be relativised to 'an information-base defined in some objective way (e.g. *the world's state at time t*)' (Finlay 2020: 10). Note also that despite appealing to a sort of (substantially revised) Deductive Nomological understanding of explanation, Finlay (2020: 10) sees explanation also as context-sensitive and for simplicity assumes 'by default that in statements about normative reasons, explanation and probability/goodness are relativized to the same background information'. With all these remarks and specifications in mind, we are now in a position to reproduce Finlay's complete analysis of normative reasons (i.e. of normative reasons statements):

> [Reasons as Explanations of Goodness + End-Relative Theory of Goodness, REG+ERT] To say in a world *w* that R is a 'reason' for S to do A is to say, of some end *e* and information-base *b*, that R is an explanation in *w* why *given b* it would be good/probability-raising for *e*, if S does A. (Finlay 2020: 10)

Given the specifics of the view, I suggest referring to this Reasons as Explanations of Goodness + End-Relative Theory of Goodness view as the Axiologic Contextualist Explanation view (or Axiologic Contextualist Explanationism, for short).

So, to recapitulate, why is the consideration that my kids are hungry a normative reason for me to prepare some food for them? Well, this is so because (or it just means that) in a world *w*, there is some end *e* and an information base *b* and that my kids are hungry is an explanation in *w* why given *b* it would be good/probability-raising for *e*, if I make my kids some food. Presumably, the end here is that they don't starve (or perhaps, less dramatically, that they just have a 'healthy' dinner), and the information base is that what I know and/or believe at this time in *w*, including that preparing food for dinner normally helps reduce hunger (if I make an effort) or something similar.

Arguments in favour. A number of considerations speak in favour of axiologic contextualist explanationism. First, and perhaps foremost, it appears to have a straightforward account of a central constraint for a theory of normative reasons, namely it respects the 'gradable' aspect of normative reasons. Indeed, it can explain where the 'weight' of normative reasons comes from. Thus, the comparability, combination, outweighing, and cases of additivity/subtraction of normative reasons (when applicable) can be easily accounted for within this account. This is done within this account by reference to the gradable property of goodness. Goodness comes in degrees. This much seems uncontroversial. The 'weight' of a reason to F within axiological explanationism is tied to the degree or 'weight' of (relative) goodness of F-ing. Thus, that there is an injured person in front of me is a normative reason for me to stay and help. And this reason outweighs my reason to leave, which is grounded in my promise to meet a friend for a coffee, because the degree of goodness of helping is higher than the degree of goodness of meeting a friend for a coffee in this context. Presumably, the further explanation of why this holds would appeal to the difference in the 'weight' that is a function of the importance of the end of helping and the conditional probability of achieving that aim by staying, and the 'weight' that is a function of the importance of the end of keeping my promise and the conditional probability of achieving that end given my going to the coffee shop instead of staying. At any rate, axiological explanationists seem to have at their disposal means to the gradable aspect of normative reasons. By definition, it will be tied, one way or another, to the degree of goodness of the relevant F-ings. Note that this may be one of the most important advantages that axiological explanationism has over deontic explanationism. As we saw in the previous section, the existing deontic explanationism proposals seem to have trouble with the gradability aspect of normative reasons. (Recall that contrary to what, for example, John Broome suggests, the appeal to the special sort of explanations, the 'weighing explanations', doesn't really fit our pre-theoretical judgments about how outweighed reasons work.)[9]

Second, like deontic explanationism, the Axiological Explanation view is also perfectly situated to explain the intuitive connection between explanation and reasons. In general reasons, be they normative or not, seem to be associated in a sense with explanations. It is natural for us to say that global warming is both an explanation and a reason why patterns of bird

---

[9] Finlay also makes a more specific point that axiological explanationism fits perfectly with the observation that apparently at least some normative reasons don't respect the additivity constraint on combining the 'weight' of reasons. It seems that at least sometimes having r1 and having r2 as distinct reasons to F doesn't add up to having more 'weight' for F-ing than having only r1 or r2 as a reason to F. Axiological explanationism accounts for this, given that '(i) it accounts for the weights of reasons by the degree and kind of goodness they explain and (ii) we can have non-competing correct explanations of the same thing' (Finlay 2020: 3). I take this feature as being a specific instance of the more general point made in the text, namely that, given the central role of the goodness in the axiological explanationist view of reasons, and goodness being paradigmatically gradable and flexible in the relevant ways, the view is well suited to account for all aspects of the gradability of normative reasons. Non-additivity seems to be just one specific feature of the sort of gradability involved in reasons that the flexibility of axiological explanationism can take care of without any difficulty.

migration are changing. That is, that global warming is occurring can be referred to *interchangeably* in this context as the reason or explanation for the fact that bird migration patterns are changing. It seems there is no difference in the meaning of (a1) 'that global warming is occurring is the explanation why patterns of bird migration are changing' and (a2) 'that global warming is occurring is the reason why patterns of bird migration are changing'. 'Reason why' and 'explanation why' can be interchanged in this context without any change in meaning. And it would seem that a similar observation can also be made in the context of normative reasons. It seems that 'reason why' and 'explanation why' in the following two sentences can be interchanged without affecting the meaning of either of the two: (b1) 'that my kids are hungry is a reason why it would be good (for me) to prepare them a dinner' and (b2) 'that my kids are hungry is an explanation why it would be good (for me) to prepare them a dinner'. Crucially, it seems that (b1) can also be paraphrased by (c) 'that my kids are hungry is a reason for me to prepare them a dinner'. Arguably, (c) just corresponds to a standard way of expressing normative reasons. Thus, the argument goes, accounts of normative reasons that don't appeal to explanation in defining/characterising them have an extra burden of explaining why it can be natural to use 'reasons' and 'explanation' interchangeably in both non-normative *and* normative contexts. The proposal here is not that there cannot be an independently plausible story why this is happening that non-explanationist accounts could offer but rather that such accounts will be necessarily more complex than explanationist accounts on which reasons just are explanations in *all* contexts. Non-explanationist accounts will probably involve appeals to the ambiguity of 'reasons' (perhaps by suggesting that only in non-normative contexts do 'reasons' express explanations). No such assumptions are needed on explanationist accounts, which are simpler in this aspect (cf. Finlay 2020: 2).

Third, again, as in the case of deontic explanationism, axiological explanationism is also well suited to explain why mere enabling considerations are not normative reasons (see also Finlay 2020: 2–3 for a suggestion along sufficiently similar lines). Again, this is an advantage of any explicationist view over, say, alternative views that define reasons in terms of reasoning or evidence alone (see Chapters 2 and 4). Being (more or less) able to prepare my kids a dinner seems to matter with respect to why it would be good for me to prepare the dinner. But, again, it certainly doesn't matter as a normative reason, since that I am able to prepare the dinner is not a reason to prepare the dinner. That is, if my ability matters at all with respect to the goodness of *me* preparing the dinner for my kids, it should matter otherwise than it constituting a normative reason for me to prepare the dinner. It should matter as a mere enabling condition. Explanationists have an easy way of explaining this: exactly as in the case of non-normative explanations, we can also distinguish in the normative case between *explanans* and mere background conditions (e.g. that there was oxygen is a enabling condition, that the match was lit was an *explanans* of the *explanandum* that there was fire). My ability to cook (even if rudimentary) is a mere enabling condition, but that my kids are hungry is a reason for me to prepare the dinner. Similar considerations apply for, say, not F-ing under duress as a mere enabling condition rather than a normative reason to F. It should be noted, though, that I am not suggesting here that for all normative reasons there have to be some enabling conditions, or that ability to F is universally an enabling condition for some F-ing having a normative aspect. The point is only that if there are cases where some conditions seem to matter normatively but appear to be more like enabling conditions rather than reasons, then axiological explanationism has an easy account for that, since with respect to all sorts of explanations, it makes sense to distinguish between enabling conditions and the *explanans*.

A fourth general advantage of axiological explanationism is that it also has the means to explain why entailing conditions are not normative reasons. A fact that entails that F-ing would be good (say, in virtue of being conclusive evidence that F-ing would be good) needs not be a normative reason for one to F. That a highly reliable newspaper reports that it would be good (for people living in cities) to go to the mountains this weekend need not be a normative reason for me, a city-dweller, to go to the mountains this weekend. Now, axiological explanationism can explain why this is so. Typically, p cannot be an explanation of why p. This is just another aspect of explanations in general that helps to account for why mere entailing conditions are not [always] normative reasons. By the same token, this is a problem for non-explanationist views, like the Reasoning view of reasons (see Chapter 2) and the Evidence view (see Chapter 4). Hence, this constitutes an advantage for axiological explanationism (and the generalised point, for all explanationist views) over these rival accounts of normative reasons.

Fifth, axiological explanationism might have another advantage over some alternative views – for example, the Reasoning view of normative reasons. I say 'might' because, as will become clear, this depends on which further assumptions axiological explanationism takes on board. Once more, similarly to deontic explanationism, it might account for the possibility of cases where Moore-paradoxical considerations (and self-undermining considerations more generally constitute normative reasons for one to F). On axiological explanationism, that the building is on fire but I am unaware of the fire is a reason for me to check the state of the building given that that there is a fire of which I am unaware is an explanation why it would be good (presumably for the aim of self-preservation) for me to check the state of the building. Axiological explanationism might explain such a possibility if it is not also committed to the view that one needs to be able to reason in a fittingness-preserving way from reasons as contents of true beliefs (and other states) to the relevant F-ing. That is, axiological explanationism has an advantage here if it doesn't require that all explanation has to be understood as a valid/good pattern of reasoning that the subject has to be able to follow.

So, this raises some questions about the specifics of Finlay's axiological explanationism, and in particular about the nature of his commitment to a version of the DN model (i.e. the Deductive-Nomological model of scientific explanation; cf. Hempel and Oppenheim 1948; Hempel 1965) as applied to explanations in general. On a standard understanding of the DN model of *scientific* explanation,[10] scientific explanation ultimately just is an argument of a specific sort. It has, in particular, among its premises a reference to universal laws (universal generalisations) and concrete conditions from which the relevant *explanandum* can be deduced. One of the well-known worries with it (cf. Salmon 1971) is that by definition, arguments can be valid and even sound and yet (explanatory) irrelevant; whereas good explanations cannot be irrelevant (see Chapter 5 for more on the fundamental differences between explanations and arguments). For instance, adding some (law-like) necessary truths to a valid argument will not undermine the validity of the argument. But, of course, adding some random necessary truth to an explanation would typically undermine the goodness of the explanation.[11] Finlay (2020: 5) tells us that on his account: '*p* is a *complete explanation* of *q* in case *p* is a set of true propositions that

---

[10] DN models as elaborated and defended by logical positivists have been proposed as models of scientific explanation.

[11] Consider Salmon's (1971: 34) well-known example that illustrates the problem of irrelevant truths for the DN model of scientific explanation (a case that is different from the necessary aforementioned truth case in our main text): 'John Jones avoided becoming pregnant during the past year, for he has taken his wife's birth control pills regularly, and every man who regularly takes birth control pills avoids pregnancy.' The example satisfies the constraints imposed by the DN model on scientific explanation (the explanandum is entailed by the universal generalisation and specific conditions), but of course no one would accept that the universal generalisation together with the specific conditions in this example constitute a genuine, good explanation of why John Jones is not pregnant.

logically entails q but doesn't include q.' He then adds that '[l]ogical entailment may seem too strong here, but p should be understood as including any relevant conceptual truths or essential definitions, occupying the role played by scientific laws in Hempel's theory of scientific explanation' (Finlay 2020: 5). Of course, to avoid the objection from irrelevant truths, Finlay needs not only to say that complete explanations not only include 'any conceptual truths or essential definitions' (Finlay 2020: 5) but also that it should *not* include any irrelevant conceptual or other truths. And Finlay does seem to make a remark along these lines. See the relevant passage in Endnote 20, where he claims that the standard objections against the DN model will not apply to his account: 'Although this DN theory is admittedly too broad, the problems of irrelevancies and asymmetries don't arise because the explanantia I'll propose will be clearly both relevant and metaphysically prior to their explananda, given my reductive account of goodness' (Finlay 2020: 33). There is a reading of this remark on which it just amounts to an ad hoc move in the light of the problem of explanatory irrelevancies. To see that reading, compare two sets of considerations. The first, R1, contains merely the claim that I promised to call a friend of mine. Clearly R1 entails that with respect to some background conditions b and an end e (say, the end of respecting one's promises), the probability that e is achieved given that I call my friend and given b is higher than the probability of e without me calling my friend (given b). Now, consider R2, which contains the claim that I promised to call my friend later today and the claim that I am 1.89 m tall. R2 also clearly entails that with respect to b and e (e.g. respecting one's promises and background conditions), the probability of e being achieved given that I call my friend and b is higher than the probability of e without that I call my friend (given b). Thus, on the face of it, both R1 and R2 seem to satisfy the DN model of explanation. This would, of course, be problematic for Finlay's proposal, since it doesn't seem that R2 is a genuine, good explanation of why the probability of respecting the promise by calling my friend is higher than the probability of respecting the promise without me calling my friend. It contains irrelevant information that undermines the goodness of the explanation. Compare R2 to R1, which doesn't contain such irrelevant information. R1 is a good candidate for explaining the relevant explanandum, not R2. On the DN account, however, both should be understood as equally good explanations of the explanandum (e.g. that the probability of respecting a promise given that I call my friend is higher than the probability of respecting the promise without me calling my friend). Now, one might think that a proper treatment of this problem is not just to add a general remark that the version of the DN account that we have here is such that it doesn't allow there to be irrelevant information among its explanatia. Of course, strictly speaking, Finlay is not making such a move. However, what he suggests might sound like it comes dangerously close to such a move. He suggests that the *specifics* of explanatia that we have in the case of normative reasons are such that the possibility of cases of irrelevant information in explanatia doesn't even arise. It is not clear why this should be so, however. One might want to see *why* exactly this is so. My aforementioned case about promises and promises conjoined with some irrelevant information seem to be just such a case that respect the entailment condition: both R1 and R2 entail the relevant explanandum (the goodness of an end given the F-ing of promise keeping). But R1 seems to be able to genuinely explain the explanandum, since R2 contains some irrelevant information. It is not clear *on what theoretical grounds exactly* R2 is ruled out on Finlay's account from counting as an explanatia.

However, let us assume here for the sake of the argument that there probably is a way to fix this and to give an independently plausible story of why our R2 cannot be an explanatia on Finlay's account. Returning now to the point about whether Moore-paradoxical cases will count as another line of argument in favour of axiological contextualist explanationism, or instead will constitute counterexamples to it, will ultimately depend on what is meant by 'entailment' in Finlay's version of the DN theory of explanation (recall: '*p* is a *complete explanation* of *q* in case *p* is a set of true propositions that logically entails *q* but doesn't include *q*'; Finlay 2020: 5). For instance, if it is required that the subject (for whom there is a reason) is able to reason [properly] following the relevant pattern of 'entailment' in a truth-preserving way, then Finlay's general account might actually collapse into a version of the Reasoning view seen earlier (Chapter 2). If so, Moore-paradoxical cases will count as counterexamples for this view as well, for general reasons explored in Chapter 2. If, on the contrary, the 'entailment' here is not understood as corresponding to a pattern of reasoning/argument that the subject should be able to instantiate in her reasoning, but be rather of subject-independent, metaphysical sort, then Moore-paradoxical cases may well be accounted for within this approach. Note, however, that this latter option might appear somewhat alien to the initial neo-positivist motivation for the DN model. One might reasonably wonder in what sense the view here is really a 'version' of the DN theory after all. In what follows, I leave this exegetical worry aside. On such an understanding, the Moore-paradoxical cases (e.g. (a) 'the building is on fire but I don't know that the building is on fire') can be categorised as cases of normative reasons to F (e.g. checking the state of the building), since Moore-paradoxical considerations (e.g. (a)) explain or ground/constitute why the probability of achieving some end *e* (e.g. self-preservation), given the F-ing (e.g. checking the building), is higher than the probability of achieving *e* without F-ing. Now, if this interpretation is on the right track, then axiological contextualist explanationism doesn't predict that contrary to our pre-theoretical judgments, Moore-paradoxical considerations can never be normative reasons for one to F. Respecting the pre-theoretical judgments that they can be reasons to F is then another prima facie consideration in favour of axiological contextualist explanationism (given that the aforementioned assumptions are in place).

Worries. Finlay (2020) considers five objections ('puzzles') to the explanation of goodness-based accounts of reasons (axiological explanationism in general). He suggests that given the specifics of his more elaborated axiological contextualist explanationism, all these objections can be dealt with. That is, even if these objections undermine the plausibility of some more rudimentary versions of axiological explanationism, his contextualist version of it can be maintained. If this is right, then, of course, this would also constitute an additional argument in favour of axiological contextualist explanationism – namely, it has an advantage over other axiological explanationist accounts.

Among the five objections that Finlay considers are (i) the problem of the 'right kind' of reasons (in short: how are the 'right kind' of reasons for attitudes even possible, that is, reasons connected to the fittingness of an attitude rather than to, say, some benefit of holding it, on a value-based account of reasons?); (ii) the objection from normative facts being themselves reasons (in short, if that it would be good to F is a reason to F, then axiological explanationism would predict that some considerations are auto-explanatory, which is problematic); (iii) the objection from evidence being sometimes a reason to F (in short, normative testimony/evidence that F-ing would be good may sometimes constitute normative reasons to F without explaining why F-ing would be good); (iv) the objections from subjective; and (v) motivating reasons (in short, the existence of problem cases where an agent seems to have a reason to F but unbeknownst to the agent F-ing would actually not be good, and the existence of problem cases where F-ing would be good but unbeknownst to the agent the relevant reasons apparently constituting consideration R are false and thus cannot explain why F-ing would be good). We will not go through the details of *all* these 'puzzles' and Finlay's treatment of them here. Instead, let me merely sketch the general recipe of Finlay's responses to these. The guiding idea in Finlay's responses to all these is his appeal to contextualism about either the relevant ends in a situation or the contextualism about the relevant base-information or the contextualism about both of these. Among the elements that can 'move' in axiological contextualist explanationism are, for instance, the focus on the agent's desired/preferred outcome as the relevant end, the focus on a [potential] adviser's preferred outcome as the relevant end, the focus on some of the agent's subagential aims (as is suggested with respect to the problem of the 'right kind' of reasons, for instance; see ahead for discussion), the focus on the agent's knowledge/beliefs as the relevant information-base, the focus on the knowledge of a better-informed [potential] adviser as the relevant information-base, and so on. In short, according to Finlay, selecting the right focus, the right interpretation of the relevant end and information-base can account for all the apparent 'puzzles' in (i)–(v) without giving up value-based explanationism. The high flexibility of the account is fundamentally what does the job in dealing with these objections, according to Finlay.

However, it is also this high flexibility that one might find somewhat problematic with this account. The first general worry for axiological contextualist explanationism is a worry that any contextualist approach with respect to any normative concept has to tackle. Namely, one needs to explain how we are supposed to make sense of a view on which normative concepts are always relativised to some further aspect and even the relevant normative concept *sans phrase* has to be understood as relative to some aspect, say, a common ground. This is a very general worry and may just conceal differences in fundamental theoretical commitments that metanormative theoreticians might have. Someone who is not attracted to contextualism in the normative domain in general may also find Finlay's fine-grained contextualism about normative reasons unattractive.[12] The worry here is the apparent lack of independent theoretical motivation for such an extreme contextualism given that our pre-theoretical judgments about reasons to do something or to have an attitude don't seem on the face of it to be so radically context-dependent. At least on the surface, they don't always appear to be relative to some given end or some given information-base. At any rate, a contextualist about reasons, axiological or not, may need to provide some error theory to explain why we are

---

[12] Thanks to Jacques Vollet for the suggestion that this may indeed be a serious problem with axiological contextualist explanationism.

wrong in pre-theoretically thinking that reasons are not so *radically* context-sensitive. Granted Finlay's contextualism can account for both 'the intuitions of Humean internalists about reasons as the result of privileging the *agent's* preferences for outcomes (e.g. Hitler may well have had "no reasons" to refrain from genocide, assuming that none of his preferred ends were threatened by it)' (Finlay 2020: 7) and 'the intuitions of externalists, and the categorical nature of moral claims, as the result of privileging the *speaker's* or *audience's* preferences for outcomes (*of course* Hitler had reasons to refrain from genocide, given the harm it inflicted on innocent people!)' (Finlay 2020: 7). But I doubt that either Humean internalists or externalists would agree with Finlay's proposal. Humean internalists would not accept 'reasons' in the externalist sense as genuine reasons at all, nor would externalists accept 'reasons' in the internalist sense as genuine reasons.[13] Contextualism has the burden of explaining not only why both are right in a sense but also why strictly speaking both are wrong. The worry here is not that it cannot be done but that it is an extra challenge for a theory of reasons that has to be met.

Our second and more specific worry concerns the account's treatment of reasons for attitudes and beliefs in particular. To see this worry, I would like first to return briefly to Finlay's response to the 'puzzle' of the 'right kind' of reasons (cf. aforementioned (i)). First of all, the observation that simple value-based explanationist accounts of reasons cannot explain why there would be any right kind of reason for attitudes at all seems right.[14] Finlay captures the worry precisely when he writes:

> Something is a reason of the 'right kind' for an attitude if and only if it makes the attitude fitting, but raising the probability of an end desired by the speaker, audience, or agent is neither necessary nor sufficient for fittingness. (Finlay 2020: 8)

Recall that that someone's threatening me to admire them as contrasted to them being admirable is a 'wrong kind' of reason to admire them (cf. Section 1.4); believing *p* being practically advantageous is also often seen as being the 'wrong kind' of reason to believe that *p*. According to evidentialists about reasons to believe, considerations of this sort are not normative reasons at all to believe that *p*; pragmatists reject this and see practical considerations as possible genuine normative reasons to believe (see

---

[13] And this seems to be exactly what we find in the literature. See, for instance, Williams (1989) for internalism and Parfit (2011: 58–110) for arguments against internalism.

[14] And a little further, we will see briefly a value-based view of reasons that bites the bullet and endorses this conclusion.

Chapter 6 for more on the evidentialist–pragmatist debate about reasons to believe). Now, even if we put aside for a moment the debate over whether the 'wrong kind' of reasons are genuine reasons, the fact that simple value-based explanationist accounts of normative reasons entail that there are no 'right kind' of reasons for attitudes (e.g. belief) is already dramatic. For it would be a dramatic cost to a view if it were to entail that that a consideration makes *p* more probable or entails its truth cannot be by itself a normative reason to believe *p* and that a consideration that entails that someone is admirable cannot be by itself a normative reason to admire them.

How exactly is Finlay's contextualism supposed to help axiological explanationism to respond to this problem – that is, to make axiological explanationism compatible with the existence of the 'right kind' of reasons? The move is to treat what has been known in the literature as constitutive norms of attitudes as possible salient ends in a situation, thereby making the 'right kind' of reasons fall within the definition provided earlier (REG +ERT). Thus, Finlay writes:

> [w]hen talking about reasons for *attitudes* there is a competing source of salience for ends, in the reference to the attitudes themselves. These are attitudes that are commonly said to have subagential, 'constitutive' ends of their own, which need not be ends desired or intended by anybody. It is commonly said, for example, that the constitutive end of belief is *truth* (or knowledge). How to precisify this idea of 'constitutive ends' is controversial, but for our purposes this doesn't matter.[. . .] All we need is that talking about 'belief' is sufficient, in normal contexts, to make salient an end like truth. (Finlay 2020: 8)

This then brings us to the specifics of our worry. The worry is that it is not clear in what sense, if at all, constitutive aims can count as one's salient ends and be of genuine use for a value-based account of reasons. Finlay talks about 'constitutive ends' of attitudes, but it is clear from the context (and from the references he appeals to) that this talk should be understood in the sense of the 'constitutive aim' of attitudes as it has been commonly discussed in recent debates. But in these debates, the 'aim' talk is understood at best as a metaphor. An attitude is not the kind of thing that can aim at anything at all. Let us focus specifically on the 'aim' of belief.[15] As it is commonly understood, to say that the belief aims at truth is to say that truth sets the standard of correctness or fittingness for belief, namely a belief is correct or fitting just in case it is true. It is assumed that a standard

---

[15] See Fassio (2015) for a comprehensive overview of the aim of belief debate.

of correctness of an attitude defines or is essential for the sort of attitude in question. Thus, belief is an attitude that is defined as an attitude that is correct just in case it is true. Its standard of correctness allows us to distinguish it from other attitudes that have distinct standards of correctness (e.g. guessing is not an attitude that is defined as an attitude that one can correctly have if and only if one is guessing correctly). A common way to understand the standard of correctness for belief is to appeal to a fundamental norm of belief, the norm that defines what belief is. Various proposals exist (with respect to the content and with respect to the form of the norm), but let us assume, just for the purpose of illustration, that the relevant norm is something like: (TN) one ought to [believe that p only if p] (see Velleman 2000; Wedgwood 2002, 2013; Boghossian 2003; Shah 2003; Engel 2004, 2013; Shah and Velleman 2005; among many others). Thus, the idea is that only attitudes that are subject to (TN) are beliefs; (TN) defines what sort of attitude belief is. An attitude has to be subject to the fundamental (TN) if it is to count as belief at all, according to a standard approach with respect to the aim of belief. The suggestion is that the nature, the very essence of belief, is to conform to this norm. This is, then, the sense in which beliefs are said to aim at truth (the same applies for the alternative of the knowledge norm of belief). But if we understand the aim of belief in this sense, it is not clear how it could be one of the salient ends that can be plugged into the axiological contextualist explanationist definition of reasons. Here are two more specific considerations that suggest that the aim of belief cannot be a 'competing source of salience for attitudes' (see the aforementioned quotation) for an axiological explanationist and thus cannot help Finlay's attempt to block the objection from the 'right kind' of reasons.

The first reason why the appeal to constitutive aims of attitudes as presented earlier cannot help an axiological explanationist is simply that allowing for standards of fittingness (e.g. fundamental truth norm of belief) to play an indispensable and irreducible role in an analysis of reasons is giving up on the purely 'axiological' aspect of axiological explanationism. In other terms, appealing in this way to standards of fittingness makes it unclear in what sense the view would still count as a value-based view of reasons. Of course, it is not a problem per se. Maybe fittingness is indeed fundamental and should be appealed to in explaining other normative notions. It is only that this move doesn't seem available to someone who takes values as more basic and aims to reduces reasons to goodness. At best, the resulting view would count as a hybrid view combining both value and fittingness in explaining reasons. At this point, one might think that existing alternative non-hybrid views may be preferable to this account on the basis of simplicity and parsimony. Be that as it may, the first point is that explanationists that are also value purists – that is, who want to appeal only to goodness in explaining reasons – cannot really appeal crucially to irreducible standards of fittingness in their explanatory analysis of normative reasons.[16]

The second reason why the appeal to constitutive aims of attitudes won't help axiological explanationists to deal with the worry from the existence of the 'right kind' of reasons is that it is not clear in what sense, if any, the aim of belief could be on a par with the ends that we pursue. Finlay talks about 'constitutive ends' of attitudes constituting 'a *competing* source of salience for ends' (see the aforementioned quotation, emphasis added). So the idea would be that standards of fittingness are competing and thus are on a par with one's ends or desired/preferred outcomes. But how should we understand such a suggestion? It is not clear that the appeal to constitutive aims being 'subagential' (cf. Finlay 2020) really helps here. The truth norm of belief, for instance, is not a subagential end one is having. The truth norm of belief is an *abstracta*, and as such, it is not, on the face of it, something one can properly have as an end. One could, of course, set oneself an end of believing only truths and avoiding falsehoods as an end towards which one is striving. But that's not how the constitutive aim of belief is understood in the literature. The constitutive aim of belief, as a standard of correctness, defines what belief is. It is a norm that defines the attitude of belief (belief is just the sort of attitude that is subject to the truth norm). Definitions, in terms of norms or otherwise, are not the kind of thing that one can have. There is no useful sense for analysis of reasons, it seems, in which a definition in terms of constitutiveness can be said to compete with one's desired outcomes. They are not the sort of thing that can compete, let alone be meaningfully compared. Definitions, contrary to one's ends (subagential or not), don't obtain and are not realised. Thus, our second problem here is that it doesn't seem that one can plausibly

---

[16] Note also, in passing, that Finlay's proposal that REG+ERT, together with the constitutive understanding of ends of attitudes, provides an explanatory analysis of fittingness seems overenthusiastic. Finlay (2020: 9) claims that '[a]n added bonus [of the view] is that it also offers an explanatory analysis of fittingness, which some philosophers claim to be an unanalyzable primitive:[. . .] for an attitude to "fit" its object is for that attitude to realize or promote its constitutive end when directed at that object'. The problem, however, is that given the standard understanding of constitutive aims (see the main text earlier), such an analysis would be problematically circular. For it would amount to the claim that for an attitude to fit its object is for that attitude to satisfy its fittingness conditions (= realize its constitutive end), which is uninformative and thus unhelpful as a putative explanatory analysis of fittingness.

supplement the REG+ERT account of reasons with the thought that an attitude's constitutive aim is an end whose increase in probability of obtaining, given one having the attitude, would be explained by a consideration that would count as a reason to have the attitude in question. In short, it just doesn't seem possible to plug constitutive aims (correctness conditions) into the REG+ERT analysis without making it somewhat incoherent. It would seem, then, that while running away from the 'right kind' of reasons problem, Finlay runs into the 'wrong kind' of ends problem.[17]

Now, it might still be the case, as observed earlier, that an agent has an end of believing only truths and avoiding falsehoods. Such an end could, of course, plausibly function in the REG+ERT account as a salient end in a situation. But it should be noted that this sort of end plausibly can be reduced to believing truth and avoiding falsehood being the agent's preferred/desired outcome. Such an outcome, of course, can obtain or fail to obtain, be promoted, realised, or made more probable. But it is crucial to note that focusing on this sort of end as the salient end with respect to beliefs (and, *modulo* necessary amendments, to other attitudes as well) would consist in falling back to a simpler axiological explanationism that cannot explain *why* the 'right kind' of reasons are normative reasons at all for attitudes, given that, as Finlay (2020: 8) notes, 'raising the probability of an end desired by the speaker, audience, or agent is neither necessary nor sufficient for fittingness'. The 'right kind' of reasons for attitudes are essentially connected to fittingness of the relevant attitudes. And despite it being much more sophisticated and indeed it being an ingenious move,

---

[17] See also Way (2013: 19ff) for a somewhat related objection to an arguably less sophisticated version of axiological explanationism on which reasons are defined in terms of partial explanation of goodness of F-ing for its own sake or instrumentally (Way's focus is specifically on pro-attitudes). The objection there is that such a view seems to be committed to an implausible assumption that 'pro-attitudes towards outcomes which are good in some respect are good for their own sake' (Way 2013: 22). An example concerning egalitarians illustrates the following point:

> Consider an outcome in which wealth is distributed equally, but everyone is extremely poor. If egalitarians are right, this outcome is good in some respect. But even egalitarians can admit that this outcome is not good overall. And it does not seem plausible that favouring this outcome is good for its own sake. It does not seem to be good for its own sake to hope for everyone to be extremely, if equally, badly off, or to be glad if this outcome comes about. (Way 2013: 23)

The parallel with our objection here is that on the view reconstructed and rejected by Way, an axiological explanationist aims to specify the goodness in a way somewhat intrinsic to the attitude. Finlay's account appeals to constitutive aims, whereas Way's constructed axiological explanationists focus on overall goodness of attitude for its own sake. Both versions of axiological explanationism that focus on F-ing's goodness are problematic as is shown in main text and by Way's counterexample.

the contextualist version of axiological explanationism still has the same problem of explaining the existence of the 'right kind' of reasons. I conclude tentatively that this alone is a strong argument against this approach. The rest of the present section is devoted to an exploration of an alternative recent axiological explanationism that proposes a different move with respect to this problem.

Alternative axiological explanationism: in virtue of promoting valuable states of affairs. In the light of problems met by the contextualist version of axiological explanationism, someone who is sympathetic to the idea that reasons should be understood in terms of value (e.g. a value-first proponent) might want to explore alternative options for defining normative reasons in terms of explanation and goodness. One such alternative is elaborated in a recent and promising value-based account of reasons by Barry Maguire (2016). Let us rehearse rapidly the main tenets of his proposal.

The official version of the view is as follows:

> Value-based theory of reasons: Some fact of the form [φ would promote S] is a reason to φ if and only if and if so in virtue of the facts that φ would promote S and that S is valuable. (Maguire 2016: 237)

There are a few things to note before comparing this view to Finlay's account. First, without going into too much exegetical detail, it may nonetheless be useful to unpack the proposal slightly. On Maguire's account, reasons are for options.[18] Options can be understood in a variety of ways, according to him, so 'our options are the things we choose between or rationally control – whether these are actions, omissions, activities, or plans' (Maguire 2016: 239). That F-ing would promote S is on Maguire's account a 'canonical fact'.[19] F-ing is the option that one may take (choose/rationally control). S is a placeholder for 'state of affairs'. Not all canonical facts promote valuable states of affairs, and not all canonical facts are reasons (cf. Maguire 2016: 236). Value on this account is 'a gradable monadic property of states of affairs' (Maguire 2016: 237). Value is understood in a neutral way and not as 'value-relative-to-me-or-you' – for example, 'the disvalue of the drowning of the small child in Peter Singer's pond has nothing to do with you or me, the passers-by, and *a*

---

[18] He writes: 'The central claim is that to be a reason for an option is to be a fact about that option's promoting some state of affairs, on the condition that that state of affairs is valuable' (Maguire 2016: 237).

[19] More precisely: a canonical fact is 'a fact of the form [φ would promote S], where φ is some agent's taking some option in some situation and S is a state of affairs' (Maguire 2016: 236).

fortiori not to any reasons we might have to care or want to help. It has entirely to do with the child, his suffering, his loss of life prospects, and so on' (Maguire 2016: 238–239). Note equally that value here is supposed to be final, not instrumental. Promotion is also characterised in neutral terms. Maguire wants his view to be compatible with a number of possible interpretations of promotion: 'an option *promotes* a state of affairs by instantiating it, causing or partially causing it, constituting or partially constituting it, preventing the preventing of it, or non-superfluously probabilifying it' (Maguire 2016: 238) (here it is important that '[t]he relevant valuable state of affairs may be instantiated by the action itself'; cf. Maguire 2016: 239).

Second, the view qualifies as a version of explanationism given how its details are worked out. An important thing to note in this respect is that Maguire's proposal is a revisionary one in the sense that he doesn't take the surface structure exhibited by our ordinary statements or reasons ('reasons talk') to correspond exactly to metaphysics of reasons. Strictly speaking, on his account, only canonical facts can be reasons; canonical facts have the form of 'F-ing would promote state of affairs S'. Our ordinary talk of reasons doesn't reflect this form, at least not on its surface. We commonly say 'that it is raining is a reason to take an umbrella'. But 'that it is raining' doesn't have (on its surface) the form 'taking an umbrella would promote state of affairs S'. This is no problem, according to Maguire (2016: 254), since '[q]uite generally, the considerations we actually offer as reasons are those that are saliently needed, in the specific conversational context, to pick out a larger explanatory structure'. Maguire (2016: 254, fn 37) also notes, referring to a point from David Lewis, that '[t]his is an instance of a more general distinction between metaphysical explanations and consid-erations that one can give as an answer to a "why" question in a specific context'. So, we can imply here that canonical facts that are reasons are these larger explanatory structures or, in other terms, genuine metaphysical explanations. Thus, for Maguire, our common reasons' statements are '*good representatives* [...]' either for the basic reasons themselves or for other significant chunks of this overall structure' (Maguire 2016: 255; the term 'good representatives' is attributed to Fogal 2016). Two examples illustrate Maguire's point. First,

> [s]uppose that Frank enjoys flowers because they remind him fondly of his grandmother, or because he likes to marvel at the fragile beauty of nature, or because he likes their smell. Any one of these facts – the fact that flowers remind him of his grandmother, for instance – may be said to be a reason to give him flowers. Each is part of an explanation of why giving him flowers

would make him happy with some intensity, for some duration – which is the basic reason. (Maguire 2016: 255)

And, second, '[t]ake the fact that Teresa's tyre is flat. Since Teresa drives to work, the fact that her tyre is flat partially explains the fact that giving her a lift will realise the state of affairs of her being in work on time. That's a reason to give her a lift to work' (Maguire 2016: 255, fn 39). Thus, given how the details of the account are worked out (and, in particular, given the specifics of his proposed metaphysics of reasons, as opposed to our common and somewhat loose talk of reasons),[20] Maguire's proposal qualifies as a version of axiological explanationism. *Metaphysical* explanation is a key element in his analysis of normative reasons.

Turning now more specifically to a comparison of Maguire's account to Finlay's, we can note that a major difference between these two is that where the latter appeals to R explaining the goodness *of F-ing* for some end/outcome e (i.e. F-ing increasing the probability of e obtaining), the former appeals to the value *of an end/outcome* (e.g. state of affairs) that would be promoted by F-ing (cf. Maguire 2016: 234, fn2) in defining reasons. Adapting a distinction from Way (2013), we can say that the former sort of value-based account of reasons focuses on F-ing-based goodness (in Way's original terminology: attitude-based); whereas the latter's focus is on object-based goodness/value (the goodness of the relevant end).

The focus on neutral value in the case of Maguire versus a fine-grained contextualism of end-relative goodness/value in Finlay's account is another notable difference between the two. Thus, someone having the sort of worry we alluded to the aforementioned about Finlay's contextualism being, well, too relativised (to ends and information-bases) need not have a parallel worry for Maguire's object-based value-neutral approach. Maguire's proposal doesn't involve that level of context-sensitivity (given that F-ing would promote a neutrally valuable state of affairs, the canonical fact of the form [F-ing would promote S] just is a reason *sans phrase* to F, and this need not be relativised to some further parameter on Maguire's account).

---

[20] See also: 'Strictly speaking, only the basic reasons play a grounding role in determining the total weight of reason favouring each option, and hence (by way of further principles not defended here) in turn, in determining what you ought to do' (Maguire 2016: 254). For matters of brevity we haven't defined what's meant by 'basic reasons' here, but it has to do with the value of distinguishable states of affairs (cf. Maguire 2016: 252). For our purposes this may be left unspecified here.

Yet another, even more important difference for our purposes between the two views is that Maguire, contrary to Finlay, baldly rejects the very existence of genuine 'right kind' of normative reasons for attitudes. Finlay attempts to provide an explanation of these within the framework of axiological contextualist explanationism, while Maguire embraces the consequence that his account may rule out the 'right kind' of reasons for attitudes, where the 'right kind' of reasons are understood as 'facts that make attitudes *fitting*' (Maguire 2016: 240). Maguire suggests that this consequence need not be a problem, for it is not clear that there is a unified reasons relation anyway. The suggestion is that the focus of his account – namely, the 'reason-for-an-option relation' – may well not be the same relation as the '"right-kind" of reason for an attitude relation' (cf. Maguire 2016: 240).

In a more recent publication, Maguire (2018) provides a further argument against the unity thesis (i.e. that a reason for an option and the 'right kind' of reason for an attitude are relations of the same sort). Before examining whether this more elaborated argument undermines the 'unity thesis', note the details of Maguire's dialectic here with respect to the objection from the 'right kind' of reasons: '[h]owever, whether we should accept any such "unity" argument [e.g. argument against his value-based account relying on the premise that the "right kind" of reasons for attitudes are genuine normative reasons], or rather reject the relevant "unity" premise, will depend in part on the strength of the case for the Value-Based Theory of Reasons itself' (Maguire 2016: 240). I tend to think that the qualification 'in part' is doing the heavy lifting here. Of course, if there is a strong prima facie case in favour of the value-based account of reasons, it will matter for the overall assessment of the view; however, at the end of the day, if the 'right kind' of reasons objection hasn't received an independently plausible response *and* there are alternative initially plausible accounts of reasons that don't have this problem (and are not subject to some further unanswerable challenges), then the conclusion should be clear: the value-based account cannot be rationally upheld. So, it is crucial for our overall assessment of the view to focus specifically on whether Maguire's suggestion that the 'unity thesis' should not be accepted really works out. This is specifically what we will now focus on in the concluding part of this section. (The details of an alternative, new theory of reasons that is not subject to the objection from the 'right kind' of reasons and is independently plausible will be elaborated in Chapter 5.)

The main argument in Maguire (2018) is an argument against the possibility of the 'right kind' of reasons for affective attitudes. The argument there is silent about the 'right kind' of reasons for beliefs (cf: 'I take no stand on whether my arguments can be generalized to conative attitudes (the action-oriented attitudes such as preference and intention) or epistemic attitudes'; Maguire 2018: 782). However, a reference is made to a distinct manuscript where a 'related account of normative support for epistemic states' (cf. Maguire 2018: 782, fn 5) is defended, which is, presumably, Maguire and Woods (2020). However, note, crucially, that the proposal defended in that paper is highly contentious; it is basically a rather radical version of pragmatism about reasons to believe. A very popular view in contemporary epistemology – namely, evidentialism – according to which normative reasons to believe are evidential (i.e. truth-conducive) – is clearly incompatible with the account defended in that paper. Thus, one should be advised that taking on board the value-based explanationist response to the 'right kind' of reasons objection in general might have, at the end of the day, a rather high theoretical cost. It is far from being neutral with respect to substantive theoretical options. However, for the sake of the argument, let us put the 'right kind' of reasons for beliefs question aside for the time being. We will return to the debate about the nature of reasons to believe and the pragmatism–evidentialism opposition in Chapter 6.

The overall structure of the argument in Maguire (2018) is really simple and straightforward. Indeed it may appear to be rather appealing at first sight. It can, I think, be summed up as follows:

1. Normative reasons are non-strict, essentially contributory, and essentially gradable in a sense to be explicated.
2. For all x, such that x is a 'right kind of reason' consideration that normatively supports an affective attitude A, x is a fit-making consideration for A.
3. Necessarily, no fit-making consideration is non-strict, contributory, and gradable in the relevant sense.
4. Necessarily, no 'right kind of reason' consideration for an affective attitude A is a normative reason for A.

In other terms, Maguire identifies what he thinks are essential features of normative reasons; he, then, distinguishes normative reasons from fit-making considerations and argues that fit-making considerations have none of the essential features of reasons (an alternative that seems to be evoked in the last section of the article is that fit-making considerations don't have *all* of the essential features of reasons). Crucially, the considerations that qualify as the 'right kind of reasons' for affective attitudes are all fit-making considerations. It is concluded on this basis that no consideration that qualifies as a 'right kind of reason' for an affective attitude is a genuine normative reason for the affective attitude in question.

What exactly are these allegedly essential features of normative reasons? According to Maguire, these are being non-strict, being contributory, and being gradable. Being a non-strict normative consideration is basically to satisfy the constraint of holism (cf. Dancy 2004: chapter 5) – that is, a constraint according to which considerations that are reasons to F never 'justify or require anything on their own' (cf. Maguire 2018: 784). The idea here is that reasons on their own don't imply anything about what normative considerations – for example, reasons against F-ing, there might be. To illustrate the idea, consider the following: '[t]he fact that the child will drown, for instance, would fail to justify wading into the pond if the alternative were defusing a bomb on dry land, set to destroy Chicago' (Maguire 2018: 784). Reasons are not assumed by Maguire to be essentially non-strict (see Maguire 2018: 801); however, fit-making considerations are assumed to be essentially strict. Maguire (2018: 785) claims that 'facts about what you overall ought to do are the paradigmatic strict facts' and '[so called reasons of the right kind for affective attitudes] are themselves, if you like, a kind of ought fact' (Maguire 2018: 780).

The gradability constraint on reasons, according to Maguire (2018: 783), just is that a reason 'has some gradable property that is usually called its weight'. That is, 'reasons are essentially *gradable*' (Maguire 2018: 785). Again, Singer's drowning child example is supposed to illustrate the gradability constraint: 'the "saving the child" reason has more weight than the "getting your clothes muddy" reason' (Maguire 2018: 783).

The contributory constraint on reasons is the idea that it is essential for reasons to contribute – that is, to interact in determining the overall normative status of F-ing. According to Maguire (2018: 785), '[c]-ontributoriness is the property of playing a specific role in a "weighing explanation" of an overall normative fact.' How exactly does this work? The idea is that reasons have 'weights', and that the net weight of reason supporting an option is somehow explained by the weights of all reasons for and against that option and the fact that 'these are all the reasons bearing on the given option' (Maguire 2018: 784). It is assumed that '[t]hese facts about the net weight of reason supporting each option (together with some fact about what options there are) in turn explain the fact that there is *most* reason in support of some option' (Maguire 2018: 784). And this, then, is supposed to explain that one *ought* to take the relevant option (it is assumed that one ought to do what one has most reason to do). The ought fact – that one ought to take the relevant option – is on Maguire's view an overall normative fact. 'It obtains in virtue of all the contributory normative facts together with a "normative totality fact" to the effect that these are all the relevant normative facts' (Maguire 2018: 784). Finally, Maguire (2018: 785) specifies that typically reasons fulfil this function of contributoriness 'by combining or by competing with each other'.

Now, what about Maguire's argument then? It does appear to be valid, the conclusion seems to follow if the premises are true, and there doesn't seem to be any equivocation going on – the terms used in the premises do seem to have the same meaning as in the conclusion. How about soundness? I would like to submit that there are reasonable and distinct considerations speaking against each of Maguire's premises. Let me elaborate on these a bit.

The first, and arguably the most problematic, consideration concerns premise 1. To see the problem, recall the overall dialectic we are facing at this point. The fundamental question that we are addressing in this part of the present section is whether any axiological version of explanationism is plausible overall and, in particular, does better than deontic explanationism, which we have already put aside due to a number of problems it faced. Now, we observed that a major problem for any axiological explanationism is the so-called right kind of reasons problem – it is not easy to see how any value-based explanationist proposal can account for normative reasons for attitudes, beliefs, and emotions in particular. Maguire's proposal on this matter has a radical boldness. He seems to suggest that the problem can be avoided, since according to him there are no genuinely normative reasons for attitudes. But on the face of it, attitudes are paradigmatic examples of F-ings that can be supported by reasons. So his argument for that specific conclusion has to be convincing. However, note that his argument for that conclusion – that is, that there are no reasons for attitudes – relies on the assumption that (arguably, broad) explanationism about reasons is true, namely it is part of his premise 1. He assumes that reasons are essentially contributory, and as we saw earlier, this property just is an instance of a broad explanationist approach – that reasons are things that play a 'role in a "weighing explanation" of an overall normative fact' (Maguire 2018: 785). But to presuppose the truth of explanationism at this point would amount to begging the question in the context of the present discussion. The supposed truth of explanationism *is* what's under question in our discussion. One could, of course, reply that that's not the context of Maguire's discussion. This might be correct and that's why

I only claim that the move we are discussing *would* commit a proponent of explanationism to begging the question, not that Maguire is actually begging the question against us in the present context. However, note that the 'right kind' of reasons problem is a problem for any axiological explanationist account, including Maguire's proposal. And consequentially, presupposing the truth of general explanationism at any point within the context where the 'right kind' of reasons problem is discussed, is problematic, especially in the context where other, non-axiological versions of explanationism have already been set aside as not fully satisfactory.

One could reply to this by pointing towards the very general aspect of Maguire's contributoriness constraint on reasons. It does not assume *axiological* explanationism in an argument against an objection to axiological explanationism; it only assumes the truth of explanationism in general. One could insist that it is not a flaw to assume the truth of the general theory X in one's argument in favour of a theory XN and then argue in favour of the specific version XN. Surely, it is true that taking on board this sort of assumption need not *always* constitute a flaw in an argument. However, again, recall the present dialectic. We are investigating explanationism about reasons, in all its forms. Thus, within our present context, assuming that normative reasons essentially are things that play a role in a sort of explanation of overall normative facts would constitute begging the question. We have already put aside other versions of explanationism. Thus, we cannot at this moment in our discussion merely presuppose that a version of explanationism has to be true.

Moreover, some of the objections that we have explored against deontic versions of explanationism, and in particular against the very idea of there being a special sort of 'weighing explanation' of normative facts, can be brought up again in the present context. It is not really clear how the supposed weighing explanation works. If it is an explanation at all, it has to be radically different from any other explanations we know. Maguire doesn't propose an argument for the claim that the 'net weight of reason' supporting an option is explained by facts about all the reasons for and against that option, and thus that the facts about reasons for and against an option explain the facts about most reason for an option. It is not clear, in particular, in what sense the fact that a friend of mine offers me his beach house for free for the holidays (and we can add to this the fact that spending my holidays at a beach house would promote my happiness) *explains* or *partially explains* the fact that I have most reason and indeed ought not to go on holiday to that beach house. (Recall, I ought not to go on the holiday, since I just broke my leg.) It is not clear in what sense we talk about explanation at all when we talk about the alleged 'weighing explanations' of normative facts (compare to the arguments from Brunero 2013, 2018). At this point, appeal to the metaphors of 'weight', 'weighing', and 'balance' only makes the discussion more obscure.

Another objection against what we have identified as Maguire's premise (1) comes from a different angle. As David Faraci (2020) has recently observed in his critical discussion of Maguire's article, the difference between reasons for action and 'right kind' of reasons considerations for attitudes might be explained by the difference between action and attitudes. More specifically, the contexts where there are reasons for action tend to be such that the subject cannot take several options at the same time. There is an actual limitation in terms of what the subject can do. Hence, it is not surprising to observe a competition among reason considerations. However, in contexts where we have 'right kind' of reasons considerations, we do often have, as Maguire himself observes, the possibility to have a number of distinct attitudes. Therefore, it is not surprising that we observe the absence of the competition aspect with respect to 'right kind' of reasons considerations.[21] In short, we can take this to show that the aspects that Maguire takes to be proper aspects of normative reasons, indeed, as being essential characteristics of reasons, are merely side effects of his focus on reasons for action (and given certain background assumptions; see the previous paragraphs). But the fact that reasons for actions are always non-strict, gradable, and contributory (let's grant this for the sake of this line of thought) doesn't yet allow us to conclude that these features are features of normative reasons in general. All that follows is only that these might be features of normative reasons for actions. The fact that we are able to have various distinct attitudes with respect to some relevant objects may well explain why reasons for attitudes don't have these same features that reasons for action have. In other terms, we don't have sufficient grounds for holding that the characteristics that Maguire identifies are

---

[21] See Faraci's point:

> What Maguire's cases illustrate, I submit, is not that FMCs [that is, fit-making considerations] are not reasons but rather that the contexts in which we tend to think about reasons for action and reasons for attitudes differ, in part because actions and attitudes themselves differ. We tend to think about how we and others should act in contexts where the reasons for them compete, because actions are frequently in tension, and we need to pick one. By contrast, as Maguire's cases show, we often consider how we and others should feel in contexts where there are no relevant tensions, because we can feel many different ways about different things, or about different aspects of the same thing. In such contexts, there is no reason to expect competition amongst the relevant FMCs, and therefore no reason to think they are not reasons. (Faraci 2020: 230)

essential to reasons as such, as opposed to being aspects of reasons for action, because of specifics of action as opposed to attitudes.

Second, and independently from our discussion of premise (1), one might also question the claim (i.e. premise (2)) that all 'right kind' of reason considerations that normatively support an [affective] attitude are fit-making facts, which are 'if you like, a kind of ought fact' (Maguire 2018: 780). If this verdict is on the right track, then we have a case where a consideration – say, the general, abstract consideration that it is raining – is a reason that speaks in favour of holding an attitude, namely feeling pessimistic about the prospects of a pleasant run, without also being a fit-making consideration for one to feel pessimistic about the prospects of a pleasant run. Given that it is also really hot outside, it is not a fitting attitude for the subject in this case (one can, of course, vary the case by changing the attitude of feeling pessimistic to being sad, being disheartened, unhappy, demoralised, and so on, without affecting our assessment of it). Of course, Maguire is free to deny that this sort of case is even possible. However, if one does this, then it is not clear how one could maintain the possibility of parallel cases involving action – for example, running/intending to run in the heat and the rain; see Nair (2016) and our discussion in Section 3.2, where we took these cases as showing that the additivity/accrual of reasons to F can fail. If this is on the right track, then reasons for attitudes might not always be fit-making facts, whatever exactly this implies.

The third and distinct complaint concerns premise (3) – that is, the claim that no fit-making consideration can be non-strict, gradable, and contributory (alternatively: at least have one of these characteristics). If we stick with a fairly common view within the rich literature of contemporary philosophy of emotions – with which oddly enough Maguire never engages, but really should have, given that the debates about fittingness of emotions and reasons for emotions have gone on in that field for decades and well before they made an appearance in general normative philosophy – an emotion is fitting when it respects its *formal object*. Here is a classic contemporary statement of this idea, applied to the example of fear: 'The formal object of fear – the norm defined by fear for its own appropriateness – is the Dangerous' (de Sousa 2002: 251; see also de Sousa 1987; Deonna and Teroni 2012: 1–12; Scarantino and de Sousa 2018 for an introduction of the relevant distinctions and further overview of the relevant literature). Thus, on a common view in philosophy of emotions, an emotion E is fitting if and only if 'its intentional object o [e.g. the thing *about* which the emotion is, as for example the dog in the case of fearing a dog] exemplifies the formal object that E (re)presents o as having' (cf. Echeverri 2019: 543). Crucially for us and without going into too much detail, whether the emotion's intentional object *o* indeed exemplifies the formal object that the emotion is supposed to present *o* as having depends on a number of factors. Among these will figure background conditions, cultural influences, personal history, and so on. Take the case of the dog and fear. It will be only in virtue of some specific features of the dog, say, that the dog has big teeth and it moves erratically, that the dog exemplifies the formal object of fear – that is, the dangerous/the dangerousness (cf. Deonna and Teroni 2012: 1–12; Echeverri 2019). To put it in Maguire's terminology then, it is in virtue of some aspects that the fact about there being a dog makes the fear of the dog fitting (is a fit-making fact). However, that these features – for example, the teeth and erratic movements – exemplify the danger is not a 'strict' fact. It depends on the context, on background aspects and assumptions. For example, it may do so only in virtue of us having the background knowledge of there being some sort of correlation between dogs with big teeth moving erratically and one getting bitten by a dog. But consider, for instance, a community where no erratic dogs with big teeth have ever been observed biting people, and no reports about such incidents have ever been heard about from other places. Arguably, in such a community, that the dog in front of one has big teeth and is moving erratically *doesn't exemplify* the formal object (i.e. the dangerous/the dangerousness) that the emotion of fear represents its intentional object as having. Thus, the fact that the dog with big teeth in front of one moves erratically exemplifies the formal object of fear – the dangerousness that my fear represents the dog as having, holds *only* provided that I/we have the background knowledge of the correlation of dogs with big teeth moving erratically and one getting bitten by a dog. But this crucial aspect does sound very much like a 'non-strict' fact in Maguire's sense. That the dog has big teeth and moves erratically doesn't 'justify or require anything on their own' (cf. Maguire 2018: 784). We need the additional knowledge that in this community it is well known that dogs with big teeth who move erratically tend to bite. Only given this background assumption is the dangerousness present.

Now, with respect to the contributoriness, the abovementioned case of running can be taken as putting pressure on Maguire's idea that fit-making considerations are not contributory. And with respect to gradability, as contemporary discussions on gradable adjectives show, it is far from established that adjectives exhibiting a sort of crispness and absoluteness are not gradable (see for linguistics Kennedy 1999; Kennedy and McNally

2005; Kennedy 2007; Lassiter 2017; Logins 2020a, 2020b contains discussion of these points with respect to *correct/appropriate*, *confident*, and
supported).[22] Thus, overall we might well have sufficient grounds for
doubting premise (3) as well.

Given the aforementioned discussion, I think we have good reasons for
doubting the soundness of Maguire's argument that we schematised
earlier – that is, (1)–(4). The claim that there are no genuine 'right kind'
of reasons for affective attitudes doesn't withstand scrutiny. Given that the
'right kind' of reasons for attitudes are genuine normative reasons,
Maguire's version of axiological explanationism is back at square one.
That there are genuine 'right kind' of normative reasons for affective
attitudes speaks against this version of axiological explanationism. And
its proponents still don't have a satisfactory answer to this problem.

Two quick remarks before concluding are in order. First, it may be
useful to note that contrary to what axiologists like Finlay and Maguire
seem to think, their views do have problems not only with accounting for
the 'right kind' of reasons for attitudes but *also* with accounting for the
'wrong kind' of reasons for attitudes. More precisely, their view seems to
rule out the possibility of at least some sorts of normative reasons for
attitudes that are not directly related to fittingness of attitudes ('fit-making') *and* are not directly related to promoting valuable states of affairs.
The key case here is *epistemic reasons* for emotions – that is, reasons that
contribute to making an affective attitude/emotion reasonable from an
epistemic point of view. It is a commonly held view within philosophy of
emotions – indeed, I would say it's more or less orthodoxy today – that
emotions can be assessed from a number of perspectives. And in particular,
it is a very popular view that, besides emotions, being fitting or not (i.e.
meeting their formal objects), emotions can also be evaluated from a
purely epistemic point of view (see Gordon 1987; Greenspan 1988;
Mulligan 1998; Goldie 2002, 2004; Deonna and Teroni 2012; Pelser
2014; Epley 2018; Meylan 2018; Scarantino and de Sousa 2018;
Drucker 2019; Echeverri 2019; Na'aman 2021; for a non-exhaustive list

---

[22] Faraci also puts forward similar considerations against Maguire's claim that fit-making
considerations lack non-strictness, contributoriness, and gradability. See in particular his
suggestion that fit-making considerations for emotions might well combine: 'And it seems
perfectly possible that while neither the sharp claws nor the murderous look alone is sufficient to
outweigh the dragon's claim to be only interested in friendship, in combination they are; you ought
to run. Most importantly, this is no less plausible if we take these to be reasons for and against
fearing her' (Faraci 2020: 231). And with respect to non-strictness: 'arguably it is always fitting to
feel disappointed when someone gets a promotion you deserve, whereas it is not always fitting to
fear something with sharp claws' (Faraci 2020: 231, fn 11).

of philosophers who appear to endorse this idea).[23] Robert Gordon puts the idea about the epistemic status of emotions being distinct from their fittingness states explicitly in terms of different sorts of reasons one can have for an emotion. He writes: '[i] Tom is worried that his wife was on the two o'clock flight, because that's the one that was hijacked (attitudinal). [ii] Tom is worried that his wife was on the two o'clock flight, because she said she'd be arriving early in the evening (epistemic)' (Gordon 1987: 35). The example in (i) is a case of an attitudinal reason for an emotion (e.g. connected to the formal object of emotions, fit-making), whereas example (ii) illustrates an epistemic reason for an emotion (e.g. connected to the purely epistemic status of an emotion). In a sense, then, epistemic reasons for emotions are of the 'wrong kind', understood in the specific sense that only fit-making considerations (e.g. related to an attitude's formal object) can be the 'right kind' of reasons. But, given that epistemic reasons are connected to attitudes' epistemic status, and an attitude's epistemic status is not dependent on promoting some valuable state of affairs, the value-based accounts have trouble explaining why these 'wrong kind' of reasons – that is, epistemic reasons for emotions – are genuine normative reasons. The value-based accounts have trouble explaining not only the 'right kind' of reasons for beliefs and emotions but also in accounting for some (i.e. epistemic) 'wrong kind' of reasons for emotions.

Second, and in fact connectedly to the first point, this further weakness of the account seems to elicit a more fundamental problem with axiological explanationist accounts and, arguably, explanationist accounts *tout court*. While they do capture one important aspect of our common understanding of reasons – that is, that there is, in a sense, a connection between reasons and explanation of normative facts – they have hard time explaining another equally fundamental aspect of our common understanding of reasons, namely that there has to be some connection between reasons and reasoning broadly understood. In a sense, reasons are understood to be right foundations on which our attitudes can be based; that is, reasons are often perceived as considerations that can lead us to hold fitting responses, e.g. attitudes in a given situation. Somehow, views that limit their accounts of normative reasons only to their explanatory functions fail to appreciate this important aspect of our common view.

---

[23] If a quotation is needed, here is one paradigmatic statement of this idea: 'standards of correctness so conceived should be distinguished from epistemological standards by which we assess the justification of emotions' (Deonna and Teroni 2012: 6).

3.4 Concluding Remarks

This chapter has focused on views that analyse/define reasons in terms of their explanatory role for some normative facts. The two major approaches within this broad explanationist camp comprise those who appeal to the role of reasons in explaining deontic facts (e.g. ought facts), and those who appeal to the role of reasons in explaining axiological facts (e.g. value facts – either F-ing-based or object-based goodness). We looked at the details of what appear to be the most promising versions of both general approaches. We considered the positive arguments in their favour. A major advantage of these approaches is that they do indeed seem to capture an important insight, namely reasons have to be connected in a sense to explanation of normative (deontic or axiological) facts. However, we also saw that none of the more specific versions of the general explanationist approach withstands scrutiny. Both deontic and axiological versions of explanationism run into fundamental difficulties. For one thing it is not clear how exactly outweighed reasons can function in explanation of ought facts (deontic explanationism); for another, it is not clear how the 'right kind' of reasons for attitudes are even possible if reasons are supposed to explain value promotion or the value of an end. More specific worries were elaborated along the way. Thus, the conclusion we reached is that while explanationist views do seem to point towards an important insight in understanding reasons, they also seem to leave substantial aspects of reasons unexplained. Reasons matter for us not only in virtue of their explanatory roles but, sometimes, also for their role in reasoning/argument towards a fitting response.

CHAPTER 4

The Evidence View

4.1 Introduction

In what precedes, we have explored two major reductionist approaches to normative reasons. And the implicit assumption with which we have been working was that all existing reductionist views could be reduced to one or the other of two camps: the Reasoning view camp that appeals to good/ fitting patterns of reasoning from fitting premise-responses to fitting conclusion-responses in order to define reasons; or the Explanation view camp that appeals to the role of reasons in explaining some normative facts (ought-facts or value-facts). However, one might reasonably protest at this way of partitioning the debate, for a very prominent view within the reasons, literature doesn't seem on the face of it to fit into this picture, namely the Evidence view of reasons, which doesn't seem on the face of it to fall into either the Reasoning view camp or the explanationist camp. According to this view, as defended most notably by Stephen Kearns and Daniel Star in a number of publications (Kearns and Star 2008, 2009, 2013, 2015), normative reasons to F are evidence that one ought to F.

The focus of the present chapter is on the Evidence view of reasons. In what follows, we explore the details of the view along with arguments in its favour that appear to make it quite promising. But we also consider some of the most popular objections to the view. We will conclude, however, that contrary to what one might initially think, the Evidence view, when fully developed, reduces to a version of the Reasoning view. And thus the view also suffers from some of the same problems that we have observed with respect to that approach. In this way, it will miss out some of the aspects of normative reasons as we commonly understand them, the aspects for which reasons actually matter for us. Nevertheless, working through the details of this view will also help us to see what exactly a theory of reasons should be able to do. A new proposal that builds on the conclusions from this and discussions in the previous chapters will be elaborated in the chapter after this.

4.2   The View

According to a prominent version of the Evidence view of normative reasons, a normative reason for one to F just is evidence that one ought to F. This version of the view has been notably defended by Stephen Kearns and Daniel Star in a number of publications (see Kearns and Star 2008, 2009, 2013, 2015). Before assessing the merits of the view, let us first see in a bit more detail what exactly the view suggests.

The official version of the view that we will focus on in what follows reads as follows:

> **R** Necessarily, a fact F is a reason for an agent A to φ iff F is evidence that A ought to φ (where φ is either a belief or an action). (Kearns and Star 2009: 216)

The first thing to note about the view is that it is presented as a simple bi-conditional, which, of course, need not be taken as presenting an explanatory analysis/definition of reasons. Kearns and Star are clear that their arguments in favour of the Evidence view support, strictly speaking, only this bi-conditional. However, they do commit themselves to a stronger position: 'we also believe that the *best* explanation of the truth of all these principles [e.g. the genus principle R and more specific reasons as evidence principles applied to reasons for beliefs and reasons for action] is that the property of being a reason and the property of being evidence of an ought are identical' (Kearns and Star 2009: 219).

Another thing to note is how Kearns and Star characterise evidence. An important element in that characterisation is being a reliable indicator. But they don't endorse the somewhat strong and unqualified claim that evidence that p just is a reliable indicator that p. They suggest that the possibility of there being misleading evidence for necessary truths is one reason why such a view should not be accepted, and that that a generally reliable source of information (e.g. a phone book) can be wrong about some specific p (e.g. the number of someone in particular) is another reason why evidence is not just a reliable indicator of p. Some facts can be evidence that p even without it reliably indicating that p (see Kearns and Star 2009: 229–230). Nonetheless, they maintain that something similar enough to the 'reliable indicator' conception of evidence should hold. For instance, they write:

> We may therefore conclude that a fact is evidence for a proposition if and only if relevantly similar facts reliably indicate relevantly similar proposi-tions. In the normative case, then, we can say that a fact F is evidence that one ought to φ if and only if facts relevantly similar to F reliably indicate propositions relevantly similar to the proposition that one ought to φ. (Kearns and Star 2009: 230)

The phone book example illustrates this idea. The normally reliable phone book is wrong about John's number. Thus, Kearns and Star concede that the book indicates that such and such is the person's number (a fact) doesn't reliably indicate that such and such is the person's number. But that fact is evidence that such and such is the person's number. It is so because, according to Kearns and Star (2009: 230), 'there are many relevantly similar facts that do reliably indicate relevantly similar propositions (e.g. the book does reliably give the correct numbers for Mary and Henry and many others).'

Another aspect of their view of evidence is that they endorse a probabilistic conception of evidential support. This is apparent from their treatment of the strength of evidence. They write: 'The strength of a piece of evidence E for a proposition P depends on the degree to which E increases the probability of P' (Kearns and Star 2009: 231–232). And more specifically, they tell us that appeal to increase of probability also captures the ways in which one piece of evidence is stronger than another, outweighs other evidence, and can combine with further evidence:

> The more probable P is given E, the stronger evidence E is that P is true. E is stronger evidence than another piece of evidence E* for P if and only if E makes P more probable than E* makes P. E outweighs a piece of evidence E* if and only if E is evidence for P, E* is evidence for ∼P and E makes P more probable than E* makes ∼P. Two pieces of evidence, E and E* can combine to form stronger evidence if the probability of P given the conjunction of E and E* is greater than both the probability of P given E and the probability of P given E*. (Kearns and Star 2009: 232)

The kind of probability that they have in mind here is 'evidential or epistemic probability' (cf. Kearns and Star 2009: 232, fn 10). They refer to Williamson (2000, chapter 10) for an exploration of this kind of probability.[1] A question that one might have at this point is how exactly the quasi-indicator understanding of evidence is supposed to fit with the increase of evidential probability understanding of evidential support.

---

[1] Note, however, that the conception of evidential probability that they seem to suggest is not uncontroversial. In particular, some have found it difficult to accept the idea of there being one prior P function as characterized by Williamson (2000: 211):

> The discussion will assume an initial probability distribution P. P does not represent actual or hypothetical credences. Rather, P measures something like the intrinsic plausibility of hypotheses prior to investigation; this notion of intrinsic plausibility can vary in extension between contexts. P will be assumed to satisfy a standard set of axioms for the probability calculus [. . .]. P(p) is taken to be defined for all propositions; the standard objection that the subject may never have considered p is irrelevant to the non-subjective probability P. But P is not assumed to be syntactically definable.

For one thing, one might wonder whether it is always the case that when relevantly similar facts to F reliably indicate relevantly similar propositions to p, it is always the case that the probability of p given F is higher than the probably of p without F (say, given some other facts). Maybe the afore-mentioned example of the possibility of misleading evidence for a neces-sary truth (that Kearns and Star themselves provide as a genuine instance of evidence) is one case in point. Given that it is a necessary truth, nothing can increase nor decrease its probability (which is 1), be it quasi-reliable indicator or not. See also Logins (2016b) for a related objection from necessary truths to a version of the probabilistic conception of evidence. But let us not dwell on this specific potential worry. Arguably, there might be ways to fix the problem of necessary truths (for instance, by giving up the idea that there is evidence for necessary truths at all or to alter the probabilistic conception of evidential support, or to add a clause about special treatment for necessary truths).

4.3 Arguments in Favour

Kearns and Star offer a battery of considerations in favour of their view. I suggest we focus here on what appear to be the four strongest arguments. The first line of thought that, I think, provides a good prima facie case in favour of the evidence is based on the simple observation that, typically, in standard cases it does make sense to explain normative reasons in terms of evidence for oughts. Often we can simply paraphrase the reasons state-ments with evidence for ought states, which, of course, gets a straightfor-ward explanation if something like the Evidence view is on the right track. Kearns and Star suggest that considerations of this sort offer a good inductive argument in favour of their view.[2] In support of the claim that standard situations where one has reasons to F are also situations where one has evidence that one ought to F, Kearns and Star provide two examples. But they also suggest that there are many more standard cases, indeed a large number of situations that would provide fitting examples to illustrate the point (see Kearns and Star 2009: 222–223). The first example

---

It is in particular the assumption that there really is 'something like the intrinsic plausibility of hypotheses prior to investigation' is something that some have found questionable. See for instance Kaplan (2009), Hawthorne (2005), and Hawthorne and Magidor (2018) for related worries.

[2] The exact wording of the argument is as follows:

(1) Standard cases of practical reasons to φ are cases of evidence that one ought to φ, and vice versa.
(2) Therefore, RA is true (argument from induction).

(Kearns and Star 2009: 222)

is a case where a subject sees a friend who is in terrible pain; his foot is stuck under the wheel of a car. The suggestion here is that the fact that the friend is in pain is a reason to help the friend, and also it is a reason to believe that the subject ought to help his friend. Crucially, the same fact is also evidence that the subject ought to help the friend. As the subject is helping the friend, he remembers that he has promised to meet another friend in two minutes' time for a philosophical conversation. That he has promised to meet the other friend is a reason to leave and go to meet the other friend. It is suggested that it is also evidence that the subject ought to rush to meet that other friend. Of course, the first friend's pain provides much stronger evidence that the subject ought to stay and help than the evidence that the subject ought to rush to meet the other friend. Finally, it is suggested that the reason to stay and help (pain) is much stronger than the reason to rush away (promise).

The second example concerns someone who likes to spend evenings either reading some scientific book to better understand the world or by relaxing and watching TV. It is suggested that the fact that reading a book would lead him to better understanding of world is a reason for him to read the book, and it is also evidence that he ought to read the book. And the fact that watching TV would provide the subject with some pleasure is a reason for him to watch TV, and it is also evidence that he ought to watch TV. In this example, it is then suggested that the subject weighs his reasons and determines that he ought to read the book, which is taken to be just the same as 'saying that he weighs the evidence that he ought to read a book against the evidence that he ought to watch television, and judges that he ought to read a book on this basis' (Kearns and Star 2009: 223). These are only two examples of a much larger number of standard cases (i.e. cases of transparent facts and no misleading evidence; cf. Kearns and Star 2009: 223) where a fact is both a reason to F and evidence that one ought to F. On the basis of induction, one seems to be warranted, then, to conclude that being a reason to F just is being evidence that one ought to F (or at least to hold the corresponding bi-conditional about being a reason and being evidence that one ought to F).

The second argument that I would like to rehearse here appeals to considerations about deliberation. The official version of the argument can be summed up as follows: reasons to F have to be able to play a role in reliable reasoning about whether one ought to F or not; only evidence that one ought to F can play that sort of role in reliable practical reasoning. Thus, normative reasons to F are evidence that one ought to F (cf. Kearns and Star 2009: 224). As such, this argument might be a bit of an overstatement. One might think that things other than evidence can play a role in reliable reasoning. For instance, unless you think that all premises in reliable/good reasoning about whether one ought to F are pieces of evidence, you might think that a non-evidentialist Reasoning view might account for the reasons–reasoning connection just as well as, if not better than, the Evidence view. We will come back to this, or something close enough to this, thought when examining the worries faced by the Evidence view of reasons. For now, we can agree that a toned-down version of the argument that appeals to reasoning can be taken to provide *some* support for the Evidence view, namely the argument that the Evidence view is well suited to account for most of the reasons–reasoning connection, given some further assumptions about the role of evidence in reasoning. One way of filling out the details here would just be to say that by definition playing some crucial role in reasoning just is being evidence, and being evidence just is playing a role in reasoning. If so, then of course, by definition, the Evidence view would provide straightforward explanation of the most relevant aspects of the reasons–reasoning connection and its simplicity alone would constitute a basis for preferring it to potential attempts by rival non-reasoning-centred views to account for the observed connection. But let us not anticipate our discussion on the Evidence view as a version of the Reasoning view.

The third argument concerns another aspect in which the Evidence view seems to have an advantage at least over some of the rival views. The Evidence view has the advantage (over some views) in terms of the simplicity of the explanation that it can provide of why reasons appear to have various degrees of 'strength' or 'weight'. On the Evidence view, the explanation is straightforward and hence theoretically powerful: it's just because evidence (for a proposition) by definition comes in various degrees of strength, given the probabilistic gloss over the strength of evidence. Given Kearns and Star's understanding of evidence, it is only a consequence of their view that reasons (to F) are gradable; their degree of 'strength' is inherited from the degree of increase of probabilistic support for the proposition that one ought to F provided by the corresponding piece of evidence. Again, the official version of the argument might be a bit too ambitious, since, strictly speaking, Kearns and Star claim that the Evidence view is 'the best explanation' of the gradability of reasons,[3] which

---

[3] They write:

    (1) Reasons can have different strengths.

might be contested, for instance, by proponents of some alternative views that we have seen earlier. But even if one tones down the argument slightly, and only claims that the Evidence view of reasons provides a straightforward and theoretically powerful explanation of the gradability of reasons, it is already a good prima facie reason for taking the Evidence view seriously. For it is at least among the best possible potential explanations of the gradability of reasons, and certainly it does better in this respect than some of the alternatives. Note, however, that unfortunately Kearns and Star only compare their view in this respect to reasons-first and Broome's version of deontic explanationism. But, of course, a fuller picture would also need to compare it to other versions of explanationism (e.g. value-based accounts and Reasoning views), in which case it is not clear that the Evidence view would constitute *the* best (e.g. the simplest) possible explanation of the gradability of reasons. Nevertheless, that the view can easily account for the apparent gradability of the 'strength' of reasons is certainly a point in its favour.

The fourth consideration in favour of the Evidence view is that it does respect the theoretical unity constraint on a theory of reasons. More precisely, the account applies perfectly both to normative reasons for actions and normative reasons for attitudes. Strictly speaking, Kearns and Star only explain how it applies to beliefs, but they stipulate that the view can be easily extended to other attitudes as well (cf. Kearns and Star 2009: 216, fn2).[4] Kearns and Star assume that the default position should be that normative reasons for attitudes and normative reasons for action are of the same kind. They do provide considerations in favour of taking this to be the default position, namely, the consideration that we can refer to one and the same fact as being a reason both to act in a way and to believe a proposition, something that becomes difficult to explain if reasons for action and attitudes are of a totally different sort, and

(2)   RA is the best explanation of how this is possible.
(3)   Therefore, RA is true. (*inference to the best explanation*).

(Kearns and Star 2009: 230)

Note also that in unpacking this argument they tend to switch between the talk of the Evidence view providing the 'best explanation' of the gradability of reasons and the talk of the Evidence view providing a 'very attractive account of what it is for [normative] reasons to have strengths' (cf. Kearns and Star 2009: 232). I suggest that the latter reading is more realistic.
[4] See the official formulation of the argument:

(1)   Epistemic and practical reasons are of a kind.
(2)   RA provides the only plausible account of reasons according to which (1) is so.
(3)   Therefore, RA is true (inference to the best explanation).

(Kearns and Star 2009: 219)

the consideration that apparently reasons to believe and reasons to act can be weighed against each other (see Kearns and Star 2009: 220–221). The suggestion, then, is that the Evidence view has a straightforward explanation of this. Again, let us focus on this interpretation of the argument, rather than the bold claim that the Evidence view provides *the* best possible explanation of the apparent fact that reasons for attitudes and reasons for actions are of the same kind. On the Evidence view of reasons, normative reasons just are evidence, in the belief case, reasons to believe that p are evidence that p and also/or evidence that one ought to believe p (depending on whether one wants to leave the pragmatism option about reasons to believe open), and in the case of action, reasons to F are evidence that one ought to F. The unifying principle in reasons to believe and reasons to act is that both are evidence for some proposition. Given this common element, the Evidence view is perfectly placed to explain why reasons to believe and reasons to act are of the same kind. This explanatory power in complying with a natural constraint on a theory of reasons is then another prima facie consideration in favour of the Evidence view of reasons.

4.4   Worries

Despite its prima facie plausibility, the Evidence view has attracted a number of critics. A non-exhaustive list of publications that contain objections to the Evidence view of reasons includes Broome (2008), Brunero (2009), McNaughton and Rawling (2011), McKeever and Ridge (2012), Fletcher (2013), McBride (2013), Setiya (2014), Littlejohn (2016), Schmidt (2017), and Hawthorne and Magidor (2018). In what follows, we will not cover all the existing objections, however. We will focus only on some of the most problematic aspects of the view.

Testimonial evidence. To begin with, let us consider what seems to be the most popular line of objection against Kearns and Star's Evidence view of reasons, namely the line of thought that some examples clearly demonstrate that not all pieces of evidence can be normative reasons. Consider the example that Kearns and Star (2009: 233) actually discuss themselves as a possible counterexample to their view (the example is attributed to James Morauta). A reliable newspaper states that there are people starving in Africa. That this reliable newspaper says it, is clearly evidence that one ought to give money to a charity, say, Oxfam (presumably, the assumption here is that this would somewhat help to alleviate the suffering of starving). Now, the suggestion is that while that the reliable newspaper repeats that there are people starving in Africa is evidence that one ought to send money to Oxfam, it is not by itself a reason for one to send money to Oxfam. That people are starving is a reason. Not that someone, reliable or not, says so. However, the Evidence view of reasons predicts that the mere report from the newspaper is a reason for one to send money to Oxfam. Thus, the case seems to present a counterexample to the Evidence view of reasons.

The initial reply that Kearns and Star offer to this sort of potential counterexample contains two possible ways of dealing with the objection. One line of reply is to bite the bullet and to claim that in the normative domain, when something is evidence that one ought to F, it has a potential to create effectively an obligation, the moral obligation in the case of Oxfam, to give money. The mere fact that the newspaper reports the starvation can create a reason to give money to Oxfam. They write: 'The fact that the newspaper says that people are starving in Africa may in itself be enough to create an obligation to send money to Oxfam' (Kearns and Star 2009: 233). This is, of course, a bit too quick. For this is exactly what is at issue here (assuming that, at least typically, having an obligation to F entails having a reason to F, and assuming that those who propose this counterexample would also put forward the intuition that a mere report by a newspaper doesn't yet create by itself a moral obligation). To say that the newspaper's report creates an obligation without providing further theoretical grounds for why this is so would amount to begging the question against those who offer the newspaper example against the Evidence view of reasons.

One might also want to know what exactly is 'enough' in the example 'to create an obligation to send money to Oxfam'. Is it the fact that people are starving in Africa, or is it that the newspaper reports it? If the former, then the creation of obligation has nothing to do with there being evidence that one ought to do the relevant thing and so this is still a counterexample to the Evidence view. But if the mere fact that the reliable newspaper publishes something is enough to create an obligation, then, arguably, we have many more moral obligations than we could ever suspect that we have (e.g. today's newspaper published all sorts of things, some bad, some not; is there a moral obligation for me corresponding to each of the assertions? If not, why not? What's so special about the starvation case?). Anyway, we need more theoretical considerations if we are to take the first response to be anything more than just begging the question against the objection from the newspaper counterexample.

The second line of response is based on the idea that implausible consequences will follow if the newspaper's report is not a reason to send money to Oxfam. On the face of it, this line appears to be more promising.

Kearns and Star's published version of this response is relatively short. I attempt here to work out the implicit details of the argument. The suggestion seems to be that we only have the relevant pre-theoretical judgments in the newspaper case (i.e. that the mere report is not a reason to send money) because the fact that even a reliable newspaper can be mistaken is somehow made salient. And it is made salient mainly because of the focus on the non-conclusive aspect of the newspaper's report. But denying that the newspaper's report is a reason on the basis that it is non-conclusive (or non-entailing) leads to a slippery slope, according to this line of objection. If one denies that the fact that the newspaper says that people are starving is a reason to F, because of the non-entailing character of the report (i.e. that a reliable newspaper says that p doesn't *entail* that p), then one will also have to deny that the fact that people are starving is a reason to donate to a charity that can help them. For even the fact that people are starving doesn't on its own *entail* that these people are in a terrible condition. Even starving is only a non-entailing condition with respect to suffering. They write: 'After all, the fact that people are starving *need* not mean that they are badly off. In some distant possible worlds, starving might be extremely pleasant and not life threatening at all' (Kearns and Star 2009: 234). And they add: 'Indeed, *most* of the facts we cite as reasons merely indicate what we ought to do. Therefore, unless one wishes to deny that most facts that we think of as reasons really are reasons, the fact that the newspaper says there are people starving in Africa is really a reason to send money to Oxfam' (Kearns and Star 2009: 234).

So, this line of reply seems to have two elements. The first is the error-theory element – that is, we only have this common-sense pre-theoretical judgment because we focus on the non-entailing aspect of the newspaper report, not because it is not a reason. And the second is the counter-argument element – the *reductio* argument according to which if the newspaper report is not a reason, then the fact that people are starving in Africa isn't one either, but, of course, that people are starving in Africa is a reason to send money to Oxfam; hence the newspaper report is a reason to send money to Oxfam too.

Despite being somewhat more promising than the first reply, this line of objection is nonetheless unsatisfactory. For one thing, as John Hawthorne and Ofra Magidor (2018) have observed, the judgment about testimonies being mere evidence that one ought to F without being a normative reason doesn't seem to be tied to the non-entailing aspect of the testimony in this sort of case. Indeed, as they have showed, the same sort of pre-theoretical judgment seems to be elicited even when we focus on cases of testimony that cannot be wrong (in the relevant sense of 'cannot'). The case that Hawthorne and Magidor offer to illustrate the point focuses on a far-away hermit who *knows* the relevant facts. Knowing that *p* entails *p*. Moreover, given that knowledge is safe, it couldn't easily be the case that *p* is false (i.e. the worlds where *p* is false are not among close possible worlds to the world where the hermit knows that *p*). Here are the details of the case from Hawthorne and Magidor (2018: 131).

> To our ears, if a hermit in a cave on the other side of the world knows that the apple is poisonous, it remains hard to recover a context where it seems true to say 'That someone knows that the apple is poisonous is a reason for the agent not to eat it' (though of course the fact about knowledge is evidence that the agent ought not to eat it).

Thus, neither the error-theoretical aspect nor the *reductio* part of Kearns and Star's second response to the objection from the newspaper case seems to be well motivated. It's simply not the case that our pre-theoretical judgments in this sort of case stem *specifically* from the focus on the non-entailing aspect of the relevant considerations, since the hermit case doesn't have this aspect. Some facts that constitute entailing evidence that one ought to F don't constitute a reason to F, contrary to what the Evidence view states.[5]

Elsewhere, Kearns and Star (2008: 48–49) discuss a somewhat similar objection suggested by John Broome in correspondence (Broome 2008 repeats and modifies the objection) that appeals to a case of normative testimony in particular. The objection is similar to, and yet also crucially different from, the newspaper example objection. It focuses on a putative counterexample, discussed earlier, where a reliable book says that one

---

[5] Another argument against Kearns and Star's second reply to the newspaper counterexample is to reject the idea that the fact that a reliable newspaper says that people are starving in Africa and the fact that people are starving in Africa are relevantly similar. If the analogy is not well motivated, the *reductio* can be blocked, since from the fact that the newspaper's report is not a reason to send money, it doesn't follow that that people are starving in Africa is not a reason to send money. Indeed, as Mark McBride (2013) has argued against Kearns and Star, there is a substantial disanalogy here. According to McBride, both the fact that the newspaper says that people are starving in Africa and the fact that people are starving in Africa reliably indicate that people are starving in Africa, and both can be accepted as evidence that one ought to send money to Oxfam. The relevant difference – that is, the difference that makes it the case that only the fact that people are starving in Africa is a reason to send money to Oxfam and not the fact that a reliable newspaper reported it – is that only the former entails that people are starving in Africa (see in particular McBride 2013: 232). Thus, denying that that the newspaper says that people are starving in Africa is a reason to send money to Oxfam doesn't lead us to deny that the fact that people are starving in Africa is a reason to send money to Oxfam.

ought to eat cabbages. The suggestion is that that the book states that one
ought to eat cabbage is evidence that one ought to eat cabbage, yet on its
own it is not a reason to eat cabbage. And, of course, for Broome, it is not a
reason to eat cabbage, because it is not [part of] an explanation of why one
ought to eat cabbage (but see also our discussion of constitutive deontic
explanationist view in Section 3.2, where a similar observation about meta-
ethical theory saying that one ought to F was taken to speak against
Broome's own deontic explanationism). The objection is similar, since it
is also a case of testimonial evidence, yet it is different because it is a case of
evidence for an ought fact and, crucially, the objection assumes that
reasons are right-makers – that is, that they have to play a role in explaining a normative fact. And Kearns and Star make it explicit that they are not
committed to reasons being centrally right-makers (e.g. *explanans* of
normative facts): 'as we have mentioned, we are *not* committed to the idea
that all reasons are right-makers. Thus even if the fact that a reliable book
says one ought to eat cabbage is not part of an explanation of why one
ought to eat cabbage, we are still open to its being a reason' (Kearns and
Star 2013: 73). But they also provide further considerations against
Broome's argument by granting for the sake of the argument that reasons
are right-makers. The line of reply there is to put forward a dilemma. They
write: 'Either facts such as the fact that the book says you ought to eat
cabbage *are* parts of explanations of what one ought to do, or many other
facts (such as the fact that cabbage helps the digestive system) are *not* parts
of explanations of what one ought to do' (Kearns and Star 2008: 48). This
is so because explanations, according to Kearns and Star, can be fundamental or non-fundamental. Fundamental explanations of normative facts
would appeal to correct normative theories (e.g. utilitarianism, deontolo-
gism). Many things that we offer as reasons don't appeal directly to
fundamental normative theories (e.g. 'that cabbages are good for the
digestive system'; Kearns and Star 2008: 49). So, again, the line of
objection is that if the normative testimony of the book is not a reason
(because it is not a part of an explanation of why one ought to eat
cabbage), then many other considerations that we typically take to be
reasons will not count as reasons after all. For they too will not count as
fundamental explanations of why one ought to eat cabbages. But, of
course, all these considerations (e.g. that cabbages are good for the digestive system) are reasons, so, by *reductio*, the normative testimony from the
book is one too. If we focus on non-fundamental explanation as the mark
of reasons, then normative testimony too, exactly like many other non-
fundamental considerations, should count as reasons for one to eat cabbage

according to this line of thought.[6] I would like to suggest that this line of reply is, however, problematic. The main problem is that Kearns and Star themselves recognise that they are not committed to reasons being right-makers. And indeed it seems they shouldn't, given that on the face of it evidence that *p* and *explanans* of *p*/*p*-maker can commonly come apart. But would Kearns and Star even avoid the counterexample by *endorsing* the claim that reasons are always right-makers? Actually, we might doubt that. For one thing, as we saw earlier, when discussing explanationist views, not all normative reasons are parts of explanation of deontic facts. It is also not the case that evidence that one ought to F is always a part of an explanation why one ought to F. We have seen some of the relevant cases already in our discussion of the Reasoning view and will return to this shortly (e.g. undercutting defeaters, self-undermining considerations, Moore-paradoxical considerations). Thus, it is still not clear why we should accept the idea that cases of testimony, like the newspaper case or the reliable cabbage book case, don't constitute straightforward refutation of the Evidence view of reasons. Some considerations are evidence that one ought to F but don't seem to constitute reasons for one to F.

If the reader is not convinced by the aforementioned simple examples of testimony (of the descriptive or normative variety), here is another, somewhat more sophisticated counterexample. It constitutes a basis for an objection against the right-to-left direction of the Evidence view of reasons (i.e. the claim that if *e* is evidence that one ought to F, then *e* is a reason for one to F). Consider the following example reconstructed from a recent counterexample to the Evidence view proposed by Eva Schmidt (2017). A student ought to do his best in his upcoming biology exam. In order to do his best, he has to study all Sunday. As it happens, the student goes to a party on Saturday night and gets totally drunk. As a result, he remembers

---

[6] I note here also that it doesn't seem absurd to deny the relevant similarity assumption in this version of Kearns and Star's argument as well – that is, to deny the assumed similarity between the fact that the book says that one ought to eat cabbage, and non-fundamental considerations contained in the book, such as that cabbage helps the digestive system. It doesn't seem that that the book says that one ought to eat cabbage is any part of an explanation of why one ought to eat cabbage at all. Fundamental or not, that the book says that one ought to eat cabbage just doesn't seem to work as part of an explanation of why one ought to eat cabbage. That cabbage is good for the digestive system, on the other hand, does seem to be able to play a role in an explanation of why one ought to eat cabbage. For one thing, that the book says that one ought to eat cabbage doesn't seem to presuppose that it is a known fact that one ought to eat cabbage. To the contrary, it is natural to think of that fact as a piece of a potential argument towards the conclusion that one ought to eat cabbage and not as a part of an explanation of the *fact* that one ought to eat cabbage. On the other hand, it is natural to bring up the fact that cabbage helps the digestive system specifically when one is in the business of explaining why one ought to eat cabbage.

absolutely nothing about the exam, studying, or biology upon waking up on Sunday morning. He notices, however, a note from his dad that enjoins him to study for his biology exam. Despite the heavy hangover, he nevertheless manages to infer from this note (correctly!) that he ought to study for his biology exam. Now comes the crux. From this he then further infers by an inference to the best explanation that he ought to do his best in the exam (we assume here that indeed there is no other equally good or better explanation for him at this point). This case is a problem for the Evidence view, since the Evidence view predicts that the fact that the student ought to study for the exam is a reason for him to do his best in the exam. But this just seems wrong. Schmidt (2017: 712) writes:

> But the fact that Henry [e.g. the student] ought to study for the exam is clearly not a normative reason for him to do his best in it: It does not count in favor of his doing his best in the exam. If anything, that he ought to do his best in the exam is a fact that counts in favor of his studying for the exam, or a normative reason for him to study for the exam

Schmidt further suggests that the fundamental problem that this sort of example reveals is that the Evidence view misconstrues the symmetry relations. According to Schmidt, the evidence that one ought to F is symmetrical in the case of evidence in favour of fundamental ought facts and in the case of evidence in favour of derivative ought facts. However, roughly, the normative 'favouring relation' between derivative and fundamental ought facts is asymmetrical (cf. Schmidt 2017: 716). This verdict seems to speak in favour of views that define reasons as right-makers of some sort. Without entering into details of the proposed verdict, we can nonetheless agree that in the exam case, the derivative ought fact (i.e. that the student ought to study) can be evidence in favour of the [more] fundamental ought fact that the student ought to do his best in the exam (the hangover amnesia case illustrates this), while the derivative ought fact cannot be a reason for one to do the thing ordered by the fundamental fact (i.e. doing one's best in the exam). Thus, it is another case where the right-to-left direction of the Evidence view seems to fail.[7]

---

[7] Still other cases of testimonial evidence that one ought to F that don't amount to reasons to F exist. In a recent article, John Brunero (2018) proposes two such cases: a case where a reliable book, written by an expert on Lincoln, says that Lincoln had conclusive reason not to eat cabbage. This then constitutes evidence that Lincoln ought to have abstained from eating cabbage. Given this, the Evidence view predicts that the book's testimony is in itself a reason for Lincoln to have abstained from eating cabbage. But such a verdict is highly implausible and on the face of it speaks against the Evidence view. The other case is a case of a friend A telling a friend B that their mutual other friend

Enabling conditions (again). Another substantial set of worries for the Evidence view comes from considerations about enabling conditions (and the worry is similar to a worry we observed earlier for the Reasoning approach; see Section 2.5). The Evidence view seems to be unable to distinguish on theoretically well-motivated grounds mere enabling conditions for appropriate F-ing (or enabling conditions for some other facts to be reasons to F) from genuine normative reasons for one to F. For in certain situations, enabling conditions may constitute evidence that one ought to F (especially assuming the increase in probability conception of evidential support) without constituting reasons to F. A notable illustration of an argument against the Evidence view of this form within the recent literature can be found in Brunero (2009) (but see also Fletcher 2013 for an argument that appeals to a different sort of enablers; see also Brunero 2018). Brunero relies on Jonathan Dancy's insightful discussion on enablers versus reasons (see Chapter 2 for details). In particular, Brunero asks us to consider a case of a promise. Let's say that I have promised to F. My promise to F is a normative reason for me to F. But consider the fact that there is no reason for me not to F. From a pre-theoretical point of view, this second consideration is not a reason for me to F. However, this consideration matters in a normative sense. It enables me to move, in an instance of deliberation, from the fact that I have promised to F to F-ing (i.e. to move to F-ing in an appropriate/fitting way); alternatively, it allows me to conclude [appropriately] that I ought to F (see Brunero 2009: 544). The worry is that the Evidence view predicts that this second consideration, the enabling condition, is a genuine normative reason for me to F. For, presumably, the probability that I ought to F, given that there is no reason for me not to F and given that I have promised to F, is higher than the probability that I ought to F, given merely that I have promised to F. This is problematic for the Evidence view, since, as we observed earlier, that there is no reason for me not to F doesn't seem to be a genuine reason for me to F.

In more recent writings, Kearns and Star reply to Brunero's argument from enabling conditions. Their response is to try to put some pressure on the assumption in Brunero's argument that the fact that there is no reason for me not to F is not a genuine normative reason to F. Their argument

C has a weighty reason to get divorced. That friend A says so does constitute some evidence that friend C ought to get divorced (at least this seems so on the increase in probability conception of evidential support). If so, the Evidence view predicts that that friend A tells B that C has a weighty reason to divorce is a reason for C to divorce. But such a consequence is implausible. The possibility of such cases is another prima facie reason to reject the Evidence view.

proceeds by considering a different case, where they claim it is natural to admit that an enabling condition can constitute a genuine reason to F, in virtue of there being some further facts. Once this is accepted, they argue, it is difficult to see why the same sort of move cannot be appealed to in the case of the promise. That is, it is difficult to see, according to Kearns and Star, why the fact that there is no reason for me not to F cannot count as a reason to F, given that some further facts about F-ing are in place, in particular, given that I have promised to F. Consider the following passage that captures the central aspect of their response to the objection from 'no reason not to F' enablers:

> Bob gets depressed by various facts. In particular, Bob gets very depressed by the fact that he has no reason not to take anti-depressants. Given that Bob gets very depressed by the fact (when it is a fact) that he has no reason not to take anti-depressants, the fact that Bob has no reason not to take anti-depressants (when it is a fact) is a reason for Bob to take anti-depressants. (Kearns and Star 2013: 84)

The line of thought here seems to go as follows: the fact of the form 'there is/S has no reason not to F' is a reason for S to F in the depression case; the depression case is a standard case (and is sufficiently similar to the promise case); hence, the fact that one has no reason not to F (e.g. the promised thing) may be a reason for one to F. Kearns and Star (2013: 84) write: 'Similarly, we would suggest that the fact that I have no reason not to Φ can be a reason to Φ *in virtue of* the fact that I have promised to Φ.' Thus, according to this response, as I understand it, it can be plausibly maintained that the fact that I have no reason not to F is not a reason for me to F, only if it can be shown that this latter fact (i.e. that I have no reason not to F) is relevantly different from the fact that Bob has no reason not to take anti-depressants. However, according to this line of thought, it hasn't been shown that the two are relevantly different. The parallel here is supposed to go as follows: as that Bob gets depressed when he has no reason not to take anti-depressants explains that the fact that Bob doesn't have a reason not to take anti-depressants is a reason for Bob to take anti-depressants, the fact that I have promised to F also explains that that I have no reason not to F is a reason for me to F (cf. Kearns and Star 2013).

However, this line of response is unsatisfactory. The major problem here just is that the rejection of the parallel between the anti-depressants case and the promise case *is* theoretically well motivated. Indeed, the two cases are relevantly different. The fact that Bob gets depressed when he realises that he has no reason not to take anti-depressants (*ceteris paribus*) *explains* why Bob ought to take anti-depressants. And this (i.e. the fact about this deontic explanation) is fundamentally why that Bob has no reason not to take anti-depressants is a reason (in a sense) for Bob to take anti-depressants. Nothing similar happens in the promise case. It is simply not a fact that I promise to F when I realise that I have no reason not to F. Contrary to the case of being depressed and realising that one has no reason not to take anti-depressants, there is no connection whatsoever in this latter case between me realising that I have no reason not to F and me promising to F. I may well realise that I have no reason not to F but never even think about promising to F. So, it simply cannot be the case that the fact that I promise to F when I realise that I have no reason not to F (*ceteris paribus*) explains why I ought to F. It cannot be the case because the left-hand side of the purported explanation is plainly false: it is not a fact that I promise to F when I realise that I have no reason not to F. That I have no reason not to F in the promise case is not a normative reason for me to F. It is crucially different from the fact that Bob has no reason not to take anti-depressants. Despite having the 'there is/S has no reason not to F' surface form, the fact that Bob has no reason not to take anti-depressants is not a mere enabling condition. It does speak in favour of Bob taking anti-depressants. Plausibly it does so in virtue of being part of an explanation of why Bob ought to take anti-depressants (together with the fact that Bob gets depressed when he realises that he has no reason not to take anti-depressants). No such deontic explanation is available in the promise case. That I have no reason not to F doesn't speak in favour of me F-ing in the promise case. Plausibly, this is so because it is not part of an explanation of why I ought to F. Thus we can conclude that the response from Kearns and Star to the objection from enabling conditions is misguided. The Evidence view does seem unable to respect the plausible distinction between mere enabling conditions and normative reasons.

Moreover, note that the discussion here has been centred only on *one* sort of enabling conditions. As we have learned from Dancy, there are various other sorts of enabling conditions. And these may constitute further potential counterexamples to the Evidence view. Think for instance of the fact that a promise was not made under duress. In certain contexts this fact may well constitute evidence that I ought to respect the promised thing. However, it would be odd to accept that the mere fact that the promise was not made under duress is a reason for me to respect the promised thing. Or think of ability considerations. That I am able to F may well constitute an enabling condition for a fitting F-ing, and it may also increase the probability of the claim that I ought to F. Yet it is a considerable cost for a theory that entails that the mere fact that one is able to F is a normative reason for one to F.

Undercutting defeaters. Until now our critical discussion has been focused on the objections to the right-to-left direction of the bi-conditional of the Evidence view (i.e. the claim that if X is evidence that S ought to F, then X is a reason for S to F). Objections to this part of the Evidence view have constituted the majority of objections to the Evidence view in the literature and we have presented only some of the most promising ones. Let us now turn briefly to the worries that arise for the left-to-right part of the Evidence view, i.e. the claim that if X is a reason for S to F, then X is evidence that S ought to F. The first line of objection to this part of the view appeals to the existence of undercutting defeaters. Some considerations might function as a defeater for a piece of evidence that one has for the proposition that one ought to F, without defeating one's reason to F. Consider the following case that may be taken to illustrate this sort of possibility. You see a toddler drowning in front of you in a shallow pond as you go through a park. That the toddler is drowning is clearly a reason for you to jump into the pond. It is also at this point evidence that you ought to jump in. But now, here is a twist. As you prepare to jump in, an employee of the park approaches you and says: 'Oh, please, don't! It's not a child. It's just a hologram of a child. We are conducting a social experiment here, measuring the percentage of people ready to jump in when it appears to them that a child is drowning. Thanks for your participation and sorry for any distress caused'. Arguably, this new information functions as an undercutting defeater for you. That a child is drowning in front of you is no longer evidence for you that you ought to jump into the pond. Now, the twist is that the employee didn't tell the truth (we can fill in the details in more or less evil ways: the employee is a sadistic serial killer, or alternatively they are indeed conducting a social experiment, but as it happens by an incredible and unlucky turn of events there is a real child in the place of the hologram in the pond today). In such a dramatic scenario, that the child in front of you is drowning is still a reason for you to jump in, but arguably it is not a piece of evidence for you that you ought to jump in. Even more can be said: the fact that you see a child drowning (even if you don't know that a child is drowning) is a reason for you to jump in, but not a piece of evidence for you that you ought to jump in.

Now, Kearns and Star might reply that what happens in the case of undercutting defeaters is that while the new information defeats *one's* evidence – that is, in our case, the testimony from the employee effectively makes it the case that *you* no longer *have* evidence that a child is drowning in front of you – there is still a sense in which that the child is drowning in front of you is evidence that you ought to jump into the pond. And it might even be maintained that there is a sense in which that you see a drowning child is evidence that you ought to jump in. It is evidence, according to this line of thought, in a more objective, reliable indicator sense of evidence. Also, they might insist that, given some further specification about the relevant background information, that a child is drowning in front of you does increase the probability that you ought to jump in, even if you don't know that the child is drowning.

The problem with this move, however, is that it appears arbitrary, or even incompatible, given Kearns and Star's other theoretical commitments. A major selling point of the Evidence view was that it was said to accommodate perfectly the guidance function of reasons in reliable/good reasoning (see in particular their argument from the role of reasons in deliberation; Kearns and Star 2009: 224–226). In other terms, reasons have a function of guiding one to justified actions and attitudes through reasoning. Now, if the normative reason for you to jump into the pond in our case corresponds to a piece of objective evidence (e.g. reliable indicator), then we may ask how the guidance function of reasons that Kearns and Star have advertised can be really satisfied. It is well known now that the concept of *evidence*, as we typically understand it both in common usage and in theoretical practice, is associated with various roles or functions. Timothy Williamson identified three crucial functions of our ordinary concept of *evidence* as (i) the function of ruling out hypotheses that are incompatible with it; (ii) playing a role in inferences to best explanation; and (iii) playing a role in probabilistic reasoning (see Williamson 2000: 194–207). Thomas Kelly (2016) goes a step further and suggests that the four main functions that we associate with *evidence* stand in tension. According to Kelly, it is doubtful that any single sort of thing could play all of the roles that we standardly associate with *evidence*. In particular, and of most interest for our present discussion, Kelly argues that one and the same sort of thing cannot always play the role of *justifying evidence* and at the same time the role of *reliable objective indicator evidence*. The relevant point for us is that Kearns and Star do insist on the justificatory function of evidence in the guidance of reasoning; this is what allows them to claim that their view accounts for the guidance role in reasoning of reasons. But if Kelly's suggestions are on the right track, this would rule out, on the pain of accepting an incoherent conception of evidence and reasons, that reasons on their account can also correspond to the more objective, reliable indicator sense of *evidence*. In short, insisting that in the pond case the relevant unknown fact that there is a child drowning in the pond is still evidence that you ought to jump in stands in tension with the professed claim of Kearns and Star that their account of reasons fully respects the guidance in good reasoning, that is, the justifying function of reasons.[8]

Moore-paradoxical considerations and self-undermining beliefs. Another set of worries that the Evidence view shares with the Reasoning view of reasons comes from Moore-paradoxical considerations and self-undermining beliefs. We have seen above (cf. Chapter 2) that these cases appear problematic for the views that define reasons as (fitting) premises in good/fitting patterns of reasoning. Here is how these cases also cause trouble for the Evidence view. Consider first the following Moore-para-dox-style affirmation: (m) 'the building is on fire but John doesn't believe that the building is on fire'. We argued above (cf. Chapter 2) that considerations of the form (m) can be reasonably taken to be a reason for one to F in a sense. In this case, (m) can be reasonably taken to be a reason for John to investigate/check/reconsider etc. the state of the building (more precisely, consider the hypothesis (h) 'the building is on fire'). It does appear to speak in favour of John's checking the state of the building. Here, I would like to suggest that (m) is not evidence for John that he ought to check the state of the building (e.g. reconsider the hypothesis h). More specifically, (m) is not evidence that John ought to check the building, if we endorse Kearns and Star's proposal that a central function of evidence is to guide one's reasoning towards justified F-ing. The following quotation sums up that apparent commitment:

> Premise (4) [of the Deliberation Argument] says that evidence that an agent ought to φ can help this agent conclude that she ought to φ. The plausibility of this idea stems from the very notion of what it is for a fact to be evidence for something. We use evidence precisely to work out which propositions are true. If a fact is evidence that one ought to φ, then such a fact is able to help an agent conclude that she ought to φ. [...] If the agent is reasoning well, she can use this fact to conclude that she ought to φ on those occasions she ought to φ. (Kearns and Star 2009: 225)

---

[8] One might also think that there is a distinct objection to the evidence view coming from the higher order defeat cases applied to normative reasons. Working out the details of this objection will be left for another occasion.

They also write:

> We conclude, then, that reasons to φ are evidence that one ought to φ and that evidence that one ought to φ is a reason to φ. This is equivalent to RA. Because a fact's being able to play a certain important role in practical reasoning is both necessary and sufficient for this fact to be a reason and for it to be evidence, we conclude that reasons are evidence. (Kearns and Star 2009: 226)

Elsewhere they also commit themselves to the specific characterisation of evidence as facts that can be knowable:

> More plausibly, a fact can be evidence only if it is *knowable*. There is evidence that P only if someone is able to have this evidence. (Kearns and Star 2008: 52)

I take these passages to constitute sufficient evidence for the claim that Kearns and Star are committed to the understanding of evidence according to which a consideration that is a piece of evidence for a subject has to be able to play a role in one's practical reasoning, and, in particular, it has to be able to guide one's practical reasoning towards a justified F-ing (e.g. one has to be able to F on the basis of evidence and be able to do it justifiably).

And this sort of thing, evidence as knowable and being able to guide us in the specific way, is precisely what we don't have in Moore-paradoxical cases. The Moore-paradoxical considerations are not able to guide one's reasoning towards justified F-ing. One cannot F *on the basis* of the Moore-paradoxical considerations. At the heart of the paradox lies the very fact that the subject of Moore-paradoxical beliefs *cannot* know the Moore-paradoxical consideration. John cannot know [that the building is on fire but he doesn't believe that the building is on fire]. Knowing one of the conjuncts of 'the building is on fire but John doesn't believe that the building is on fire' would undermine the truth of the other. Thus, given Kearns and Star's understanding of evidence, Moore-paradoxical considerations cannot be evidence for one that one ought to F, and yet, plausibly enough, they are still reasons in a sense for one to F.

Similar considerations apply for self-undermining beliefs. Consider: (d) 'I just took a drug that erased all my memories of the last 5 minutes'. It seems that (d) can well be a reason for me to suspend judgment about what I did during the last 5 minutes. But, again, I cannot use (d) in my reasoning towards suspending judgment about what I did during the last 5 minutes. It seems that (d) cannot play a role in reasoning that Kearns and Star expect evidence to be able to play. Hence, (d) seems to be a reason for me to suspend judgment without being evidence for me that I ought to suspend judgment about what I did during the last 5 minutes. Thus we have identified another sort of case where *pace* the Evidence view, a consideration can be a reason to F without being evidence that one ought to F.

These critical considerations lead us to a somewhat more general observation about the Evidence view, an observation that points to a more fundamental flaw within this approach. The Evidence view faces many if not all of the problems of the Reasoning view of reasons that we have discussed above (and some additional ones as well). A natural thought at this point is that the Evidence view just is a variation of the Reasoning view. This interpretation is supported by the above observation about the central aspects of evidence according to Kearns and Star. It is implicit in much of Kearns and Star's theorising. They clearly think that an important and good thing about their view is that it can account for the intuitive feature of normative reasons in guiding one's deliberation/reasoning towards an overall-ought (Kearns and Star 2009: 224–226, 2013). Thus a reasonable interpretation of the Evidence view is that it is a version of the general Reasoning approach to reasons.

Daniel Star (2018) actually explores the topic of the compatibility of the Evidence view with Jonathan Way's version of the Reasoning view. Star thinks that the Evidence view is superior to the Reasoning view, given that it appeals to a more easily graspable, more robust notion of *ought*, as compared to the notion of *fittingness* that figures centrally in Way's version of the Reasoning view. Note, however, that the purported difference in this respect might be more artificial than Star seems to think it is. For fittingness just is, as we saw above, the property of F-ing that complies with an ought. Thus a fitting action just is an action that one ought to do. If so, the difference between the Evidence view and the fittingness version of the Reasoning view really seems to be a minimal one, if any. Now, realising that the Evidence view just is a version of the Reasoning view allows us to see a central flaw in the view. As is the case with the Reasoning approach in general, the Evidence view focuses on one of the functions of a common-sense notion of being a reason to act or have an attitude, at the expense of another crucial function of our common-sense notion of a reason to act/have an attitude. It focuses on the role of reasons in reasoning and guiding towards justified F-ing at the expense of the role of reasons in making F-ing fitting or more specifically explaining why one ought to F.

At any rate, even if my suggestion that the Evidence view reduces to a version of the Reasoning view is wrongheaded, the above objections stand. And many of the same problems that the Reasoning view faced also apply to the Evidence view – which should lead us to investigate the prospects of alternative options in our attempt to define normative reasons.

4.5 Concluding Remarks

In this chapter we have seen another major approach within the recent debates about the nature of normative reasons. We have presented Kearns and Star's influential Evidence view of reasons, according to which a fact is a reason for one to F if and only if that fact is evidence for one that one ought to F. We rehearsed some of the main positive arguments in favour of the view. And we then spent some time exploring the pitfalls of this original proposal. At the end of the day we concluded that it is reasonable to see the Evidence view just as another version of the Reasoning view of reasons. Thus the substantial worries that we identified with the Reasoning view re-surface with respect to the Evidence view as well.

Can someone sympathetic to the Evidence view try to provide a different version of a view that maintains the insights of thinking about reasons in terms of evidence but still avoids its problems? I haven't shown that this cannot be done. And indeed some recent proposals might be more promising in this respect than Kearns and Star's original view (see, for instance, the view presented and defended in Whiting 2018). Unfortunately, however, a full-blown analysis of further variations of the Evidence view lies beyond the framework of the present discussion. At this point, I would like only to suggest that, given the poor track record of existing monist reductionist views, the views that appear to be close to either a version of the Reasoning view or a version of explanationist views might not be the most promising alternative to explore. I would like to suggest that we rather focus on a radically different proposal, a view that doesn't commit itself to the idea that there is only one sort of normative reasons and that it should be understood either to be more like a [fitting] premise in good reasoning or more like an explanation of why one ought to F/why it would be good for one to F. Rather, the alternative, towards which I would like to turn now, combines the best insights from both of these general views without inheriting their respective pitfalls. Without further ado let us now turn to our positive proposal about normative reasons.

CHAPTER 5

New Proposal
The Erotetic View

5.1 Taking Stock

The purpose of the present chapter is to elaborate and motivate a new account of normative reasons. The view in question takes on board the insights from the views discussed earlier. In particular, it relies on the pre-theoretically plausible claims that (i) reasons, in a sense, are somehow connected to reasoning and (ii) reasons, in a sense, are somehow connected to explanation. Before going into details of the view, however, let us take stock.

We began with a pre-theoretically plausible assumption that reasons are considerations that speak in favour of an action or an attitude (cf. Scanlon 1998). So, for instance, if I promised my friend to come to the party at his place tonight, then my promise – that is, the fact that I promised – is a reason for me to (intend to) go to his place tonight. Or if Michael tells me that he saw Thomas at the concert last Wednesday, Michael's testimony is a reason for me to believe that Thomas went to the concert.

We also agreed that reasons in this sense are normative and have to be distinguished from considerations that are mere bases on which we act or form/maintain an attitude. In this sense, reasons for one to F (e.g. to act or to hold an attitude) are to be distinguished from reasons *for* which one acts or holds an attitude. Our focus is on the former, the *normative*, and not on the latter, the *motivating*, reasons.

A fundamental question in the debate on reasons is whether there is anything more substantial and positive that can be said about normative reasons. This is also the guiding question of the present work. In the stage-setting chapter (Chapter 1), we assumed that the *reasons-first* approach (cf. Scanlon 1998; Schroeder 2007; Skorupski 2010; Parfit 2011), according to which we cannot say anything more substantial – for example, analyses about normative reasons (by appeal to normative properties) than the aforementioned mere characterisation but can appeal to reasons in defining/explaining other normative notions – is problematic. For one thing, the reasons-first programme cannot really avoid the so-called wrong kind of reasons problem. Part of the reasons-first programme is a buck-passing account of value, according to which values are defined/explained in terms of reasons. For instance, according to this account, that someone is admirable just amounts to there being sufficient reasons for one to admire the person. The buck-passing account is an important part of the reasons-first approach since it is supposed to show how reasons are more fundamental than values. However, as the wrong kind of reasons problem shows, there are cases where one seems to have considerations speaking in favour of admiring someone while, clearly, the person in question is not admirable (e.g. a demon who threatens to kill everyone unless one admires it; cf. Rabinowicz and Rønnow-Rasmussen 2004). The problem is that in order to explain why the threat is not a reason, while still being a consideration that speaks in favour of admiring the deplorable person (i.e. the demon), a proponent of the reasons-first programme undermines her account by accepting that there has to be, after all, something more substantial that can be said about reasons in order to distinguish these from considerations that merely speak in favour of F without being reasons. In other words, it is unclear how one can maintain at the same time the idea that normative reasons are undefinable and fundamental while also avoiding the counterintuitive consequences of the wrong kind of reasons type situations.

Moreover, it has been increasingly acknowledged that the reasons-first approach is less parsimonious than its alternatives, and hence, if a viable, more parsimonious account of reasons becomes available, it should be preferable to the reasons-first view. A recent wave of reasons anti-fundamentalism doubts the need for an undefinable notion of reasons as a mysterious entity in the normative realm.

The bulk of the present work, then, was to explore the most promising *reductionist* alternatives to the reasons-first approach, according to which normative reasons can be reduced to a combination of some normative property and *other* elements. We have classified the existing reductionist views into two categories. The difference between the two amounts to how exactly the 'other elements' are understood here. Two competing views seem to emerge. According to the approach of the first broad category, the other elements here appeal to the function of reasons in reasoning. Thus, according to this sort of approach, r being a reason for one to F just amounts to, roughly, r being part (of a premise) of good/fitting/appropriate [depending on the preferred normative property] reasoning for S that concludes in F-ing. According to the second broad category, normative reasons roughly are parts of an explanation of why one ought to F (or why it's fitting for one to F) or, alternatively, it is an explanation of why promoting F-ing would be good/valuable/fitting.

In assessing the existing views, we have been guided by what many take to be constraints on or desiderata for a plausible account of normative reasons. Some of these desiderata are implicit in the debates. Different authors focus on different aspects of these. Here is a brief reminder about what might be seen as the main desiderata for a theory of normative reasons in the literature. *First*, a theory of normative reasons should be extensionally adequate.[1] That is, a theory of normative reasons should count as normative reasons all and only considerations that are normative reasons. This, of course, raises the question of how we should go about determining what counts and what doesn't count as a normative reason. The risk is that in assessing whether something is a normative reason, we are already influenced by our background theory of normative reasons and so we don't have a theory-neutral 'method' for establishing what counts and what doesn't count as a normative reason. A promising proposal here is to focus on the pre-theoretic, rough characterisation of reasons to F as considerations that count in favour of F-ing (see Scanlon 1998). Thus, a plausible theory of normative reasons should fit our pre-theoretical judgments about considerations that speak in favour of F-ing.

Second, a viable theory of normative reasons has to respect the motivating–normative reasons distinction while also being able to explain their supposed connection. Often this is taken to imply that there has to be some sort of connection between reasons and reasoning, as we saw in Chapter 2.

Third, a theory of normative reasons has to be tolerant/general enough. That is, it has to apply to reasons to act, but also to reasons to believe, to fear, and other attitudes.

Fourth, the most economical theory is to be preferred. In other words, a simpler theory (i.e. a theory that appeals to a lesser number of entities and principles) that can explain all reasons (reasons to act, to believe, to fear, etc.) is, *ceteris paribus*, preferable to more complex views.

Fifth, a theory of normative reasons has to respect the 'currency' aspect of reasons. Namely, it has to fit well with the observation that normative reasons are useful tools for rough, prima facie characterisation of normative

---

[1] I take the idea of extensional adequacy being a constraint on a theory from a recent article by Dutant and Littlejohn (on a somewhat related topic of epistemic defeat); cf. Dutant and Littlejohn (2021).

notions in a domain. Think, for instance, of the naturalness of describing a moral ought in terms of what one has most (moral) reasons to do (which is not to say that moral oughts can be fully reduced to what one has most (moral) reasons to do). According to Parfit (2011: 269), '[i]n the conflict between [. . .] various [meta-ethical] theories, reasons provide the decisive battlefield'. This can be understood as a claim that whether, say, naturalism is the right normative theory can be determined by debating the nature of normative reasons. We need not be reasons-first proponents to accept the general point that reasons seem to have this 'currency' aspect that enables us to express (roughly) and debate various normative theories in somewhat neutral terms. The currency aspect is also illustrated in the context of domain-specific debates. For instance, appeal to normative reasons seems to allow us to present clearly the possible view of pragmatism in epistemology (as opposed to evidentialism). Arguably, this currency aspect can also be understood as the idea that reasons have to be somehow connected to the explanation of normative properties/facts. If there are explanations of why, say, one ought to F, then, plausibly, such an explanation is best provided in terms of normative reasons.

Sixth, a theory of normative reasons is supposed to respect the 'gradable' aspect of normative reasons. It is easy to observe that reasons admit of comparisons, combinations, outweighing, and so on (for example, my promise to go to the party is a 'weightier' reason than my desire to binge-watch *BoJack*). Many think that this comparative aspect is best captured by the talk of 'weight' of reasons or, at any rate, by an appeal to some sort of scale and the idea that reasons are scalar properties.

In the previous chapters, Chapters 1–4, we have seen how exactly the Reasoning view and the Explanation view cope with the aforementioned constraints/desiderata. We have seen that the best versions of both approaches fit easily with some of the constraints, while failing to respect others. So, for instance, versions of the Reasoning view can account straightforwardly for the motivating–normative reasons connection and distinction (the reasons–reasoning connection is at the very core of that approach). They are also tolerant and economical (and, arguably, can deal with the currency aspect). Yet they (at least some of them) have a hard time accounting for the gradable aspect of reasons. Some sophisticated accounts manage to deal with outweighed reasons, and yet the more fundamental question of what the 'weight' of reasons amounts to exactly remains largely unexplained by even the most promising versions of the Reasoning approach.

The Explanation views are tolerant and economical, and they respect the currency aspect. They also respect, at least on the face of it, the gradability aspect. But they are not really apt to account for the reasons–reasoning connection.

Moreover, neither the Reasoning approach nor the Explanation approach fully manages to respect the extensional adequacy constraint. They both, in their own ways, over-generate and under-generate normative reasons. The Reasoning approach has a hard time explaining why mere enabling conditions (e.g. that one is able to F) and entailing conditions (e.g. that one has a reason to F) are not normative reasons. It also predicts that some considerations that speak in favour of F-ing are not normative reasons (e.g. Moore-paradoxical considerations and self-undermining beliefs). The Explanation views that distinguish *pro toto* from *pro tanto* reasons as sorts of explanation of why one ought to F, but accept that both are considerations that count in favour of F-ing, are bound to double-count reasons that there are for one to F. They also predict that considerations that don't seem to speak in favour of F-ing are nonetheless partial explanations of why I ought to F (e.g. against-F considerations in weighing explanation of why one ought to F). Other versions of the Explanation approach (e.g. value-based versions) have a hard time explaining how there might be normative reasons for attitudes (e.g. on some of these views, there are no reasons to fear, or to be happy, and they have difficulties in explaining reasons to believe). They predict that there are no reasons where our pre-theoretical judgments imply the contrary and thus they face the 'right kind' of reasons problem. Thus, we have seen that both the Reasoning approach and the Explanation approach in their most promising forms capture important aspects of our pre-theoretical notion of reasons, while both also have some substantial and, in my view, insurmountable difficulties.

This dialectical situation, then, leads us back to square one. We had better not accept reasons-first and look for a plausible reductionist account, but, at the same time, we don't have any satisfying reductionist account available. The best existing reductionist accounts of reasons are problematic. Is there any other viable approach to reasons available at all? At this point, one might think that we should really be sceptical about reasons altogether. One might be tempted at this point to endorse an eliminitivism about *normative reasons*. One can observe that there is no one single thing that would respect all the constraints/desiderata that philosophers have imposed on *normative reasons*. There is no one single sort of thing that could satisfy all the supposed functions of the concept of *normative reasons*.

Thus, an eliminitivist might conclude that it's not really meaningful to talk about normative reasons. On such a view, there are no normative reasons, reducible or not. Talk about reasons just is not meaningful on such an extreme approach.

In this chapter, I propose to elaborate a view that avoids such a radical eliminitivist/sceptical conclusion while sharing some of its premises. I agree with the eliminitivist on the observation that there is no one single sort of thing that corresponds to normative reasons. Indeed, we should reject the monist assumption that dominates the debate about normative reasons. And yet we should not be eliminitivists. It's still meaningful to talk about normative reasons. On the view elaborated a little further, there are two fundamentally distinct and yet somehow connected sorts of normative reasons – connected in that both are normative reasons. There is a unified element of the two that has been overlooked in the debates. But this element is essential to understanding reasons and to understanding why the two sorts of normative reasons are indeed two species of a genus. The key element of our account is a shift in the focus on *normative questions* and reasons as possible answers to a normative question. The aim of the next section, Section 5.2, is to put the new proposal on the table.

5.2 The Erotetic View of Reasons

According to the view developed in this chapter, a normative reason to F is, roughly, a possible appropriate answer to the normative question 'Why F?'. This view, I suggest, is able to respect the desiderata/constraints on a theory of reasons, introduced earlier. It integrates the best aspects of both the Reasoning and the Explanation views while avoiding their respective pitfalls. Before looking at the details of the view and the arguments in its favour, let me take a step back and describe two major insights on which the present account builds.

The first insight comes from Pamela Hieronymi's treatment of reasons. In her influential paper on the wrong kind of reasons problem, Hieronymi (2005) notes that we should approach the question of what reasons are by focusing on reasons as considerations that bear on a question. According to Hieronymi, the reasons-first view about reasons cannot be maintained. The reasons-first proposal that reasons just are considerations that count in favour of an action or an attitude generates robust ambiguity in certain sorts of cases. The problem, according to Hieronymi, is that the proponents of the reasons-first approach are focusing on the wrong kind of relation in characterising reasons. Instead of thinking of reasons (exclusively) as considerations that count in favour of an action or an attitude, Hieronymi (2005: 438) suggests that 'we would do better to think of a reason as *a consideration that bears on a question*'. Now, as we saw earlier when we classified Hieronymi as a proponent of the Reasoning view, she also thinks that reasons are things that play a role in reasoning. She writes: 'To start reflection, we can note that, most generally, a reason is simply an item in a piece of reasoning' (Hieronymi 2005: 443). Hence, the relation of bearing on a question, according to Hieronymi, is to be understood in a reasoning-centred sense. The bearing on a question relation that captures normative reasons, according to Hieronymi, is a relation of bearing on a question that one aims to answer in a piece of reasoning (or deliberation). Bearing on a question is closely related, if not equal, to bearing on a conclusion (of reasoning), according to Hieronymi (2005: 444, fn 16): 'One could say [that a reason is], "a consideration that bears on a conclusion." I do not think there would be any relevant difference [between this proposal and the claim that a reason is a consideration that bears on a question], though I find the idea of answering a question more intuitive for capturing the activities of rational agents'. Now, the relevant point for us, the foundational insight for our new account, is that we can take on board Hieronymi's point about reasons being considerations bearing on a question without accepting her other point about reasons always being items in a piece of reasoning. How exactly this can be done will appear more clearly in what follows.

The second insight on which the present account builds comes from a well-known, indeed classic, observation in theory of argumentation, informal logic, and rhetoric. According to this observation, a 'Why?' question can be interpreted in at least two different ways. When someone asks 'Why is such and such the case?', one may be in the business of asking for an *explanation* of why such and such is the case, or, alternatively, one may be in the business of asking for an *argument* for why such and such is the case. For a *locus classicus* on this distinction, see Whately's erotetic logic (cf. Whately 1827, 1828; see also Prior and Prior 1955 on Whately's erotetic logic). For example, when one asks why dolphins are not fish, one may be in the business of asking for, say, an evolutionary explanation of how swimming mammals evolved and so on. In such a case, typically, one is not challenging the assumption that dolphins are indeed not fish. One is only asking for an explanation of this fact. Presumably, in most typical cases, the aim of asking for an explanation is to gain a better understanding of the relevant fact (except, of course, in the context of exams, quizzes, and suchlike). Alternatively, one may ask the question 'Why are dolphins not fish?' in a more challenging way. By posing such a question, one may ask for an argument that would establish and support the conclusion that dolphins are not fish. In such cases, one is typically challenging the relevant supposition. In our case, one would be asking in such a context for premises that deductively, inductively, probabilistically, or abductively would support the conclusion that dolphins are not fish. A proper answer to this reading of the 'Why are dolphins not fish?' question might consist, for example, in one replying that dolphins are not fish because they are not cold-blooded, because they are mammals, or because that's what biologists have shown to be the case. In short, every 'why is such and such the case?' seems to be interpretable as either an explanation-requiring question or an argument/reasoning-requiring question.

This observation is closely linked to a well-known distinction in philosophy of science, namely the orthodox assumption that there is a substantial distinction between explanations and arguments/reasoning. *Pace* Hempel (cf. Hempel 1965) and logical positivists, it is widely admitted that scientific explanations and scientific arguments/reasoning are not the same. One well-known argument comes from Salmon (1971), who notes that while one can, in principle, add any number of true premises to a sound argument without spoiling it, the same cannot be done in the case of an explanation (see also Section 3.3 for a discussion). An explanation containing, say, irrelevant but true claims (say, necessary truths) is not as good as a simpler explanation that doesn't appeal to the irrelevant truths.

For a recent treatment of the distinction in the theory of argumentation, see McKeon (2013), who interestingly enough sees the distinction between explanation and argument as less substantial than has sometimes been assumed in the post-positivist literature. Interestingly, the common element between explanation and arguments for McKeon is that they both offer reasons: 'For purposes of this paper, arguments and explanations are taken to be products of reason-giving activities: in presenting an argument or an explanation, one gives reasons for a proposition' (McKeon 2013: 284). Another interesting observation is that McKeon doesn't doubt at all the distinction between the speech acts of explaining and the speech acts of arguing, which is, again, entirely in accord with what we suggest here.

It has to be stressed that the explanation–argument distinction is not limited to the scientific domain only. It seems pretty commonsensical to assume that there are two distinct speech acts involved here. The speech act of explaining anything seems to be quite different from the speech act of arguing (presenting a pattern of reasoning/argument). One is in a different sort of linguistic business when one is aiming for one's interlocutors to understand something and when one is in the business of aiming to convince one's interlocutors of something. These are distinct intentions, corresponding to two distinct speech acts: explaining versus arguing (presenting premises in an argument/pattern of reasoning).

Now, putting together these two aforementioned insights – that is, question centrality and the explaining–arguing distinction – a new proposal about normative reasons emerges. On this account, normative reasons are to be understood as appropriate answers to the normative 'Why F?' question in one or the other of its possible readings (as per usual 'F' stands for verbs referring to actions or attitudes that can have reasons in their favour). Hieronymi is right in focusing on questions in thinking about reasons. But her account fails to integrate the crucial observation that some instances of questions require as an answer an explanation, while others require an argument/reasoning. Once we integrate this observation about the duality of 'Why?' questions, a new version of a question-centred (*erotetic*) account of normative reasons emerges. To see the view in detail, let us start by putting on the table a succinct general statement of the view:

> The Erotetic View of Reasons: For that p to be a reason to F for S is for that p to be (a part of) the content of an appropriate answer to a (S directed) question 'Why F?'.

This formulation needs some unpacking and further specifications. The first thing to note is that for a consideration to be a normative reason on this account, it has to be (a part) of the content of a response to a question, but it is not required that the response has been actually given or even entertained by someone. It is not required that the question be actually asked by anyone. There only needs to be an appropriate response to the relevant 'Why F?' question. We are focusing on questions and possible responses as context-sensitive *abstracta*. A subject need not be aware that there is any possible 'Why F?' question directed at her.[2] (In this respect, the proposal here is similar to the proposal of the proponents of the Reasoning view; cf. McHugh and Way 2016 who suggest focusing on the *patterns* of reasoning, the abstract entities.) We could similarly say that

---

[2] The 'S-directed' clause is supposed to capture the fact that the subject of the question is S. That is, the question 'Why F?' is about S's potential F-ing. Note that one can pose the 'Why F?' question (concrete question asking) to someone about someone else. That is, A may ask a question to B about the standing of S's potential F-ing. Of course, S can also ask the 'Why F?' question about herself to herself (or to someone else). The relevant point for us is the abstract question (the *pattern* of the question) 'Why F?' that is about, involves S, independently of whether anyone is concretely aware of there being such a question. This is the sense of 'S-directed'.

the focus here is on *patterns* of questions, not the concrete pieces, episodes of asking questions. So, for instance, that there is a drowning child in the pond next to me is a reason for me to jump into the pond. I may be unaware of the fact that there is a drowning child in the pond. Thus, arguably I don't possess the reason to jump into the pond. Yet this doesn't change that that a child is drowning next to me is a reason for me to jump into the pond. The present proposal can account for this aspect easily: there is a normative question that can be addressed to me, namely 'Why jump in the pond?' and that the child is drowning in the pond is an appropriate response to at least one reading of the question. That no one concretely asks me this question doesn't alter the fact that there is a question that someone could ask me: 'Why jump in the pond?'

The aforementioned statement of the view appeals to 'Why F?' questions. But we should not put too much weight on the exact formulation of the question. As far as I can see, nothing substantial would be lost if we paraphrased the question in the statement of the view as 'Why should/ought S to F?' question. In what follows, I take 'Why F?' as addressed to S to be roughly equivalent to 'Why should/ought S to F?'[3]

We've observed earlier that 'Why?' questions admit of two distinct readings. Consequently, there are two distinct possible appropriate ways to answer 'Why?' questions. Plugging this observation into our account of normative reasons, we now have a consequence that there are two possible readings of the normative 'Why F?' question and consequently two distinct ways to answer the normative 'Why?' question. Let's start with questions.

According to one reading of the 'Why F?' question, the addressee is required to provide (or to point to) an *explanation of the normative fact*, namely of the fact that the subject of the question should/ought to F. One cannot provide an explanation of X unless X. Thus, the 'Why F?' question on this reading presupposes that it is the case that the subject of the question ought to/should F. In conversational contexts where this reading

---

[3] As noted earlier, 'F' here is a placeholder for action or attitude verbs. But note, also, that we may want to maintain that we are talking about normative reasons without appealing to an action or attitude verb, but by using, say, an adjective instead. For example, one may ask things like 'Why is BoJack unforgivable?'. 'Unforgivable' is an adjective, and hence, on the face of it, restricting 'F' in our account to verbs only may appear problematic. For one may think that the question 'Why is BoJack unforgivable?' requires a statement of reasons as a proper answer. However, I think the problem is not really a substantial one. For constructions like 'Why is BoJack unforgivable?' can be naturally transformed into constructions using verbs. For instance, it is natural to understand this question as a question: 'Why should one not forgive BoJack?' or: 'Why should one think that BoJack cannot be forgiven?'. Alternatively, we can easily amend the formulation of the view to include adjectives and their referents without altering the substance of our proposal.

is the relevant one, both the addresser of the question and the addressee take it for granted that the subject of the question ought to/should F. That the subject ought to F is not challenged and stands in no need of defence. The addresser of the question is asking for an explanation of what makes it the case that(alternatively, on what grounds) the subject ought to F. In standard explanatory 'Why F?' contexts, the addresser of the question aims to arrive at a better understanding of the normative fact that S ought to F.

According to the other reading of the 'Why F?' question, the addressee is required to provide a (appropriate) *premise of a good argument/pattern of reasoning* that would support as a fitting conclusion S's F-ing or the claim that S ought to F. Roughly, in contexts of conversation where this reading is the relevant one, the addresser of the question is asking for any (appropriate) consideration that S could use in a sound reasoning towards S's F-ing (the conclusion that S ought to F). The 'Why F?' question on this reading doesn't presuppose that it is the case that S ought to F. That is the thing that needs to be shown to be the case. Typically, the addresser of the question is either challenging or in a position to challenge the claim that F-ing is fitting (or that S ought to F). Arguably, in typical contexts of conversation where this reading of the 'Why F?' question is the relevant one, the addresser aims to know whether S ought to F or not by asking for an argument that would support such a conclusion.

This dual life of the 'Why F?' question leads naturally to the view that there are two distinct sorts of appropriate answers to the 'Why F?' question. One way (pattern) is to provide an appropriate answer to the explanation-requiring reading of the 'Why F?' question. The other way (pattern) is to provide an appropriate answer to the argument/reasoning-requiring reading of the 'Why F?' question. These are distinct ways (patterns) of replying, since, as we have seen earlier, providing an explanation and providing an argument are two distinct things (corresponding to two distinct speech acts).

Given these specifications, we can provide a more explicit statement of the Erotetic view of normative reasons:

> The Erotetic View of Reasons (explicit): For that p to be a reason to F for S is for that p to be either (a) (a part of) the content of an appropriate explanation providing (pattern of an) answer to a (S directed) question 'Why F?/Why ought S to F?' in its explanation requiring reading; or (b) the content of an appropriate premise in a good argument/reasoning providing (pattern of an) answer to a (S directed) question 'Why F?/Why ought S to F?' in its argument/reasoning requiring reading.

We can also read the first rough statement of the aforementioned Erotetic view as a way to point to the common element in considerations that count as normative reasons, and the second, more explicit statement as a way to specify the exact differences between the two sorts of normative reasons.

Finally, a very general comparison to the existing approaches is in order (we will see more specific comparisons in a moment). The Erotetic view agrees with the reasons-first view that the best way to pre-theoretically characterise normative reasons is by focusing on considerations that speak in favour of F-ing, something that we seem to be able to grasp without a theory. This is the best way to be clear about the phenomena that we are interested in theorising about. Yet the Erotetic view rejects the reasons-first presupposition that normative reasons cannot be explained/defined in more basic terms. There is a reductionist account of reasons available; hence, reasons are not prime. The Erotetic view agrees with the Explanation approach in that normative reasons are, in a sense (parts of), explanations of deontic facts (e.g. that S ought to F). Yet the Erotetic view disagrees with the Explanation approach in that it doesn't assume that normative explanatory reasons are the only sort of normative reasons. The Erotetic view agrees with the reasoning reductionist approach in that normative reasons are, in a sense, contents of premises in good patterns of reasoning. Yet the Erotetic view disagrees with the Reasoning approach in that it doesn't assume that normative reasoning reasons are the only sort of normative reasons. The Erotetic view agrees in a sense with the reason sceptics/eliminitivists that there is no one single notion of normative reasons that could play all the theoretical roles that one might think are the roles of our common-sense concept of *reasons to act/have an attitude*. Yet the Erotetic view disagrees with the sceptics/eliminitivists in that this would show that the very concept of *normative reasons* is incoherent or that there is no meaningful way to appeal to it in our (meta-) normative theorising. According to the Erotetic view, there is a common core in the two sorts of normative reasons, and this common core makes it the case that we are not lumping together two completely unrelated concepts under a common label of 'normative reasons'. The common core is that of being an appropriate answer to the normative 'Why F/Why ought S to F?' question. Now, given that there are two ways of understanding this normative question, it is inevitable that there are two appropriate ways of replying to it, depending on which is the relevant reading. We have two sorts of reasons, because we have two possible readings of the normative, fundamental question 'Why F?'. This duality of readings of the fundamental normative question, I think, has been largely overlooked in the contemporary debates about normative reasons. But it is precisely because of this duality that all the trouble and opposition arises.

The Erotetic view not only shows what is right and what is mistaken in existing views but also has the resources to provide a reasonable error-theory of why philosophers might have accepted mistaken conceptions. Roughly, it is because the distinction between asking for/providing an explanation and asking for/providing an argument can be easily overlooked, and one may easily focus only on one of these. The proponents of the Reasoning view have focused on the providing arguments aspect, whereas the proponents of the Explanation view have focused on explanation at the expense of reasoning. But it suffices to think about the difference between these two to see that the two are distinct and cannot be reduced one to another. Thinking about the non-normative 'Why?' questions might prove itself to be especially helpful for grasping the robust difference between requiring and providing an explanation and requiring and providing an argument. There is no reason why this robust distinction should not apply to the normative 'Why?' question. The Erotetic view works out the implication of this distinction for our theorising about normative reasons.

Before turning to some more detailed arguments in favour of the Erotetic view, let me first provide some toy examples to illustrate the two sorts of the normative 'Why F?' questions and correspondingly two sorts of normative reasons that the Erotetic view describes.

Soup. Consider the normative question 'Why eat soup tonight?' directed at my kids. That is, consider the question that one (for instance, the kids themselves) might ask about whether my kids ought to or should eat soup tonight. The Erotetic view predicts that there are two possible readings of this possible question. On the first one, the question is about the explanation, indeed the grounds of the normative fact that my kids ought to eat soup tonight. On this reading, one is asking what makes it the case that my kids ought to eat soup. This reading of the question takes it for granted that it is the case that my kids ought to eat soup tonight. Typically, this reading of the question is relevant in contexts of conversation where one wants to acquire a better understanding of the grounds of the normative fact that my kids ought to eat soup tonight – namely, in contexts where one wants to know: where does this ought come from, or in virtue of what other considerations/facts does this ought hold?

On the second reading of the question, it is about an argument/ reasoning for the conclusion that my kids ought to eat soup. On this reading, one is asking whether it really is the case that my kids ought to eat soup tonight. It is in no way assumed that my kids ought to eat soup tonight. Typically, this reading of the question is relevant in contexts where one (perhaps the kids themselves) is challenging the claim that my kids ought to eat soup.

These two readings of the 'Why eat soup tonight?' question give grounds to two distinct sorts of reasons for my kids to eat soup tonight. The first corresponds to the explanation-requiring reading of the 'Why eat soup?' question. The normative explanatory reasons for my kids to eat soup tonight correspond to appropriate answers to this explanation-requiring reading of the question. What are these? Note that, arguably, mere appeal to healthy aspects of soup, vegetables, and vitamins will not work. For there are tons of healthy foods that contain vegetables, vitamins, and so on. What makes it the case that my kids ought to eat soup and not, say, salad, broccoli, or kale tonight? In virtue of what ought my kids to eat soup and not plain kale? It seems that an appropriate answer to the explanation-requiring 'Why eat soup?' question here will appeal to my parental decision to buy soup for the kids' dinner (yes, I buy rather than prepare soups). The fact that I have authority over and responsibility for what my kids eat for dinner (and, presumably, that eating soup isn't anything bad for my kids) constitutes the relevant background conditions for this explanation to be appropriate. Thus, the fact that I chose and bought soup for the kids' dinner is a normative reason for my kids to eat soup tonight. (Another consideration that can be a normative reason of this sort in this context is that there is fresh soup at home, and unless we eat it, it will be wasted, or that there is simply nothing else at home apart from the soup, and so on.) That I bought soup speaks in favour, in a sense, of the kids eating it tonight. This reason is a normative explanatory reason, the sort of reason that is salient in contexts where participants of a conversation are not challenging the claim that my kids ought to eat soup. It is a content of an answer to an explanation-requiring question of 'Why ought my kids to eat soup tonight?'.

The second sort of normative reasons for my kids to eat soup corresponds to an argument/reasoning-requiring reading of 'Why eat soup?'. The normative argumentative/reasoning-centred reasons for my kids to eat soup correspond to appropriate answers to the argument/reasoning-requiring reading of the 'Why eat soup?' question. What are potential examples of these? Note, first, that, typically, that I bought soup will not constitute an appropriate answer to the 'Why eat soup?' question in its argument-requiring reading. If kids are in the mood to challenge the claim that they ought to eat soup, then bringing up the fact that I bought the soup will not provide any support for that conclusion, and rightly so. It is not (*pace* special circumstances) a premise in a good pattern of argument/reasoning towards the conclusion that the kids ought to eat soup. That I bought it doesn't support on its own the claim that they have to eat it. That it contains vegetables and is good for their health seem to be more appropriate responses to the argument-requiring question. It is the argumentative/reasoning reason for my kids to eat the soup. That the soup is good for their health is a consideration that can be a content of a fitting premise-response in a good pattern of reasoning/argument from this premise-response (together with other premise-responses, presumably, such as that my kids desire be healthy) to the conclusion-response of them eating soup (or the conclusion of a sound argument that they ought to eat the soup). Thus, there are two sorts of reasons for my kids to eat soup tonight. One is explanation-centred, and the other is argument/reasoning-centred. Both correspond to patterns of appropriate answers to the normative 'Why F?' question.

Army.[4] Consider the question 'Why go North?', as concerning soldiers in a battle – that is, the question 'Why ought soldiers to go North?'. On the explanation-requiring reading, this question asks for considerations that explain, ground, or make it the case that soldiers ought to go North. It is assumed that soldiers ought to go North. An appropriate answer to the question on this reading may be that a general has ordered soldiers to go North. That a general has authority on a battlefield over soldiers is part of the background considerations. That the general orders soldiers to go North seems to be a reason for them to go North. The Erotetic view explains this. That the general orders soldiers to go North is the content of (a pattern of) an appropriate answer to the explanation-requiring reading of the question 'Why ought soldiers to go North?'.

On the argument/reasoning-requiring reading, the question 'Why go North?' asks for considerations that would constitute premises in a good pattern of an argument/reasoning towards the soldiers going North (towards the conclusion that the soldiers ought to go North). It is not assumed in this reading that it is the case that soldiers ought to go North. An appropriate answer to this reading of the question might appeal to the fact that going North will surprise the enemy and will put the army in a better position to win the battle. That the general has decided that the soldiers should go North on its own need not always be an appropriate answer in this context (e.g. this is clear in a context where the general's authority is questioned). That going North will surprise the enemy and will put the army in a better position to win the battle is a reason, in a

---

[4] Thanks to Jörg Löschke for suggesting this example.

sense, for soldiers to go North. The Erotetic view explains this. That going North will surprise the enemy and will put the army in a better position to win the battle is content of an appropriate premise in a pattern of good reasoning from these premise-responses with this content to the conclusion of soldiers going North (to the claim that the soldiers ought to go North).

Hijacked flight. Consider the following example from a different context that nevertheless seems to point to the same distinction that we are drawing. '[i] Tom is worried that his wife was on the two o'clock flight, because that's the one that was hijacked (*attitudinal*). [ii] Tom is worried that his wife was on the two o'clock flight, because she said she'd be arriving early in the evening (*epistemic*)' (Gordon 1987: 35). This example comes from the context where Gordon discusses two sorts of reasons for emotions (and we've seen in Section 3.3 that this example may be used to introduce the fittingness–epistemic justification distinction with respect to possible assessments of emotions). Here I would like to suggest that this example illustrates equally well the explanation-reasons versus reasoning-reasons distinction while stopping short of a full endorsement of the idea that the two distinctions in the assessment of emotions (fittingness-justification and reasoning-reasons-explanation-reasons) are about one and the same thing. This might be so, but this is not the place to pursue this issue. The point here is a simpler one. Consider the question 'Why worry that my wife is on the two o'clock flight?' as considered by Tom. It seems that the reason provided in (i) the aforementioned is an answer to an explanation-requiring reading of that question. In this context, it is known that Tom should worry that his wife took the two o'clock flight. But the reason provided in (ii) seems to be more of an argument/premise in a reasoning sort (of course, again, the reasoning-argument here is to be understood broadly enough to encompass processes by which we arrive at emotional attitudes). In the context where (ii) is an appropriate answer to the 'Why should Tom worry?' question ('Why should I worry that my wife took the two o'clock flight?' as considered by Tom), it is not known that Tom should indeed worry. That his wife said she'd be arriving early in the evening is something that supports the conclusion that she was on the two o'clock flight. And thus it supports, in a pan-argument sense, Tom's being worried.

P therefore p. Finally, consider a case of belief. Consider the question 'Why believe that it is raining outside?' that applies to me at this moment. On one reading of 'Why should/ought I to believe that it is raining outside?', one is asking for an explanation of the fact that I ought to believe that it is raining outside. (Let us postpone the question about the nature of the ought that arguably applies to the doxastic case. Also, if you think there are no positive oughts for beliefs, the proposal here might be easily adapted by an appeal to negative obligations – for example, that it is not the case that one is required to believe that such and such is the case.) An appropriate answer to this reading of the question 'Why believe that it is raining outside?', arguably, might just be that it is raining outside (with the assumption that truth is the norm of belief or, alternatively, that knowledge is the norm of belief). On the other reading of the question, one is asking for a premise towards the conclusion that it is raining outside. An appropriate answer to this second reading might be that through the window, I see raindrops falling (that it is raining outside, arguably, will not be an appropriate answer to an argument-seeking question, the question that doesn't assume that it is raining outside). Notice an intriguing aspect of our view already (and we will come back to it later), that there is a reading on which p is a reason for one to believe that p, and there is a reading on which p is not a reason to believe that p.

The aforementioned examples (or most of them) were such that the considerations that constituted normative explanatory reasons were distinct from the considerations that were normative reasoning/argumentative reasons. These examples were supposed to make the point about the genuine distinction between the two sorts of normative reasons. Yet, of course, in many ordinary cases, the same consideration may count as both a normative explanatory reason and a normative reasoning reason in different contexts. Consider, for instance, a promise. The fact that I promise to go to my friend's party may well play a role in an appropriate answer to an explanation-requesting reading of the 'Why go to the party?' question as well as in an appropriate answer to an argument/reasoning-requiring reading of the question, depending on common knowledge and intentions of the locutors. That I made that promise is something that can play a role in explaining, grounding the fact that I ought to go to the party, as well as playing a premise content role in an appropriate pattern of reasoning from, say, my belief that I made the promise plus some other fitting attitudes (say, intention to respect the promise) towards the conclusion-response of going to the party (or the claim that I ought to go to the party). However, as the aforementioned examples showed, the fact that the same considerations can often play both roles should not mislead us into thinking that there is only one sort of normative reasons. Compare the fact that in some cases p is a proper answer to a normative explanation-requesting 'Why?' question and also a proper answer to an argument-requesting non-normative reading of the 'Why?' question doesn't show that there is no genuine distinction to be drawn between arguments and explanations. The same applies to answers to normative 'Why F?' questions.

Arguments in favour of the view. Let us now turn to arguments in favour of the Erotetic view. First, and almost platitudinously at this point, the Erotetic view fits perfectly with the observation that there are, in general, two readings of 'Why?' questions and corresponding appropriate answers to these. There are explanation-centred and argument/reasoning-centred 'Why?' questions. If this duality of 'Why?' questions were to somehow disappear when we focus on normative 'Why?' questions, it would certainly be somewhat mysterious and would stand in need of a further explanation. The Erotetic view has here a clear advantage in that it doesn't postulate any miraculous change of 'Why?' questions at the level of normative 'Why?' questions. All the 'Why?' questions have two readings and not just non-normative ones. The Erotetic view fits perfectly with this natural observation about 'Why?' questions in general.

Second, turning to the abovementioned constraints or desiderata for a theory of reasons, the Erotetic view can account for the observation that there seems to be some connection between motivating and normative reasons. As observed earlier, this intuitive link is often understood in terms of reasons being able to play a role in reasoning. The Erotetic view has it that one sort of normative reasons are appropriate contents of premise-responses in patterns of good reasoning. It is so where these (reasoning/argument-centred) contents are what is required by the corresponding 'Why F?' questions. Thus, on the Erotetic view, some normative reasons are essentially connected to reasoning (broadly construed). Assuming that motivating reasons are considerations that play the (content of the) premise role in reasoning *tout court*, the Erotetic view has it that one sort of normative reasons just are considerations that could be possible good motivating reasons. (A corollary that we will see later is that the connection between motivating and normative reasons should appear plausible only with respect to reasoning/argumentative normative reasons, which seems to be the case.)

Third, the Erotetic view satisfies the tolerance/generality constraint. That is, it can be easily applied in the case of reasons to act, but also in the case of reasons to believe, to fear, and to hold other attitudes. The aforementioned examples constitute an illustration of this point.

Fourth, the Erotetic view satisfies the desiderata of economy. That is, the view achieves great explanatory power (i.e. explaining all normative reasons) with a relatively small number of initial assumptions and without postulating new entities. The view only appeals to two possible readings of 'Why?' questions as applied to the normative (deontic) domain (e.g. oughts/shoulds), an explanation-requiring and an argument/reasoning-requiring reading and two corresponding possible patterns of answers to the readings of this question. It is a reductive view of reasons, and as such, it ultimately explains reasons in terms of other properties and entities and is not committed to any additional ontological assumptions about reasons being irreducible entities.

Fifth, the Erotetic view satisfies the gradability aspect of reasons. My promise to go to a restaurant with a friend seems to be more important than the fact that I will get some satisfaction from binge-watching *BoJack* instead of going to the restaurant. The proposal here is that we need not appeal to 'weight' to account for this apparent gradability (and outweighing). The Erotetic view inherits the strategy used by proponents of the Reasoning view who appeal to the defeasibility of good reasoning. Recall that on that view, roughly, when p is a reason to F and r is a reason to G (incompatible with F), p outweighs r, just in case adding p to the reasoning from r to G triggers the *ceteris paribus* clause and functions as a defeater but not the other way round (i.e. adding r to the reasoning from p to F doesn't figure as a defeater for that piece of reasoning). The variation in the apparent 'weight' of reasons for one and the same F-ing can be explained on the present view in a similar way. In a situation where p and r are both reasons to F, but p is 'weightier' than r, the reasoning from p to F is more resilient in the face of potential defeaters than the reasoning from r to F. The Erotetic view can thus account for our pre-theoretical judgments about the gradability of (the importance of) reasons by endorsing the existing appeal to defeasible good patterns of reasoning.

Sixth, and this is a crucial point in comparing our view to the reductionist accounts discussed earlier, the Erotetic view satisfies the extensionality constraint. That is, it classifies as reasons all and only things that we take pre-theoretically to be reasons. (Recall that our rough guide here in our pre-theoretical assessment of considerations as normative reasons appeals to the idea that reasons are considerations that count somehow in favour of an action or an attitude.) This is where the Erotetic view really has an advantage over its rivals. Both the Reasoning view and the Explanation view over-generated and under-generated reasons. They implied in their various versions that some considerations are reasons where they don't seem to be, and they failed to account for considerations that seemed to be reasons to act or have an attitude. The Erotetic view does better on this account. It is able to avoid the pitfalls of previous accounts in over-generating and under-generating reasons. Let me provide some details on this crucial point.

We observed earlier that the Reasoning view predicts that considerations that count as mere enabling conditions are normative reasons. Yet, of course, the enabling conditions, such as the fact that I am able to F, cannot (always) count as normative reasons to F. And it seems that entailing conditions, such as 'I have a reason to F', are not reasons to F. These are cases where the Reasoning view over-generates normative reasons. The Erotetic view avoids this by restricting normative reasoning reasons only to these contents of possible premises of good reasoning/argument that are appropriate answers to the relevant readings of 'Why F?' questions. The Reasoning view is committed to the claim that all contents of fitting premise-responses of a good pattern of reasoning to F (where the subject has at least some of the relevant premise-responses) are normative reasons for the subject in question. The Erotetic view is not committed to this claim. Consider the case of abilities. Certainly, there is a good pattern of reasoning such that the fact that I am able to meet my friend for lunch is a content of a premise-response of such reasoning. Yet it is not clear that the fact that I am able to meet my friend for lunch is always a content of an appropriate answer to the question 'Why meet my friend for lunch?'. Maybe sometimes it is. For instance, when I am the only one in a group of several friends who is actually able to go for lunch. We have all promised to meet him for lunch, but all except me are sick and incapable of going outside. In such a context, the fact that being unable to go for lunch is an excuse for not going is made salient. Thus, it may be appropriate to say that the fact that *I am* able to go is a reason *for me* to go even if all the other friends are unable to go. I am not relieved from my promise even if the other friends are. Maybe in such a context that I am able to go for lunch is a reason for me to go. If so, the Erotetic view can account for it: this consideration is part of a good pattern of an answer to the 'Why go for lunch?' question. But most often, appeal to the mere ability to F will not be part of an appropriate answer to 'Why F?' questions. Typically, in ordinary deliberative contexts where the salient thing is to find premises for a sound argument/good reasoning towards going for lunch with a friend, mentioning one's being able to go for lunch won't be part of the relevant considerations. Typically, in standard cases, that I am able to go for lunch with a friend will not be part of an appropriate answer to the argument/reasoning-requiring reading of the question 'Why should I go for lunch with my friend?'. It is crucial to stress that the Erotetic view explains

reasons in terms of appropriate answers to one of the two possible readings
of the normative 'Why F?' question. One of these readings is the
argument/reasoning-requiring reading. And in this last aspect, it has some
similarities with the Reasoning view (and thus it can vindicate the insights
that come from appealing to the reasoning in explaining reasons, in a
sense). But it is also fundamentally different from the Reasoning view. Its
appeal to good patterns of reasoning in explaining reasons is not unrest-
ricted, so to say. On the Reasoning view, roughly, any consideration that
can serve as an appropriate input in a good pattern of reasoning towards
F-ing can be a normative reason. Not so, on the Erotetic view. Only those
considerations that are appropriate answers to the reasoning/argument-
requiring reading of the 'Why F?' question will count as normative reasons
on the present view. These considerations surely have to be contents of
premises of an argument/premise-responses in reasoning. But being a
premise is not a sufficient condition here. These premises have to be
appropriate answers. Which answers are appropriate is also context-
sensitive, and depends on the further aims and presuppositions in a
conversation (which need not be concrete; recall that we are focusing on
abstracta, the patterns of questions and answers). Thus, the Erotetic view
doesn't treat mere enabling conditions as normative reasons (but it also
allows for considerations about, say, one's abilities to be normative reasons
in special contexts). The Erotetic view neither over-generates reasons here,
nor is it too restrictive. It is an improvement on the Reasoning approaches.
Similar conclusions also apply with respect to mere entailing conditions.

How about the cases where the Reasoning view under-generates reasons? We saw earlier (Chapter 2) that the Reasoning view had a hard time
explaining cases like the Surprise Party and Ice Cream cases, and it entailed
by definition that there are no reasons in the Moore-paradoxical and self-
undermining belief cases. And yet these cases also appeared pre-
theoretically to be cases of genuine normative reasons. The Erotetic view
has resources for treating these cases as cases of genuine normative reasons.
Take, for instance, the Moore-paradoxical considerations. That there is a
fire in the building but John doesn't know that there is a fire in the
building may well be part of an appropriate answer to the question 'Why
check on the building?'. It is an appropriate answer to the explanation-
requiring reading of that question (the question 'Why ought John to check
on the building?'). Answers on our account are *abstracta*, and neither the
inquirer nor the addressee of the question needs to be John. The mere fact
that there is a pattern of a normative 'Why check on the building?'
question that has John as a subject and that has a possible appropriate

answer 'that the building is on fire and John doesn't know that it is' is enough for the Moore-paradoxical consideration to be a reason for John to check. Sure, it is not a consideration that John could reasonably use in a fitting piece of reasoning. And thus, it is not a normative reasoning reason. But it may still be a normative explanatory reason. Thus, the Erotetic view preserves the pre-theoretical claim and is extensionally more appropriate than the Reasoning view. It doesn't under-generate the reasons in Moore-paradoxical cases. Similar considerations also apply in the case of self-undermining beliefs (e.g. a memory-erasing pill), the Surprise Party case, the Ice Cream case, and others (see Chapter 2). A consideration may still count as a genuine normative reason, namely a normative explanatory reason for why one ought to F even if the consideration is not or cannot be a premise in one's reasoning. The distinction between normative reasoning reasons and normative explanatory reasons explains how this is possible.

In a similar way, the Erotetic view also avoids the pitfalls of the Explanation view. That is, it avoids over-generating and under-generating reasons in the way that explanatory views do. We observed earlier that some explanatory views distinguish *pro tanto* and *pro toto* normative reasons (cf. Broome 2004, 2013), where the *pro tanto* reasons are supposed to be considerations that play a role in the special normative weighing explanations and the *pro toto* reasons just are explanations of why one ought to F. One worry there was that postulating the existence of two distinct sorts of normative reasons to F over-generates normative reasons (see Chapter 3 for details). The Erotetic view easily avoids this problem. On the view defended here, there are simply no such things as *pro tanto* reasons. There are normative explanatory reasons for S to F, on this view, but these are explanations (grounds) of why S ought to F and hence would rather correspond (in a sense) to *pro toto* reasons. Another worry with the Deontic Explanation view (cf. Broome 2004, 2013) was that it was unclear why considerations that appear to speak clearly against F-ing (e.g. that I can have free holiday accommodation by the sea at my disposal as speaking against staying at home during the vacation) are still on this view parts of explanation of why I ought to F (e.g. stay at home). Again, the Erotetic view avoids this worry, by not postulating the existence of *pro tanto* reasons and weighing explanation. Yet it is still able to preserve the attractive features of the Explanation view, namely it respects the intuition that reasons do appear to be connected, in a sense, to explanation. The Explanation value-centred view had a hard time explaining how reasons for attitudes are possible (some even go as far as to endorse an outright denial of reasons for emotions). Yet this is contrary to our pre-theoretical views.

On the Erotetic view, there is no problem with that. There might be both normative reasoning reasons as well as normative explanatory reasons to believe and to fear and so on.

Overall, then, the Erotetic view has a crucial advantage over its reductionist rivals. It is extensionally adequate. And it also satisfies other constraints/desiderata for a theory of reasons. Moreover, it has still further considerations speaking in its favour. It makes sense of reasons talk, it makes best sense of the dual life of normative 'Why F?' questions, and it fits best with the observation that 'Why?' questions in general can be understood either by an question-requiring or by an explanation-requiring reading. Thus, we may conclude that these considerations make the Erotetic view superior to its rivals. Section 5.3 considers some possible objections to the Erotetic view. Chapter 6 looks at an application of the Erotetic view to a well-known debate. The theoretical fruitfulness of the Erotetic view demonstrated there will constitute yet another argument in its favour.

5.3   Further Clarifications

This section anticipates some possible objections to the Erotetic view. I provide here some considerations that might seem to speak against the Erotetic view, and I reply to all of them.

First, back to enabling conditions (once more). One might worry about the strategy that we have proposed in Section 5.2, where it was claimed that the Erotetic view, contrary to the Reasoning view, doesn't predict that all enabling conditions (e.g. that I am able to go for lunch) are normative reasons even though they can be premises of good patterns of reasoning/argument. The Erotetic view avoids counting enabling conditions as reasons (in the case of normative reasoning reasons) by restricting the relevant considerations not merely to premises in good patterns of reasoning/argument but more specifically to good premises in good patterns of reasoning/argument that are appropriate answers (in a context) to the argument/reasoning-requiring 'Why F?' question. In short, which considerations will count as normative reasoning reasons depends not only on their standing as premises in good patterns of reasoning but also on the context-sensitive (yet abstract) features of conversation – whether or not they are possible appropriate answers to the relevant normative question. Now, the worry here is that one might suggest that proponents of the Reasoning view could equally appeal to context-sensitive aspects of reasoning/argument in order to restrict the considerations that would count as reasons. The idea would be that what counts as a good pattern of reasoning partly depends on the aims and presuppositions of a reasoner, and thus is also context-sensitive. In this way, one might hope, the proponents of the Reasoning view could rule out enabling considerations from counting as reasons. If so, the Erotetic view doesn't have an advantage over the Reasoning view.

In reply to this worry, I would like to note that, if successful, such a move indeed would put the Reasoning view and the Erotetic view on a par with respect to enabling conditions. But I don't think that this is so. It is not clear how exactly the appeal to the context sensitivity of good patterns of reasoning could rule out enabling conditions from being appropriate premises on the Reasoning view. It is not to say that the reasoner's aims and presuppositions shouldn't be taken into account in determining the pattern of reasoning that the reasoner is engaging in/proposing. Surely, the reasoner's intentions count. Without taking the reasoner's intentions into account, it is often difficult to establish whether the proposed argument is, say, the fallacy of affirming the consequent or an inference to the best explanation (IBE). The fact that a reasoner is aiming to provide a deductive argument, to establish the conclusion by guaranteeing its truth, will matter in classifying the argument as the fallacy or an instance of an IBE in such a case. But it is difficult to see how aims and presuppositions (or indeed other factors) could exclude enabling conditions from patterns of good reasoning. It just seems to be a core feature of any good argumentative structure that adding a true premise doesn't invalidate, *ceteris paribus*, the soundness of the argument. The proponents of the Reasoning view should show that adding a true premise expressing enabling conditions triggers the *ceteris paribus* clause. But it is not clear why this should be so. Merely postulating this would amount to an ad hoc move and doesn't have any independent theoretically satisfying motivation. It would only be motivated by avoiding the problem of enabling conditions, which is not an independently plausible theoretical consideration. The Erotetic view, on the other hand, has resources to motivate the move of the appeal to aims and presuppositions. It is a core observation about answers that their appropriateness depends on the context of the conversation in which they are proposed. They depend on the aims and presuppositions in place in the conversation. It depends on what the inquirer is asking for and on what is presupposed and so on. It depends, for instance, on the fact that typically the inquirer is asking for considerations that would convince her in endorsing the claim that S ought to F. Citing mere enabling conditions (that S can F) would not count as things that could convince the inquirer that S ought to F. Thus, the Erotetic view has an independently plausible account of why enabling conditions will not count as appropriate answers to the argument/reasoning-requiring 'Why F?' questions and can avoid the problem of enabling conditions. The Erotetic view can satisfactorily account for why mere enabling conditions are not (typically) reasons to F, whereas the same move is not available to proponents of the Reasoning view.

Second, one might have some further thoughts about the way the Erotetic view treats the question of the 'weight' of reasons and comparative judgments about reasons. The worry here is that, on the one hand, the Erotetic view postulates the existence of two different sorts of normative reasons, but, on the other hand, it explains the apparent 'weight' of reasons only in terms of defeasible reasoning. It seems, then, that on the Erotetic view, only normative reasoning reasons can have 'weight' or, more precisely, can allow for genuine comparative judgments. For by definition, normative explanatory reasons cannot be explained in terms of reasoning, defeasible or not. Yet, the worry goes, one might think that the apparent 'weight' of reasons is a common property of all sorts of normative reasons. How does the Erotetic view account for the 'weight' for all reasons?

I would like to respond to this worry in two stages. First, I would like to acknowledge that indeed, it is a consequence of the Erotetic view that genuine direct comparative judgments about normative reasons make sense only in the context of normative reasoning reasons ('direct' here excludes comparisons in terms of which normative explanatory reasons explain better the relevant ought fact – for example, explain in a simpler and more elegant way). Second, I would like to defend the proposal that this is not, contrary to what the worry suggests, an unwelcome consequence of the view. Consider, for instance, a clear case of normative explanatory reasons. Consider: (a) 'the building is on fire but John doesn't know that it is on fire'. We agreed that it is a reason for John to check (again) the building. Now, what could be an appropriate target for a comparison for (a)? That is, what could be another normative explanatory reason that we could compare to (a) with respect to their relative 'weight' or 'strength'? A proponent of this line of worry needs to find a reason that would have, for example, a lesser 'weight' than (a) but would still qualify as a normative explanatory reason. My suggestion is that there isn't really any reason that fits the bill. One might think that (b) 'that the fridge contains John's preferred ice cream, but John doesn't know that it contains it' is a reason for John to check the fridge rather than the building. But it doesn't seem to be. After all it is not the case that John ought to/should check the fridge rather than the building in the present case. Explanation is assumed to be factive. Nothing can explain *p*, when *p* is not the case. Thus, there is no genuine comparison here. In a situation where John ought to check the building and not the fridge, only (a) is a normative explanatory reason for him and not (b).

Fundamentally, in thinking about the apparent 'weight' of reasons, we should ask the question: but what's the point of comparative judgments about reasons? What do these judgments help us with? A natural answer to this question is, I think, the proposal that these comparisons help us sort things out in complicated deliberative situations. They help us order options, in particular, in situations of uncertainty. These are precisely the situations where we don't know whether we ought to F or not (or at least situations where it can make sense to challenge such ought claims). If so, then it is easy to see why talk of the apparent 'weight' of reasons makes sense only in the context of normative reasoning reasons. That one ought to F is not challenged in situations of normative explanatory reasons. Thus, I would like to suggest that the Erotetic view's prediction that the normative explanatory reasons don't have 'weight' is not problematic. Quite the contrary, it seems to be the correct consequence given the ultimate purpose of comparative judgments about reasons.

The third potential worry concerns normative questions that differ from 'Why F?' questions. Consider, for instance, the question 'Where to eat for lunch?' It is clearly a normative question, since it is best understood as a question involving an ought/should. It can be easily paraphrased as: 'where should/ought we eat for lunch today?'. The Erotetic view identifies reasons as answers to the 'Why F?' normative question. But is there an independent, theoretically well-grounded explanation of why it is limited only to 'Why F?' and not all sorts of normative questions? Isn't focusing on 'Why F?' questions ad hoc? Is there any further theoretical motivation for the choice of the specific normative question within the Erotetic approach? Note that on the face of it, it doesn't seem plausible to treat the answers to these further normative questions (e.g. 'Where should we eat?', 'What should I do tonight?') as normative reasons (e.g. 'We should eat at that new ramen place' is not straightforwardly a normative reason). Thus, the worry is not an idle one. If the proponents of the Erotetic view cannot provide an independent and theoretically well-motivated explanation of why we should focus on the 'Why F?' questions in defining reasons, the view is either ad hoc or leads to an implausible over-generation of normative reasons (this is the horn of the dilemma where all answers to all normative questions are treated as normative reasons).[5]

To this worry, I would like to reply that there is indeed a well-motivated distinction between the normative 'Why F?' on one hand and other normative questions on the other hand. We can think of 'Where to F?', 'What to F?', and similar questions as questions requiring specifications about an (alleged) ought to F. When we are asking 'Where should we eat?', we are asking for precisions about the general should/ought to eat that is (allegedly) already in place. 'Why F?' questions, on the other hand, are, so to say, more fundamental: they either question the relevant ought claim in general (or, at any rate, ask for additional arguments in their favour) or are asking for explanation of the relevant ought. They are not about asking for specification of an (alleged) ought. Of course, there might be situations where by asking a 'Where to F?' question, we are ultimately asking a 'Why F?' question, such as in a case where, after having spent an hour trying to find a parking spot, and thereby already being late for the theatre, one might utter an exasperated 'Where to park?', meaning to ask whether it is really worth continuing to search for a parking spot rather than just go back. But, typically, the other non-'Why F?' questions are about inquiring into ways to specify some general (or vague) ought into more operationisable oughts or shoulds. This, then, appears to be a major difference between the 'Why F?' questions and other normative questions. Where the latter are requiring specification or precisification of a general or vague ought, the former is asking for arguments or explanations (grounds). Thus, the focus on 'Why F?' questions seems to be justified by this crucial difference.

Alternatively, one could also explore the idea that 'Where to F?', 'What to F?', and other similar questions can, after all, be reduced to 'Why F?' questions. The reduction, according to this line of reply, would have a contrastivist flavour (cf. Snedegar 2017 on contrastivism about normative reasons in general). The idea would be that when we are asking, say, 'Where to eat tonight?', we are asking several distinct 'Why F?' questions that are lumped together, presumably, for reasons of economy and easiness of expression. The presumed 'Why F?' questions here would be of the following sort: 'Why eat at A rather than at B?' 'Why eat at B rather than at A?' 'Why eat at C rather than at A or B?', and so on. The idea would be that there is a (contextually determined) partition of options for eating out,

[5] Thanks to Jörg Löschke for making me aware of this worry as well as for suggesting some of the possible replies to it.

and there are arguments in favour and against all these options, and, presumably, one option has better arguments in its favour than others. By asking 'Where to eat?', one is merely shortcutting the longer and more tedious line of questioning about arguments in favour of each and all the relevant options for eating out tonight. If this is the case, then 'Where to F?' and similar questions can, after all, be integrated into the Erotetic view. Of course, the answer 'We should eat at that new ramen place', while completely appropriate, is also to be taken as a shortcut, a proxy to the arguments that speak in favour of eating at the new ramen place (these are the arguments that make the ramen place the winner among other options). Now, these arguments in favour of the ramen place, then, can be properly seen as normative reasons speaking in favour of eating at the new ramen place. More specifically, they can be seen as normative reasoning reasons. While this is still a very rough sketch of how this line of answer could go, it appears to be another plausible strategy that a proponent of the Erotetic view might appeal to in order to deal with the worry of non-'Why F?' normative questions.

Fourth, and somewhat connectedly to what precedes, one might think that there are normative 'Why F?' questions that cannot have an appropriate answer. More precisely, one might think that some questions are abominable and any answer to these would be insensible. Think, for instance, about questions such as 'Why kill innocent civilians with gunfire rather than kill them by torturing them to death with some archaic torture instrument?'. It's sensible to think that there is no really appropriate answer that we could give to such a question. One might think that the appropriate thing to do in the face of such a question is to say nothing and thereby reject the question entirely. Some questions just have to be refused to be answered. One should not kill innocent civilians, neither by torturing them to death nor by gunfire. Yet one might also think that in a situation where one is going to kill civilians anyway, one has reasons to kill them by relatively less-painful means – that is, by using gunfire rather than by torturing them to death. The worry, then, is that the Erotetic view predicts that there are no such reasons, since the question 'Why kill innocent civilians with gunfire rather than torturing them to death?' doesn't seem to have any appropriate answer.[6]

In response to this question, I would like to observe first that this question appeals to the classical and well-worn debate over the lesser evil. Whether and in what sense one ought to do the less-wrong thing is a

---

[6] Thanks to Jörg Löschke for making me aware of this potential worry.

debate that I think goes beyond the scope of the present discussion, and indeed beyond the scope of the Erotetic view itself. Many intricate issues pertaining to scope and sense of ought in cases of lesser evil need to be taken care of. That being said, and this is my second point, if after a careful consideration we still think that there are reasons for one to kill the innocents by gunfire in a situation where one's only alternative is to kill the innocents by torturing them to death, then there is also a reading of 'Why kill the innocent by gunfire?' that can be appropriately answered in such a context. The question may certainly appear inappropriate to us. But it is important to remember that the question is not necessarily directed at us. We are not in a situation where we are going to kill innocent civilians. Yet if one is indeed in a genuine situation where one is guaranteed to kill innocent civilians, the question may, after all, be meaningfully addressed to such a subject. One difficulty in seeing how such a question can be appropriately answered might come from our difficulty in conceiving of such a situation where there really is no other genuine option for the subject in such a case (e.g. freezing). But I would like to suggest that if it is meaningful to talk about reasons for the killer to kill by gunfire rather than by torture, then it should also be meaningful for the killer to consider the question 'Why kill by gunfire rather than by torture?'. If this is so, then contrary to what the worry suggests, the Erotetic view predicts that there may be reasons for one to kill by gunfire rather than by torture. In other words, I would like to suggest that the killer having reasons to kill by less-painful means and the appropriateness of the question 'Why kill using the less painful means?' as having the killer as its subject either stand or fall together. Thus, the Erotetic view can avoid the problem by either (i) explaining that there are neither genuine normative reasons to kill by gunfire nor an appropriate answer to the question 'Why kill by gunfire?' or, alternatively, (ii) that there are reasons for the killer to kill by gunfire (rather than by torture), and the question 'Why kill by gunfire rather than by torture?' can be appropriately answered when it has the guaranteed killer as its subject. In either way, the Erotetic view seems to avoid the alleged problem.

The fifth and final worry concerns the place of rationality within the new Erotetic view. It is a common view that rationality (or justification) in the case of both action and attitudes is the affair of reasons. For instance, one might think that it is rational for you to F just in case you possess most reasons to F. And one might think that it is rational (or justified) for you to believe that p just in case your reasons, overall, support believing that p. Now, the worry is that it seems that determining what is rational for one to do or believe (or indeed which attitude to have) is an essential feature of normative reasons. It is, according to this line of thought, a central function of reasons to determine what's rational for us to do, believe, and so on. However, the Erotetic view seems to imply that determining rationality is not that essential to reasons after all. For it postulates that there are basically two sorts of normative reasons, normative reasoning and normative explanatory reasons. But at best, only one of these may be said to play a role in determining rationality. More specifically, it is hard to see how explanatory reasons can determine what is rational for one to do, believe, and so on. It may be the case that reasoning reasons are connected to rationality. But it is difficult to see how explanatory reasons could also be linked to rationality. Think again of Moore-paradoxical cases, where one is, by definition, in no position to act *for* the relevant reason; one cannot even possess the relevant explanatory reason. Thus, one might think there is no way in which such reasons might be connected to what is rational for one to do or believe, at least not in the common-sense of rationality. Disconnecting normative reasons and rationality, then, seems to be a worrisome implication of the Erotetic view. The essential link between reasons and rationality seems to be lost on the Erotetic view.[7]

To this worry, I would like to respond by suggesting that the problem is perhaps less worrisome than it might first appear. Indeed, perhaps, the observed loosening of the link between rationality and reasons in general is not a bad feature of the view at all. This is, however, not the place to develop what a full-blown theory of rationality could look like according to the Erotetic view. Some aspects of this task (with respect to belief) will be undertaken in Chapter 6. But let me suggest only that the view according to which all normative reasons have to be essentially connected to ratio-nality may just be a mere byproduct of focusing on one sort of normative reasons only, namely normative reasoning reasons. Once one recognises the reality of normative explanatory reasons, one might see that the connection is not essential for all reasons. A proponent of the worry here could nevertheless protest. Actually, one might suggest that normative explanatory reasons shouldn't really be considered as genuine reasons if they don't have a link to rationality. One could suggest that they are not reasons, precisely because they are not connected essentially to rationality. But such a protest might come as a bit of a surprise. For such an alleged reasons–rationality connection seems to be something that is under

[7] Thanks to Pascal Engel for a discussion on the general topic of the importance of the connection between normative reasons and rationality.

question in our discussion. Surely we don't have here a knock-down argument for the conclusion that the connection is not essential, at least not for all sorts of normative reasons. Nevertheless, I would like to draw attention to something we already touched upon in the chapter on the Reasoning view (Chapter 2) when we discussed Moore-paradoxical cases (and similar ones). We observed that Moore-paradoxical considerations do appear to speak in favour of the relevant F-ing. If one is denying them the status of being normative reasons, then one has to provide an independent theoretical motivation for introducing a new, distinct category that would encompass such normative considerations (e.g. the relevant Moore-paradoxical considerations). But such a move seems to be superfluous. Seeing both normative explanatory and normative reasoning considerations as normative reasons is more economical and better motivated. For both explanatory and reasoning reasons share the basic feature, the feature by which we identify reasons pre-theoretically – namely, they both appear to speak in favour of F-ing, in a sense. It is, thus, theoretically preferable to consider normative explanatory reasons as genuine normative reasons of a sort. If so, the Erotetic view can be maintained here. All that is required is that we can provide a plausible story about rationality within the framework of the Erotetic view. This task will be partly considered in Chapter 6 with respect to reasons for belief. Let me conclude this section by comparing very briefly (a fuller comparison will have to wait for another occasion) the present proposal to an existing view that seems to rely on somewhat similar distinctions.

In a recent article, Ralph Wedgwood (2015) suggests that there are two distinct categories of concepts of normative reasons. One is that of concepts of 'normative-explanation' reasons (Broome's account of reasons is a paradigm of this category of concepts of normative reasons). The other category is that of 'ideal-motivation' reasons (Setiya's ideal dispositionalist account as well as various ideal reasoner models of reasons are taken to be paradigmatic of this second category of normative reasons). Wedgwood proposes several cases and arguments to show that there are two functions of *normative reasons*, and that these cannot be fulfilled by one single concept. There have to be two distinct categories of concepts of reasons. If we abstract from Wedgwood's specific focus on ideal or good reasoners or dispositions (and focus instead on the more general category of good patterns of reasoning), then his classification of concepts of reasons (and by extension of corresponding reasons) comes very close to our own positive proposal.

There are, however, two important differences between our proposal and Wedgwood's proposal. First, Wedgwood's main target in that article are the reasons-first views of reasons, which would like to account for both normative-explanation and ideal-motivation aspects of reasons. Wedgwood's point there is that it's impossible to maintain such a position coherently – that is, a reasons-first view that also accounts for both apparently central aspects of reasons, the normative-explanation and ideal-motivation aspects. I agree with such a verdict. However, I also suspect that proponents of the reasons-first approach would not commit themselves to taking the aforementioned two aspects, the two functions of the concept of *normative reasons*, as crucial or essential to what reasons are. After all, reasons are undefined according to the reasons-first approach. More importantly, we are not aiming here to demonstrate that the reasons-first account cannot be maintained by presenting some further problem cases. Rather our aim here is to provide a new, positive reductionist account of reasons. The second difference between our proposal and Wedgwood's is that the two proposals differ in the explanation of what the common element between the two categories of concepts is. Wedgwood appeals to a confusion of two levels: the level of a theoretician and the level of an agent. He writes: 'that is, a confusion between (a) what must be known or grasped by *the theorist* who is giving an account of a certain sort of agent, and (b) what must be known or grasped by the *agent herself*' (Wedgwood 2015: 137; Wedgwood indicates that this distinction comes from Alston). This might come close to what we propose here, but the present proposal says something more than that there is a confusion (and that proponents of the reasons-first approach who want to maintain the two aforementioned aspects of reasons are confused). On our account, there is a fundamental dual nature of normative 'Why F?' questions. And this gives rise to two distinct sorts of normative reasons. Maybe we can think of our argument-requiring 'Why F?' questions as corresponding to Wedgwood's agent's level and our explanation-requiring 'Why F?' questions as corresponding to Wedgwood's theorist's level. If so, maybe the two proposals are close and indeed compatible. However, details of the two-level distinction might need to be further specified to see how far our proposals can fit together (in particular, if the agent's level is always a level of reasoning towards a deliberative ought and never a level of explanation for the agent herself of why she ought to F).

CHAPTER 6

An Application of the Erotetic View
Overcoming the Evidentialism–Pragmatism Dispute

In what precedes, we have seen a positive case for the Erotetic view. Our discussion has been focused on how well the Erotetic approach respects constraints and desiderata for a theory of reasons in comparison to alternative accounts, and how well it integrates with general observations about normative 'Why?' questions. The overall aim of the present chapter is to provide an additional argument in favour of the Erotetic view. The argument here appeals to the advantages of adapting the Erotetic view with respect to a further debate about reasons. More specifically, the Erotetic view can shed new light on the well-known debate about pragmatic reasons for belief. This further theoretical application of the view adds an additional argument in its favour.

6.1 Pragmatism–Evidentialism Debate

An increasingly popular debate within contemporary epistemology concerns the question of whether there can be pragmatic reasons to believe a proposition – that is, whether pragmatic (e.g. practical, moral, eudaimonic) considerations may be genuine normative reasons for one to believe certain propositions. According to what until recently seemed to be a clear majority view in epistemology, only truth-conducive considerations – that is, considerations that somehow indicate, entail, or probabilify the truth of a proposition (and may or may not contain the proposition itself) – can be genuine reasons to believe the proposition. This view goes under the name of *evidentialism* within the current debates. For it is common to assimilate truth-conducive considerations in favour of p with evidence for p.[1] Explicit

---

[1] It has often been noted that 'evidentialism' is not a particularly great name for this view, since, as observed earlier, one may or may not hold that p itself can be a reason to believe p (see Berker 2018; Engel 2020b). But if it is, then clearly it has to be a truth-conducive reason (for p entails p). According to the proponents of dogmatism in epistemology (Pryor 2000) and the-warrant-approach, one may be justified to believe some propositions, perhaps, so-called hinge propositions,

defences of this view can be found, for example, in Kelly (2002), Shah (2003), Shah and Velleman (2005), Engel (2007, 2013, 2019, 2020b), and Way (2016), among others. Evidentialism is opposed to an increasingly popular view, *pragmatism*, according to which, roughly, it is not the case that only truth-conducive considerations can be reasons to believe.[2] Contemporary pragmatism comes in two forms. On the one hand, there is *radical pragmatism*, according to which, strictly speaking/ultimately, only pragmatic considerations can be genuine normative reasons to believe.[3] Versions of this view have been defended in Rinard (2015, 2017, 2018, 2019) and Maguire and Woods (2020). On the other hand, there is *moderate pragmatism* (or *pluralism*), according to which, roughly, there can be both pragmatic and evidential genuinely normative reasons to believe. Versions of this appear in Foley (1992), Reisner (2008, 2009, 2018), McCormick (2014), and Leary (2017), among others. At present, the debate has evolved to a stage where some philosophers take pragmatism to be the default position (see Maguire and Woods 2020, quote (6) reproduced in Section 6.2). Clearly, evidentialism has lost its absolute majority status. And the debate seems to be in a stalemate.

This raises a natural question: what should we really think about the possibility of there being pragmatic reasons amid the current disagreement within the field? Are there pragmatic reasons to believe a proposition or not? The debate between evidentialists and pragmatists seems to be in a deadlock. Both camps have provided positive arguments for their views, offered considerations against the opposite view, and elaborated some strategies to reply to the objections from their opponents. Yet the debate

---

even without having evidence in their favour (Wright 2004). Typically, proponents of these views call their opponents 'evidentialists'. Bearing this clarification in mind, I will, however, follow the established practice in the debate about practical reasons for belief and reserve the term 'evidentialism' for the view according to which only truth-conducive considerations may count as genuine normative reasons to believe. And for the sake of brevity, in what follows, I will treat 'truth-conducive considerations' and 'evidence' as rough synonyms. Of course, many proponents of, say, process reliabilism (cf. Goldman 1979, 2009) will, strictly speaking, not be OK with such a treatment, since on their view some belief-producing mechanisms are genuinely truth-conducive without being pieces of evidence, as the term 'evidence' is commonly understood. But I think nothing substantive hangs on this choice in the present debate.

[2] Again, the naming here is somewhat unfortunate. For not all contemporary 'pragmatists' within the debate over reasons to believe will qualify as proponents of historical (American) pragmatism (of the end of the nineteenth/beginning of the twentieth century). For one thing, contemporary philosophers don't seem to be committed to historical pragmatist distinctive views about the nature of truth and knowledge. See Reisner (2018) for more on this clarification. However, again, in what follows, we stick to the contemporary labels, even though we know that we must bear in mind this historical clarification.

[3] In Maguire and Woods's terminology – only practical/pragmatic considerations can be authoritative reasons to believe (cf. Maguire and Woods 2020).

continues, as if it were based on some deep disagreement. Neither side seems to be convinced by the arguments from their opponents. It appears that we have reached a stalemate with no clear way out in sight.

A concrete objective of the present chapter is to show that the Erotetic view of reasons can provide a way to overcome the deadlock in this debate. The key element of the proposal is that both camps within the debate are operating with a somewhat defective understanding of normative reasons. In a sense, both camps are wrong. Yet both are also right about something important. The Erotetic view enables us to give due respect to what is true in both of these approaches with respect to pragmatic reasons for belief. Finally, the implicit mistaken assumptions about the nature of reasons in these views also allows us to provide a plausible error theory about why both of the approaches may initially appear attractive. In what follows, I elaborate the details of this proposal. If successful, the proposal will constitute a concrete demonstration of how the Erotetic view can be theoretically fruitful. Before arriving there, however, we need to add some clarifications about the present dialectical situation of the evidentialism–pragmatism debate and about what plausible constraints for overcoming the deadlock in this debate might look like. We do just that in Section 6.2. Section 6.3 is devoted to presenting details of the (dis)solution of the evidentialism–pragmatism dispute by appeal to the Erotetic view. Section 6.4 contains replies to some possible objections. Finally, I conclude by drawing some remarks on the theoretical fruitfulness and further potential applications of the Erotetic view of reasons.

6.2   Present State of the Debate and Options for Breaking the Deadlock

What are the criteria that a successful approach to the debate about the possibility of pragmatic reasons to believe has to satisfy? This is the first thing that we must clarify to have any hope of moving forwards and overcoming the stalemate within the dispute over pragmatic reasons for belief. What are the constraints that every party would agree to put on a theory that could break the deadlock? Both evidentialists and pragmatists seem to put a lot of weight on being able to best explain our pre-theoretical judgments about the relevant cases. Thus, in what follows, I suggest that we take on board the assumption that all parties in the debate seem to accept, namely that being extensionally adequate (or at least having the highest degree of extensional adequacy together with a viable error theory about the rest) constitutes a key constraint for a satisfactory solution to the dispute about the possibility of pragmatic reasons to believe. In other terms, the approach that respects most of the pre-theoretical judgments about the relevant cases – that is, constitutes the best explanation thereof – should be preferred to its competitors, everything else being equal (e.g. that it doesn't lead to a contradiction).

It should be noted, of course, that while extensional adequacy is the gold standard in this debate, it is also a live possibility that no one single approach can respect all or even most of the pre-theoretical judgments in this context. If this proves to be the case, then we are warranted to follow a standard move of requiring that a successful approach be able to provide a plausible error theory of the cases that it cannot account for directly. Considerations of simplicity and theoretical fruitfulness may play a role in further assessment of competing error theories.

Now, it is one thing to agree over the theoretical constraints that should guide the discussion, but quite another thing to actually agree on how to measure whether the constraints are met or who is meeting them best. Both evidentialists and pragmatists claim that their approaches fit best with the pre-theoretical judgments about some relevant cases. Oddly enough, some of the key cases that both parties put forward are the same or, at any rate, share a disturbing number of similarities. But even if we put aside the apparently similar cases, the mere fact that our pre-theoretical judgments about some cases involving possible pragmatic reasons to believe depart in opposite directions as radically as the participants of the debate maintain is somewhat worrisome. Of course, we should not expect our best theories to fit our pre-theoretical judgments perfectly. The days of ordinary language philosophy are over. But still, such a disparity in judgments demands an explanation. In order to illustrate how dramatically evidentialists and pragmatists differ in their suggestions about what our pre-theoretical judgments are, I propose to look at some revealing passages from both camps. Let us start with three cases from evidentialists:

> (1) Imagine an agnostic who, having become convinced that the expected utility of being a religious believer is higher than the expected utility of not being a religious believer, undertakes a project designed to induce religious belief. The agnostic thoroughly immerses herself in a life of religious ritual, seeks out the company of religious believers while scrupulously avoiding that of nonbelievers and (following Pascal's advice) imitates in every way the behavior of those who do believe. [...] In time, she genuinely becomes convinced that God exists. Suppose further that a tragic irony subsequently ensues: the expected utility of belief in God suddenly and dramatically changes. (A despot bent on persecuting religious believers unexpectedly

seizes power.) Even if she recognizes that the expected utility of being a believer is now lower than the expected utility of being a non-believer, this recognition will typically not prompt the abandonment of the newly-acquired belief. (Although it might, of course, prompt an anti-Pascalian project of deconversion.) Here, the fact that the belief is not abandoned in response to the change in expected utility indicates that the belief is not based on considerations of utility. (Kelly 2002: 176)[4]

(2) Suppose a man's son has apparently been killed in an accident. It is not absolutely certain he has, but there is very strong evidence that his son was drowned at sea. This man very much wants to believe that his son is alive. Somebody might say: If he wants to believe that his son is alive and this hypnotist can bring it about that he believes that his son is alive, then why should he not adopt the conscious project of going to the hypnotist and getting the hypnotist to make him believe this; then he will have got what he wants – after all, what he wants is to believe that his son is alive, and this is the state the hypnotist will have produced in him. [. . .] [I]n the case of the 'truth-centred motives', where *wanting to believe* means *wanting it to be the case*, we can see perfectly clearly why this sort of project is impossible and incoherent.

However, he might have a different sort of motive, a non-truth-centred motive. This would be the case if he said, 'Well, of course, what I would like best of all is for my son to be alive; but I cannot change the world in this respect. The point is, though that even if my son isn't alive, I want, I need to believe that he is, because I am so intolerably miserable knowing that he isn't.' Or, again, a man may want to believe something not caring a damn about the truth of it but because it is fashionable or comfortable or in accordance with the demands of social conformity to believe that thing. Might not such a man, wanting to believe this thing, set out to use the machinery of drugs, hypnotism, or whatever to bring it about that he did? In this case, the project does not seem evidently incoherent in the way in

---

[4] Right after this passage, Kelly also proposes to consider a 'contrast' case, where one easily abandons the project of acquiring the relevant belief, given the change in expected utility, which indicates that beliefs cannot be held *on the basis* of practical considerations (i.e. that pragmatic considerations cannot rationalise beliefs, even though there might be strategies to get oneself into believing the relevant propositions):

> Now let us alter the example slightly. In the altered version, the despot seizes power at a somewhat earlier time – the agnostic has begun the project of acquiring belief in God, but the project has not yet reached fruition. Upon recognizing that the expected utility of being a religious believer is now lower than that of being a nonbeliever, she simply discontinues the project. Here, the fact that she discontinues the project in response to the change in expected utility indicates that her participation in the project is itself based on considerations of utility. The considerations on which a given belief (or course of action) is based are revealed by the circumstances which would prompt one to abandon that belief (or course of action). (Kelly 2002: 176)

which the project was incoherent for the man with the truth-centred motive. What it is, is very deeply irrational, and I think that most of us would have a very strong impulse against engaging in a project of this kind however uncomfortable these truths were which we were having to live with. (Williams 1973: 149–150)

(3) Suppose that the cuckolded husband, upon being warned of this conceptual conflation, were to reply, 'Desiring to believe that my wife is faithful does me no good, since it will not make me feel better. It is only by actually believing in her fidelity that my spirits will improve. So in fact the pragmatic consideration that I am adducing is not a reason for wanting to believe she is faithful, but rather really a reason to believe she is faithful.' If the husband were to argue in this manner, I think that we would doubt his mastery of the concept of a reason for belief, specifically his mastery of the way that truth serves as an independent standard constraining the character of doxastic reasons. [. . .] [T]he husband in the example doesn't think that this prudential consideration of the effect of the belief on his happiness is evidence of the truth of the belief, yet thinks the prudential consideration gives him a reason for the belief all the same. And this seems unintelligible. (Shah 2003: 454–455)[5]

Note that when Thomas Kelly talks about considerations on which a belief is based (in (1)), what he really has in mind is normative reasons to believe, given that he defines these considerations by appeal to basing relations and their function of rationalising a belief. Assuming that rationalising of belief is one of the jobs of normative reasons for beliefs, these basing considerations can be seen as normative reasons (and not, say, mere motivating or explanatory reasons). Kelly's (2002: 176) suggestion that the relevant aspects of the case indicate 'that the belief is not based on considerations of utility' can be understood as a suggestion that this case (or, presumably, our pre-theoretical judgments about it – for example, that we find it plausible that the religious belief is not abandoned on the basis of a mere change in expected utility for the subject) is best explained by the evidentialist view, according to which nothing apart from evidential considerations can constitute normative reasons for beliefs. In other terms, we can interpret Kelly as suggesting that if pragmatism were right, then it should be possible that considerations of utility rationalise (e.g. constitute normative reasons for the subject in this case for abandoning the religious belief. But it doesn't seem possible that mere utility considerations rationalise abandonment of the belief in this case). Thus, pragmatism (and not

---

[5] Shah elaborates here on an initial example from Gibbard (1990) of a husband who has evidence that his wife is unfaithful.

evidentialism) entails that our pre-theoretical judgments are wrong in this case and they owe us an explanation (an error theory) of why we are wrong on this account, according to this line of thought. Thus, this constitutes, according to the present reading of Kelly, a prima facie case in favour of evidentialism.

Similarly, we should note that Williams's talk of 'motives' in the quoted passage (2) should really be understood as being about normative reasons. Recall our discussion on the Reasoning view of reasons earlier (Chapter 2), where we identified Bernard Williams as an early proponent of the contemporary Reasoning view of reasons, since on his account, roughly, one has a normative reason to F only when there is 'a sound deliberative route' from one's motivational set to F-ing (cf. Williams 2001: 91). The aspect that is particularly relevant for our present discussion is that this is a definition (or characterisation) of what Williams calls 'internal reasons' which are, according to him, the only reasons that can have a normative importance for us (the relevant contrast here is with 'external reasons'). And, crucially, Williams introduces the relevant phenomena (i.e. internal reasons) by characterising these as motives. He proposes to paraphrase the relevant reading of '*A* has a reason to *φ*' as '*A* has some *motive* which will be served or furthered by his *φ*-ing' (Williams 1979: 101, emphasis added). Thus, we are warranted to read Williams's remarks in (2) as being about reasons. Crucially, these remarks have to be about normative reasons, since these are, again, the considerations that have to play a role in rendering a project, a belief, an attitude rational. Williams considers two possible (normative) reasons for the project of acquiring the relevant belief (e.g. that one's son is alive), what he calls 'truth-centred' and 'non-truth-centred' motives. These are naturally interpreted as corresponding to evidential normative reasons and pragmatic reasons for the project of acquiring belief (or, let us say, indirect pragmatic or evidential reasons for belief). The bottom line, then, of (our interpretation of) Williams's suggestion here is that while it is incoherent to even conceive of evidential indirect reasons for belief that one's son is alive such that it is essentially constituted by one's desire that one's son is alive, it may be conceived that one has pragmatic indirect reason for the belief that one's son is alive (constituted by the desire in question). But such reasons, while possible, cannot be normative reasons, since they cannot possibly render (even in the indirect sense) the belief that one's son is alive rational (or, alternatively, they cannot render one's project of acquiring the relevant belief rational). It appears that Williams sees this latter judgment as being our pre-theoretical judgment about the desperate father's case. This reading seems appropriate given the following remark from Williams: 'I think that most of us would have a very strong impulse against engaging in a project of this kind however uncomfortable these truths were which we were having to live with' (see quote (2)). Again, a proper unpacking of Williams's remarks seems to amount to the suggestion that only evidentialism can explain our pre-theoretical judgments about cases like the desperate father, and pragmatism has the burden of explaining why we are wrong in our pre-theoretical judgments.

Shah's proposal seems to follow a similar line of reasoning, but it is expressed in terminology closer to our own. According to Shah, we cannot process intelligibly the idea that there might be pragmatic genuinely normative reasons for belief. Again, the point seems to be a point about a possible case and our pre-theoretical reaction to it: the talk of genuine normative reasons to believe that are constituted by pragmatic consider-ations – for example, that believing in the faithfulness of one's partner will be comforting – is misusing the very concept of 'reason to believe'. We have to conclude then that, following this line of thought, pragmatists owe us an extra explanation of what is going on here: since their view is that pragmatic considerations are reasons to believe, they have to conclude that we are wrong in our pre-theoretical judgments that someone like the husband in Shah's case doesn't master the concept of 'reason to believe' and, crucially, they have to explain why unbeknownst to us we are wrong about that.

One might object at this point that moderate pragmatists – that is, pluralists about reasons for belief – actually can account for judgments about these cases and that they owe no extra explanation here (see, for example, Reisner 2008, 2018; McCormick 2014). More specifically, the idea is that moderate pragmatists will maintain that only when one's evidence doesn't favour *p* over not-p – that is, when evidence is equivo-cal/equipotent – one may have a pragmatic reason to believe that *p*. And, crucially, proponents of moderate pragmatism of this sort would insist that the aforementioned cases (1–3) are all cases of non-equivocal evidence. Evidentialists are right, they will insist, that in these cases the reasons are evidential and indeed our pre-theoretical judgments capture just this. But they will also insist that this is not all there is; that there are other cases, equivocal evidence cases, where judgments are different, and pluralism can directly explain the intuitions about both the non-equivocal evidence cases and equivocal evidence cases.

While such a version of moderate pragmatism may appear more prom-ising in this context (compare also to William James 1896 and his suggestions about live options), it is also unclear whether evidentialists would agree that it does fit our pre-theoretical judgments (see later for more theory-driven worries for this pluralism). It's true that key cases from evidentialists are cases of non-equivocal evidence in the sense that in these cases evidence does support p over not-p. But one might also expect that if evidentialists were to consider specifically the cases of equivocal evidence, they, or at least some of them, would insist that our judgments are the same in the cases of equivocal/equipotent evidence.[6] Indeed, this is a plausible expectation, given, for example, Williams's remark that 'a man may want to believe something not caring a damn about the truth of it, but because it is fashionable or comfortable or in accordance with the demands of social conformity to believe that thing' (see quote (2)), where the project of acquiring such a belief is described as 'deeply irrational' (Williams 1973: 149–150). The vague expression of 'not caring a damn about the truth of it' may well be understood in a general sense, where a subject who is not suspending her belief about p in a case of equivocal/equipotent evidence for p falls within the category of 'not caring a damn about the truth of' p. If so, then according to evidentialists (e.g. Williams), the moderate pragmatists' cases of alleged pragmatic reasons in situations of evidential equipoise would also fall within the category of cases where our pre-theoretical judgments qualify the subject's project of acquiring such a belief as deeply irrational. But we will return to the pluralist view later. Let us focus now on three telling passages from the pragmatist camp:

(4) Suppose that, if Joseph were to exercise regularly, it would make him a happier person. Intuitively, this is a normative reason for him to exercise: the fact that his exercising would make him happier counts in favour of him doing so. Now suppose that, if Mary were to believe that God exists, it would make her a happier person. Is this a normative reason for her to believe that God exists? [...] Given the similarities between cases like Joseph's and cases like Mary's, the alethist [that is evidentialists, in present terminology] assumes the dialectical burden in this debate. After all, the very same benefit would be conferred by Joseph's exercising and by Mary's believing that God exists. But the alethist [evidentialist] insists that, while this benefit does generate a normative reason for Joseph to exercise, it does

---

[6] Surprisingly, however, some evidentialists seem to leave such an option open; see, for instance, Shah and Velleman (2005: 534, fn 41): 'We leave it as an open question whether in cases of evidential equipoise – where the evidence equally supports p and not p – applying a nonepistemic norm to break the tie is compatible with adherence to the norm of truth'. This passage appears in the context of discussing their weak internalism about obeying norms of thought in order to explain why only questions pertaining to whether p (e.g. evidential reasons) can play a role in genuine doxastic deliberation.

not generate a normative reason for Mary to believe that God exists. The alethist [evidentialist] thus owes us an account of what the relevant difference is between action and belief, which thereby explains the normative difference between these two cases. Without such an account, we should assume that there is no such difference, and thereby accept pragmatism as the default view. (Leary 2017: 529–530)

(5) [I]magine someone suffering from a potentially fatal illness who has learned that their chance of recovery, although low regardless, is significantly higher if they believe they'll survive (around 20%) than if they don't (around 5%). This, by itself, does not constitute evidence that they will survive. But it does seem to be a good reason for them to believe that they will.

Similarly, someone might know that their athletic performance is likely to be better if they believe they'll do exceptionally well. This, by itself, is not evidence that they *will* do exceptionally well; but it does seem to constitute a good reason for them to believe it. (Rinard 2015: 2010)[7]

(6) This thesis [evidentialism in our terminology] is significantly less attractive than evidentialism [that is, pluralism or modest pragmatism according to our present terminology] since a range of different cases provide support for the idea that we have practical reasons for belief. [...] We plausibly have reasons to think better of our friends than the evidence would suggest (Stroud 2006; Keller 2004; Way and McHugh [McHugh and Way] 2016; Crawford 2019), reasons to have certain beliefs that enhance our 'self-esteem' (Kelly 2003), and reasons to be more optimistic than the evidence suggests about your chances of recovering from some challenging disease (Reisner 2008; Rinard 2015).

There are also cases where we have practical reasons to believe a certain way independently of the balance of evidence. These include believing that everyone is capable of significant moral improvement (Preston-Roedder 2013), and that there is no correlation between IQ and being the member of an oppressing class (Gendler 2011). Some beliefs are morally wrongful or unjust (Basu 2018). In a range of more or less fanciful cases, you can be offered a positive or negative incentive for being in some doxastic state (see, for example, Reisner 2008; Way 2012); Pascalian (Pascal [1670] 1995) or Jamesian (James 1896) reasons to believe that God exists may also fall into this category. [...] But anti-pragmatism is supposed to be necessarily, perhaps even conceptually, true. So any of these possible scenarios will

---

[7] Compare this to an earlier case provided by Andrew Reisner (2008: 18):

Here is another normative reason for belief. Let us say that Jill has a disease from which her chance of recovery is 10%. Let us say, too, that if she believes that she is certain to recover, her chance of getting better will improve to 15%. The fact that doing so would help her get better is a reason for her to believe that she is certain to get better. This is a non-evidential normative reason for belief.[...] The fact that is the reason is not evidence for the truth of the contents of the belief. We may call these reasons pragmatic normative reasons for belief.

yield counterexamples. Anti-pragmatists need to explain all these
cases away. (Maguire and Woods 2020: 211–213)

It's straightforward that pragmatists are suggesting in all these passages
(4)–(6) that their view fits best with our pre-theoretical judgments about
the relevant cases. They see our pre-theoretical judgments there as constituting a prima facie case for pragmatism, indeed as grounds for claiming
that pragmatism is the default view and that actually evidentialists owe us
an extra explanation of what is going on in these cases if we are to take
evidentialism seriously. An interesting observation is how close pragmatist
cases actually come to cases proposed by evidentialists. Consider, for
example, the religious belief case in (4). Belief that God exists would make
Mary happier, according to the description of the case by Leary. She
suggests that it is up to evidentialists to demonstrate that this eudaimonic
consideration is not a normative reason for Mary to believe that God exists
(the comparison with exercise is supposed to help us see the parallel).
Similarly, Rinard in (5) suggests that it does seem that belief in one's
survival contrary to evidence (see also Reisner 2008) and belief in one's
success as an athlete do constitute normative reasons to believe. Again,
Rinard seems to be in the business of putting forward what appear to be
our pre-theoretical judgments about the cases.[8] Maguire and Woods sum
up a number of cases from the literature that seem to speak in favour of
pragmatism – that is, that appear to fit best within the pragmatist framework. Note, however, a complication involving claims about friendship,
faith in humanity, and promise cases. Initially, the authors that introduced
these cases within the literature didn't conceive of them at all as prima facie
cases for pragmatism – actually, quite the contrary. When Sarah Stroud
first introduced considerations about friendship requiring beliefs against
evidence, she was well aware and made it explicit that such beliefs commonly appear to have some irrationality (cf. Stroud 2006). Similarly, when
Marušić (cf. Marušić 2013, cited in a footnote to the passage from Maguire
and Woods reproduced earlier) discusses promises and related statistically
informed cases, he is clear that he is putting forward an argument towards

---

[8] It is curious to note that Kelly actually puts forward a clearly opposite suggestion about what our pre-
theoretical judgments are in cases exactly like the athlete's case. He writes:

> An athlete who has an overwhelming amount of evidence that she is unlikely to do well, and
> bases her belief that she is unlikely to do well on that evidence, would seem to qualify as a
> rational believer – even if her rational belief frustrates, in foreseeable and predictable ways,
> her goal of doing well. (Indeed, in such circumstances her rationality would seem to be part
> of her problem.) (Kelly 2002: 165)

the conclusion that beliefs that seem to go contrary to evidence but are nonetheless necessary for sincere promises and so on are to be seen as rational after all. But his consideration here is based on an elaborated argument. He acknowledges that there is an initial tension that arises once we consider the relevant promise case. But he doesn't seem to be in the business of putting forward a simple prima facie claim that starts from an allegedly common-sense view that beliefs contrary to evidence in such cases are rational. This is, rather, his conclusion. Thus, Maguire and Woods, and also Rinard elsewhere, are mistaken in listing friendship, promises, and similar cases as prima facie cases for pragmatism, at least when they clearly refer to Stroud's and Marušić's versions and treatment of these cases. Now, having this in mind, we can still accord to pragmatists that other cases that they propose are such that they seem to indicate the possibility of pragmatic reasons for belief.

What should we make of this apparent disagreement about which position enjoys the default status and is in line with our pre-theoretical judgments? An important point to note, I think, is that a charitable reading of the debate doesn't allow us to rule out either the evidentialist claim of being in line with pre-theoretical judgments or the pragmatist claim of respecting pre-theoretical judgments and having a good prima facie case. We just don't have grounds for favouring affirmations of one side at the expense of the other on the present grounds. So, let us assume that both sides are sincere when they report that it is plausible, apparent, and so forth, that the relevant cases speak in favour of the possibility or the impossibility of pragmatic reasons for belief.

With this assumption on board, we are left with three theoretical options. First, and most radically, we can just throw the baby out with the bathwater and consider that such a disparity constitutes a defeater against any view within this debate that claims to be in accord with the pre-theoretical judgments. One might think that given that the judgments are in such disarray here, it indicates that our pre-theoretical conception is just too confused to be accounted for. There is no argumentative value in trying to fit our theory with our pre-theoretical judgments in this context, according to this line of thought. Now, this is surely a radical approach, and I think, while it is of course an option, we should regard it as the last resort. For giving up totally on the ambition to at least respect our pre-theoretical commitments might backfire in ways that might lead to a more general scepticism and the generation of theories that are completely out of touch with what commonly matters to us.

The second option is to admit that while both the authors of passages (1)–(3) and the authors of passages (4)–(6) are sincere in their affirmations, and the relevant cases do trigger the pre-theoretical judgments that the authors claim they do, one side here is nonetheless mistaken. That is, some of the pre-theoretical judgments are wrong, and there is a plausible error theory of why we might be led to hold these judgments.

So, for instance, a popular line among pragmatists is to acknowledge that evidential considerations often do appear to be the only possible candidates for the role of normative reasons in favour of believing a proposition, but such pre-theoretical judgments are explained away (i.e. explained without concluding that evidentialism is correct), according to this line of thought, by the fact that it is often practically advantageous for us to believe on the basis of truth-conducive considerations, since it is often advantageous for us to have true beliefs. The following passage illustrates this version of pragmatist error theory:

> I'll acknowledge that, much of the time, when deliberating about what to believe, we focus on evidential considerations. Although this observation may seem to lend some support to Evidentialism, the Pragmatist can point out that, much of the time, it is in our own best interests to believe in accordance with the evidence. [...] So even if Pragmatism is true, it need not be mysterious why we focus on evidential considerations much of the time. (Rinard 2015: 210)

Presumably, then, one might claim that at least some of the evidentialist cases might fit into this sort of error theory (see also Maguire and Woods 2020 for another sophisticated approach that basically treats believing as on a par with an activity of a game that has its own constitutive standards which lack the genuinely authoritative normativity). However, it is not clear whether this error theory really fits the bill with respect to all the cases in (1)–(3), for these seem to be precisely cases where one is supposed to gain something from believing against one's evidence. Hence, it is not clear how the expected utility of believing truth and the expected utility associated with believing against truth-conducive considerations should be balanced in these cases. Alternatively, a proponent of pragmatism may merely assert that the apparently evidentialism-supporting judgments about cases like (1)–(3) are wrong since evidentialism is wrong (a conclusion for which pragmatists have independent argument). On this view, they are just relics of wrongheaded evidentialist thinking. Compare Rinard:

> The objector is correct that Equal Treatment [radical pragmatism in our terminology] has this consequence [that is, that 'there are possible situations in which, according to Equal Treatment, it would be rational to believe contradictions, to violate modus ponens, to believe Moore-paradoxical propositions, etc.'; Rinard 2017: 137]. The appropriate response for a

defender of Equal Treatment, however, is simply to embrace it. The idea that there is anything inherently wrong with believing contradictions is just a symptom of evidentialist thinking. (Rinard 2017: 137)

On the other side of the debate, a popular error theory among evidentialists is an appeal to the idea of there being the 'wrong kind' of reasons for belief. Roughly, some considerations are not reasons to believe that *p*, but rather considerations that speak in favour of getting oneself to believe, or desiring to believing, or undertaking an indirect project of acquiring the belief that *p*. The proposal here is parallel to a well-known proposal by reasons-first theorists with respect to the 'wrong kind' of reasons problem, where a threat is considered to be a reason to get oneself to admire the despicable demon (i.e. the threatener), but not a reason to admire the demon (see Section 1.4). Evidentialists suggest that while considerations, such as the considerations in (4)–(6) and the like, are reasons to get oneself to believe that *p*, they are not reasons to believe that *p*. But, given that getting oneself to believe that *p* is, on the face of it, quite close to believing that *p*, it is not surprising that one might mistake the reasons to do the former for reasons for the latter. Versions of this sort of error theory or, at any rate, very similar thoughts may be found in Parfit (2011), Engel (2019, 2020a), and Hieronymi (2005), among others.

I don't intend to assess here the merits and pitfalls of the error theories introduced earlier. My objective lies elsewhere. What I want to observe at this point is that there is a third option that we may take with respect to the apparent disagreement about pre-theoretical judgments. The third option is to recognise that both those who claim that cases (1)–(3) are best explained by the impossibility of pragmatic reasons to believe and those who claim that cases (4)–(6) are best explained by the possibility of pragmatic reasons to believe are right. Of course, the trick for holding such a position, indeed for holding the view that pre-theoretical judgments both support and don't support the possibility of pragmatic reasons for belief, consistently is that 'pragmatic reasons for belief/to believe' has two possible readings. There are two sorts of normative reasons, and in one sense, there can be pragmatic reasons to believe, but in another there cannot. This option is what I elaborate in Section 6.3. Let me conclude the present section by two final remarks.

First, it should be noted that the third option is optimal, given our initial agreement on what should constitute a key criterion for overcoming the deadlock within this debate. Recall that we agreed earlier that a theory that respects most of the pre-theoretical judgments should be preferred, *ceteris paribus*, to its competitors. That is, a view that doesn't need to explain away our common intuitions about the cases (e.g. (1)–(6)) has an advantage over views that need to resort to error theories.

The second point is that the proposal to be elaborated in Section 6.3 is, of course, not the only possible way to try to respect all our pre-theoretical judgments. In particular, as observed earlier, some seem to think that versions of moderate pragmatism or pluralism with respect to reasons for belief can do just that (cf. Reisner 2008, 2018). On such a view, roughly, there are two sorts of normative reasons to believe that p. One sort is evidential or truth-conducive – considerations that constitute evidence in favour of p. Another sort is pragmatic – considerations that make believing p somehow practically, eudaimonically, or morally advantageous. Crucially, according to this view, pragmatic reasons kick in only in contexts where evidential reasons don't favour believing over disbelieving p, and rather recommend suspension of judgment.

With respect to this option, recall from the aforementioned that we may have some doubts about whether such an approach can really vindicate evidentialist intuitions. Evidentialists may well claim that going for anything else than suspension of judgment in cases of equipotent evidence is still irrational on such a view, given the rationality-normative reasons connection. They may claim that our pre-theoretical judgments indicate that no pragmatic consideration can constitute genuine normative reasons to believe even in evidential equipoise cases (recall Williams's complaint about reasoners who don't respect truth). But even if we put this worry aside, two further issues are looming in. First, such an account faces the challenge of explaining how exactly we are supposed to combine or weight pragmatic normative reasons against evidential normative reasons. It is a fundamental assumption of the pluralist proposal that they can and indeed have to be weighted against each other. I am not claiming here that no story can be provided about such weighing (see Reisner 2008 and Steglich-Petersen and Skipper 2020 for recent attempts to account for combinations). I am noting merely that it is a challenge and not everyone is convinced that this sort of project can be completed successfully (cf. Berker 2018, who provides arguments for doubts and maintains that pragmatic and evidential considerations are 'like water and oil' and don't really mix). The account that I am going to present avoids this issue altogether, since the two sorts of reasons I am going to introduce are not supposed to combine. Second, this sort of view also has the challenge of explaining why these two sorts of reasons are indeed two sorts of the same thing and what exactly their common factor is. Again, I am not claiming that no successful way of meeting this challenge can be provided, but merely that it constitutes a challenge that asks for a more substantive explanation of why there are *two* sorts of reasons for beliefs. Merely postulating that there are two sorts of reasons is ad hoc. One needs to provide an explanatory story of why there are two sorts of reasons. After all, postulating more entities (or relations) of something unified calls for an extra explanation. We should not, of course, postulate the existence of entities or relations beyond necessity. Every new distinction we make had better be grounded in independently motivated considerations. The view that I am about to elaborate avoids this challenge, since it has an independent substantial back-story about why there are different sorts of normative reasons.

Nonetheless, at the end of the day, I don't intend here to try to prove that this sort of pluralism is definitely wrong. My purpose rather is to put on the table a new option, a new proposal that can vindicate independent theoretical motivation and provide a substantive account of why there are two fundamentally different sorts of reasons that correspond to what we might call 'evidentialist' and 'pragmatist' reasons within this debate. Let us presently turn to considering this new proposal in further detail.

6.3 Explaining Pragmatic Reasons for Belief: Insight from the Erotetic View

The aim of this section is to develop and defend a new positive proposal with respect to the dispute over the possibility of pragmatic reasons for belief. This proposal applies the Erotetic view of reasons to explore the sense in which pragmatic reasons for beliefs are possible and the sense in which they are not possible. Let us elaborate this in more detail.

On the Erotetic view of reasons, developed in Chapter 5, a normative reason to F just is, roughly, an (appropriate) answer to the normative 'Why F?' question on one of its two possible readings. The two readings here are an explanation-requiring reading and an argument/reasoning-requiring reading. More precisely, when asked 'Why F?', one might be prompted to provide an explanation of why one ought to F, or alternatively one might be prompted to provide an argument/a piece of reasoning for the conclusion that one ought to F. These two readings of the normative question 'Why F?' give rise to two sorts of possible normative reasons to F, namely normative reasons as (partial) explanations of why one ought to F and normative reasons as premises of arguments/patterns of reasoning towards the conclusion that one ought to F (alternatively, fitting premises in fittingness-preserving arguments/patterns of reasoning concluding in

F-ing). The two sorts of reasons are distinct and cannot be reduced one to another. We know already from our preceding discussion that some considerations can only be reasons of one of these sorts. In particular, some considerations can constitute only explanation-providing answers to 'Why F?' questions. The example that we presented to illustrate this feature was the case already discussed in the context of objections to the Reasoning view of reasons (see Chapter 2). Namely, it was the case involving Moore-paradoxical considerations of the sort 'the building is on fire but S doesn't know that the building is on fire' in situations where S is unaware of the fire in the building where she finds herself. Plausibly, such considerations still speak in favour of S's checking the state of the building, verifying whether she is safe, and so on. The fact that she is ignorant of the fire does not matter, in a sense. Assuming that pre-theoretical judgments about a consideration speaking in favour of F-ing does indicate that the consideration in question is a normative reason, we can conclude that such Moore-paradoxical considerations are indeed normative reasons in the relevant contexts. Crucially, however, there is no way for the subject to use appropriately Moore-paradoxical considerations speaking in favour of F-ing in her reasoning or arguing towards the conclusion that she ought to F. After all, she can neither know nor properly believe such considerations. Thus, the Moore-paradoxical considerations cannot be normative reasons pertaining to reasoning; that is, they cannot be normative reasoning reasons – reasons in the sense of being appropriate answers to the 'Why F?' question in its argument/reasoning-requiring sense.

The proposal that I would like to put forward with respect to the possibility of pragmatic reasons to believe, then, is that we can respect pre-theoretical judgments of all sides and need not explain away some of these by appeal to more or less sophisticated error theories, by simply generalising the lessons from the Erotetic view's treatment of the Moore-paradoxical considerations. More specifically, we can deploy the distinction between normative reasoning reasons and normative explanatory reasons to the case of pragmatic considerations that, in a sense, sometimes seem to speak in favour of believing a proposition and, in a sense, don't seem to speak in favour of believing a proposition. In short, pragmatic considerations are another example of considerations that can be normative reasons just in one sense, but not in the other sense predicted by the Erotetic view. The thought is that pragmatic considerations, similarly to Moore-paradoxical considerations, cannot be normative reasoning reasons, but may still constitute normative explanatory reasons, as considerations that partly explain why one ought to believe that such and such is the case.

On the present proposal, pragmatic considerations cannot be appropriate answers to the argument/reasoning-requiring reading of the 'Why believe p?' question. Thus, they cannot be normative reasoning reasons to believe. And there is truth in evidentialism; this is the insight we can take from evidentialists. The problem with their view, though, is that they don't distinguish between these two sorts of normative reasons – normative reasoning and normative explanatory reasons. Thus, strictly speaking, their proposal is wrong. Evidentialism can only be the right theory for normative reasoning reasons. Note also that, interestingly, some of the paradigmatic proponents of evidentialism also seem to endorse the Reasoning view of reasons (cf. Williams 1989, and elsewhere, arguably, Hieronymi 2005). This is not surprising at all. If anything, this only makes our proposal even more plausible. For if your theory of normative reasons in general defines reasons as premises in good patterns of reasoning/arguments, then, of course, you will also reject the possibility of pragmatic normative reasons for belief. Pragmatic considerations are just the wrong kind of inputs for arguments/patterns of reasoning for believing that p. (This last observation also perfectly fits the observation that the main focus of evidentialist arguments is on the role of reasons in doxastic deliberation or reasoning towards belief.) Our view predicts that, of course, if you focus on one sort of normative reasons at the expense of the other, then some of the considerations that one might want to qualify as reasons, in a sense, will not come out as reasons on your view. We observed this with Moore-paradoxical considerations that presented a genuine worry for the Reasoning view, and we see it again with respect to pragmatic considerations that are excluded from the category of possible reasons for belief according to the Reasoning view of reasons. Thus, the present view vindicates a reinterpreted evidentialist insight: some considerations can never be normative reasons to believe, in a sense – namely, pragmatic considerations can never constitute normative reasoning reasons.

But, of course, there is another sort of normative reasons, normative explanatory reasons. And nothing prevents some pragmatic considerations from being normative reasons to believe in this sense. It is entirely conceivable that, similarly to the case of Moore-paradoxical considerations, some pragmatic considerations may in some contexts constitute appropriate answers to the explanation-requiring reading of the 'Why believe p?' normative question. That not believing p would cause tragic consequences may speak in favour of believing p. It might well be the case that in such a situation where not believing that p brings about tragic consequences, you ought (in a sense) to believe that p. That not believing brings about tragic consequences, then, explains why you ought to believe. In this sense, then, these purely pragmatic considerations about the tragic consequences of not believing p constitute normative reasons for you to believe that p. Of course, pragmatists, or at least radical pragmatists, are wrong that all normative reasons are ultimately pragmatic considerations. But the present view also takes on board their insight (or at least the insight of a reinterpreted version of pragmatism) that sometimes pragmatic considerations matter for belief. They matter, on the specification of the present view, only when (and because) they explain why one ought to believe the relevant proposition. They may constitute only one sort of reasons to believe in some situations. Note also that, interestingly, some contemporary pragmatists also appear to endorse the Explanation view of reasons in general (see Maguire 2016 in particular; Reisner also seems to be favourable towards the Explanation view but stops short of endorsing the view that reasons can be analysed, by an appeal to oughts in particular; cf. Reisner 2015: 191, fn 10). Again, this is predictable on our view. For as we saw earlier, the major motivation for evidentialism seems to come from their focus on the role of reasons for belief in doxastic deliberation, reasoning, but if from the outset you don't think that there is any essential or definitional connection between reasons in general and reasoning, then you will be less moved by the considerations that evidentialists accumulate in favour of their view. In a sense, both are right: the connection to reasoning is crucial for evidential reasons, but the connection to explanation of oughts is crucial for another sort of considerations, considerations that may well be pragmatic and constitute explanatory reasons for belief. Thus, the present view also vindicates a (reinterpreted) pragmatist insight: pragmatic considerations may sometimes constitute normative reasons to believe of a specific sort – namely, they may constitute normative explanatory reasons.

Note also that the Erotetic view contains resources for explaining why both evidentialists and pragmatists are wrong. As we saw in Chapter 5, it is relatively easy to overlook the existence of two readings of the general normative 'Why F?' question by focusing only on one of these. Sometimes we have to pay attention to discern whether one is in the business of arguing/reasoning or in the business of explanation. It is not that rare to confuse the two activities. Thus, it is not that difficult to be led to focus only on one of the readings of the 'Why believe that p?' question and relatedly on only one of the two possible sorts of answers to this question (which, of course, need not involve any conscious activity of directing one's mind to one reading of the normative question only), especially if one starts with an assumption that all normative reasons are premises in good reasoning or, alternatively, are parts of a deontic or axiological explanation. Focusing on explanatory reasons to believe at the expense of reasoning reasons, then, might easily lead one to endorse pragmatism. Focusing on reasoning reasons exclusively might easily lead one to endorse evidentialism.

Let me conclude this section by rapidly reviewing the key examples that we've introduced in Section 6.2 and that were proposed as constituting prima facie cases for evidentialism and pragmatism accordingly. Consider the example in the quote (1) from Thomas Kelly where he imagines the case of an agnostic who realises at time t1 that the expected utility of believing in the existence of God at that time is very high and thus undertakes the project of becoming a believer, and at time t2, she effectively believes that God exists, but the expected utility changes unexpectedly: it is no longer advantageous to be a believer. Kelly observes that the believer would not abandon her belief on the basis of the change in expected utility. We call this observation a pre-theoretical judgment about the case. Indeed, it seems to be a common-sense judgment. According to Kelly (2002: 176), this observation 'indicates that the belief is not based on considerations of utility'. As we saw in detail earlier, what Kelly means by this is that pragmatic considerations (e.g. considerations of utility) cannot be normative reasons to believe or to disbelieve, given that the job of normative reasons is to rationalise a belief (make it rational) by being the (appropriate) basis of belief (i.e. the considerations on which a belief is appropriately based via the basing relation). The conclusion that Kelly draws is that only evidential considerations can be reasons to believe, since only these can be (appropriate) bases and thus rationalise belief. The Erotetic view can vindicate the pre-theoretical judgment that Kelly puts forward here without endorsing the conclusion that only evidential considerations can be reasons for belief. The trick is to restrict the role of rationalising only to normative reasoning reasons to believe or rather to some proper subset of these. With this restriction in place, we can clearly and wholeheartedly agree with the observation that indeed the believer will not disbelieve in the existence of God on the basis of pragmatic considerations. We need no error theory here. But this doesn't indicate that there are no pragmatic reasons in this case for the subject to disbelieve, since this only indicates that there cannot be pragmatic considerations that rationalise a belief by being its basis. One might think that there might be pragmatic reasons to disbelieve in this case that are not bases in Kelly's sense. Nothing in the example rules this out. Moreover, this proposal receives independent support if we assume that the rationality of a doxastic state is tied more closely to the way an agent arrives at it, through, say, reasoning, rather than to an explanation of why an agent ought to be in such a state. For, arguably, explanation of why one ought to be in a state, but not one's reasoning towards that state, can be independent – that is, unconnected to one's perspective. Recall the discussion of the Monty Hall case in Chapter 1. An alternative way of seeing the case (not necessarily a way that conflicts with our initial assessment, though) is that there is an explanation of why one ought to switch in the Monty Hall situation. This explanation constitutes a reason in the explanation sense of normative reasons, to switch, even though it may not be rational from the subject's own perspective to switch; one just cannot reason towards that conclusion given what one believes and disbelieves. Thus, tying rationality to reasoning rather than to explanation of deontic facts may well be independently motivated. If so, we can see, then, that restricting the observation in the case (1) about the possible bases of a doxastic state to reasoning reasons only gives us room to admit the possibility of pragmatic reasons to believe, in the sense of normative explanatory reasons, while still accepting straightforwardly the pre-theoretical judgment that the believer will not disbelieve in this case on the basis of pragmatic considerations. On the present proposal, no pragmatic considerations can constitute a rationalising basis for a doxastic state – that is, a normative reasoning reason to believe, disbelieve, or suspend judgment.

Similarly, the Erotetic view can easily account for the cases from passages (2) and (3). Again, the move is the same; the Erotetic view can explain why we would find the desperate father's belief that his son is alive when he has strong evidence to the contrary but also has pragmatic considerations (e.g. it would make him feel less miserable) that seem to speak in favour of his belief in his son being alive. That is, we assume the content of our pre-theoretical judgment of the case. The explanation is that rationality is tied to how one arrives at a belief (i.e. basing of belief), but pragmatic considerations can never be the appropriate inputs for reasoning towards belief (they cannot be reconstructed as premises of a valid argument or pattern of reasoning towards an appropriate belief). Thus, arriving at a belief indirectly from pragmatic considerations alone can never make the belief rational. All this can be respected by the Erotetic view. But it also entails that this doesn't yet mean that there are no pragmatic reasons for belief – there might be if we understand them as restricted to explanations of why the father should/ought to, in a sense, believe that his son is alive. (Note that if everyone agrees that in this case there is no sense in which the father ought to believe that the son is alive, the present view predicts that indeed there are no reasons, not even normative explanatory reasons, to believe that the son is alive, which I think is another advantage of the view, since it gives us flexibility for different cases.) If there is a sense in which the father ought to believe that his son is alive, then the present view can clearly explain why the pragmatic considerations do speak in favour of the father's belief in his son being alive; these are normative explanatory reasons. Perhaps these are normative explanatory reasons in an objective or overall sense, given that his grief is so severe and produces so much suffering that, in a sense, he ought to maintain the belief that his son is alive. In the case discussed by Shah (in (3)), of a husband's belief that his wife is unfaithful, the explanation is the same. The present view accommodates the pre-theoretical judgment that it is unintelligible to think that the pragmatic considerations constitute a reason for the husband to believe that his wife is not unfaithful if we restrict 'reasons' to the normative reasoning reasons here. This, again, doesn't entail that these pragmatic or eudaimonic considerations cannot be normative explanatory reasons for why the husband ought to/should, in a sense, believe that his partner is faithful.

With respect to the cases from pragmatists, the explanation goes the other way but is essentially the same. Consider Leary's take on religious belief in passage (4). She seems to suggest that it is pre-theoretically plausible to see the eudaimonic considerations about the benefits of belief in God as a normative reason to believe in God, just as eudaimonic considerations about physical exercise constitute normative reasons to do physical exercise (e.g. that exercising would make one happier is clearly a reason to exercise). The Erotetic view can accommodate this intuition without endorsing pragmatism and without appealing to an error theory about pre-theoretical judgments here. If it's true that one should/ought to be happy (perhaps other things being equal), and that believing that God exists would make one happy, then that the fact that believing that God exists would make one happy is a (partial) explanation of why one ought to believe that God exists. This is, then, in a normative explanatory sense, that the eudaimonic considerations can be normative reasons for one to believe that God exists. This is not to say that there may be normative reasoning reasons of the eudaimonic variety. Indeed, admitting that eudaimonic considerations can be normative explanatory reasons for why one ought to believe something doesn't entail that all reasons to believe are ultimately pragmatic, neither that the thesis according to which no pragmatic consideration can constitute a normative reasoning reason is false.

The example of believing that one will survive (in (5)) in a situation where that belief is not supported by evidence but would nevertheless slightly raise the chances of survival can be explained without accepting pragmatism. This consideration is a reason to believe that one will survive in the sense that it partly explains why one ought to believe that one will survive – one will thereby increase one's chances of survival. This need not be a normative reasoning reason for one to believe that one will survive. And the fact that an athlete's belief that they will succeed increases the chances of success may also explain why the athlete ought to, in a sense, believe that they will succeed and thus be a normative explanatory reason without being a normative reasoning reason for the athlete to believe. The cases presented in (6) undergo the same treatment. Indeed, in all cases where one claims to have an intuition that a pragmatic consideration is a normative reason to believe some proposition, the Erotetic view can respect that intuition provided that it is a case in which the subject ought to/should believe the proposition in question and the relevant pragmatic considerations partially explain why the subject ought to/should believe it. All the cases that we have seen appear to fall into this category. The Erotetic view can explain the pragmatist intuitions without giving up evidentialist insight. There are two sorts of normative reasons to believe corresponding to an explanation of a normative fact about belief and to a premise in a reasoning/argument towards the relevant belief correspondingly. All the pre-theoretic judgments about the possibility or not of pragmatic reasons to believe seem to correspond to one or the other of these two categories of normative reasons. The mistake is to assume that there is only one category of normative reasons.

Thus, application of the Erotetic view of reasons to the question of the possibility of pragmatic reasons for belief enables us to vindicate all the pre-theoretical judgments. It has, hence, an important advantage over alternative treatments of the question. It appears that it may well constitute a constructive way to overcome the present deadlock within this debate. This theoretical fruitfulness, in turn, constitutes another argument in favour of the Erotetic view of reasons.

6.4   Replying to Potential Worries

The aim of the present section is to provide replies to some potential worries about our proposal with respect to the possibility of pragmatic reasons for belief. In providing these replies, we are also further elaborating some surprising aspects of the Erotetic view as applied to reasons for doxastic states.

My hope is that the present proposal will be seen as a serious contender for overcoming the deadlock in the debate about pragmatic reasons for belief, but, of course, we may reasonably anticipate that some proponents of evidentialism and of pragmatism will question some aspects of the view. In what follows, I consider five potential objections in particular.

First, pragmatists might actually question the assumption that we cannot believe on the basis of pragmatic reasons. In fact, some of the new pragmatists have suggested exactly this in response to older evidentialist arguments from Kelly, Shah, and Velleman, among others (cf. McCormick 2014; see also Reisner 2018). If they are right, then one might doubt whether normative reasoning reasons to believe cannot be themselves constituted by pragmatic considerations. That is, a pragmatist might accept our fundamental distinction between normative reasoning and normative explanatory reasons but question the claim that normative reasoning reasons to believe cannot be pragmatic considerations.

The first thing that I would like to note with respect to this potential worry is that, of course, strictly speaking, the Erotetic view can be made compatible with pragmatism – that is, the core claim about two sorts of reasons at any rate. However, this is not the option taken up here. On the current view, pragmatic considerations indeed cannot constitute (appropriate) bases that could be normative reasoning reasons for belief. As noted in Section 6.3, one line of thought here is that the rationality of a belief seems to be connected to the ways in which a given subject comes to hold that belief. You might, well, possess the best possible evidence in favour of a claim, but if your belief is formed by a mere hunch or via a motivated reasoning, your belief doesn't qualify as rational in the standard sense of rationality. Focusing on beliefs arrived at via reasoning or doxastic deliberation, the evidentialist suggestion that I am taking on board here is that only truth-conducive considerations can play an appropriate role in such reasoning towards beliefs. And only considerations that play an appropriate role in reasoning can be properly understood as bases of that belief. Recall also that evidentialism as it is understood in the present discussion in no way is committed to the claim that all rational beliefs are based on evidence – that is, on truth-conducive considerations (including its own content or not). Maybe there are beliefs that are not arrived at through reasoning (e.g. arguably, perceptual beliefs); evidentialism, in our sense, is not the stricter form of evidentialism that would entail that beliefs not based on independent evidence can be justified. In no way can pragmatism present the fact that possibly some beliefs are not based on evidence as an argument against our version of evidentialism (even if some pragmatists seem to appeal to this line of thought against the versions of evidentialism they are targeting). These, possibly rational, 'groundless' beliefs are, I would say, by definition not based on pragmatic considerations, since they are based on no considerations at all and hence don't constitute an argument for pragmatism. Thus, the debate about the bases has to focus on beliefs arrived at through reasoning as being based on truth-conducive considerations.

Ultimately, the motivation for excluding non-truth-conducive considerations from possibly playing an appropriate role in reasoning towards belief, as I see it, comes from the idea that good patterns of reasoning have to parallel good/sound arguments. That the fact that God exists will bring someone happiness doesn't seem to be the right kind of consideration to plug into an argument in favour of the existence of God. That the chances that a patient survives rises from 10 per cent to 15 per cent doesn't seem to constitute an appropriate input, *ceteris paribus*, into a sound argument towards the conclusion that the patient will survive (cf. Reisner 2008: 18). The examples can be multiplied. If this line of thought is on the right track, then it can explain why pragmatic considerations cannot be normative reasoning reasons to believe. They cannot be appropriately plugged into an appropriate doxastic deliberation and hence cannot be bases that would rationalise the relevant belief. This conclusion is vindicated by a plausible reading of the main claims of the Erotetic view. According to the Erotetic view, normative reasoning reasons are *appropriate* answers to the reasoning/argument-requiring reading of the 'Why F?' question. Assuming that only truth-conducive considerations can constitute appropriate answers of this sort applied to the case of belief leads to the conclusion that only truth-conducive considerations may constitute normative reasoning reasons for belief. Thus, I think that, even if the core commitments of the Erotetic view don't entail that, strictly speaking, pragmatism is false, a plausible reading of it does, and it does so on what appear to be independently plausible grounds, while also vindicating some of the key insights from broad pragmatism.

Could a pragmatist object to my argument by insisting that I endorse a too narrow view of what good reasoning is? The idea would be that good patterns of doxastic deliberation need not necessarily follow a premise–conclusion pattern but could be similar, say, to a mere list of pros and cons. Crucially, such lists would be similar to, if not a kind of, practical reasoning towards (intention to) adopting a belief. If so, practical considerations could figure in such lists and be part of appropriate inputs in doxastic deliberation (see McCormick 2014, 2019, for an argument along these lines).[9]

In reply to this further suggestion, I would say, first, that I am not entirely sure why such mechanisms would count as doxastic deliberation, as opposed to alternative belief acquisitions (e.g. groundless beliefs). And, second, I would like to insist that good patterns of theoretical reasoning – that is, of doxastic deliberation – should be connected to arguments for a hypothesis; whereas practical deliberation is connected to patterns of reasoning leading ultimately to intention/action. And it is not clear how inputs into a practical list of pros and cons for intending/undertaking the effort to get into the state of believing could be parts of the argument for the relevant hypothesis, corresponding to the content of the relevant conclusion-belief. In Logins (2021), I argue, on a similar basis, that one worry with pragmatism is that it seems to lead to the conclusion that practical incentives (e.g. bribes) could constitute good arguments for, say, a philosophical theory, a conclusion that clashes with our very understanding of how philosophy should be done (and is arguably self-undermining for pragmatists who would accept that a bribe for believing that pragmatism is mistaken can be a good argument). See also Way (2016) for a similar argument.

More generally, there is an important question we must ask when thinking about good patterns of reasoning. The question to ask is: what's the point of reasoning? As McHugh and Way (2016: 588) have convincingly argued, it is reasonable to think that the point of reasoning is to get things right and arrive at fitting responses. We value good reasoning since it is a way of arriving at true beliefs or knowledge, appropriate intentions, appropriate regret, admiration, and so on, assuming we also begin the reasoning from good, appropriate premise-responses. This kind of general picture provides an additional motivation for the idea that only truth-conducive considerations could play a role in doxastic reasoning.

The second worry might come from the evidentialist camp. Some evidentialists might object that contrary to what the present proposal admits, pragmatic considerations cannot be normative reasons of any sort. Be they explanatory or reasoning, pragmatic considerations just don't have any normative force to count as normative reasons to believe, according to

---

[9] Thanks to Sebastian Schmidt for making me aware of the need to consider this further line of objection to my proposal.

this line of objection. One way to see the worry is that the very notion of normative reasons is tied to normative force, a force that a believer who believes according to her evidence respects. But it is not clear in what sense pragmatic considerations, even if they are restricted only to being possible normative explanatory reasons, could have any normative force with respect to someone who believes. At this point, one might object that either there are no normative explanatory reasons with respect to belief in general or that there are no normative explanatory reasons of the pragmatic variety, for there is no normative force attached to pragmatic consider- ations with respect to beliefs. The normativity of reasons to believe is, on this picture, essentially attached to the rationality of belief, which in turn depends on how one reasons towards believing on the appropriate bases, bases that can only be constituted by truth-conducive considerations. A relative worry or perhaps a way to develop the general worry further is to stress that the job of normative reasons to believe is to provide material for the assessment of beliefs. But pragmatic considerations can never ground the assessment of a doxastic state. It's not the right sort of thing to ground the assessment of states of belief, disbelief, or suspension.[10]

To this worry, I would like to reply by putting forward an inference to the best explanation. Here I don't have a knock-down argument to show that strict evidentialism cannot be right. Yet I think my proposal provides the simplest overall view about the relevant phenomena. Here is my reasoning. As we have already seen in the case of Moore-paradoxical considerations, one might be tempted to exclude these (and other similar considerations which cannot constitute an appropriate basis for our rea- soning) from counting as normative reasons of any sort, especially if one is attracted to a sort of theory of normative reasons that ties normative reasons to good patterns of reasoning. However, the problem there was that if one excludes Moore-paradoxical considerations from the category of normative reasons, one still has to explain why these considerations do seem to speak in favour of the relevant F-ings. In other terms, one is left with the burden of providing a plausible and independently well- motivated error theory about our pre-theoretical judgments that would explain why we are wrong. This is not an easy task. I am not saying that it cannot be done satisfactorily; it is rather that it will necessarily involve complicating the overall picture, arguably, beyond necessity. One can, for instance, invoke the possibility of a distinct normative category that would correspond to Moore-paradoxical considerations that seem to speak in

---

[10] I would like to thank Pascal Engel for making me aware of this line of objection to my proposal.

favour of some F-ing but that fall short of counting as normative reasons. The burden, then, is to explain in a non-ad hoc way why then there is such a distinct normative category at all; what the common normative element is between these 'merely speaking in favour of F-ing' considerations (e.g. Moore-paradoxical considerations) and genuine normative reasons; and, finally, what the substantive difference is between these categories. My positive proposal was that an alternative approach that admits that Moore-paradoxical considerations are genuine normative reasons is clearly simpler. We should not postulate normative entities and categories beyond necessity. Thus, the suggestion, an inference to the best explanation indeed, was that a view that treats Moore-paradoxical considerations as reasons is preferable. The Erotetic view treats these as genuine normative reasons, more specifically as reasons of the normative explanatory sort. Now, this detour concerning Moore-paradoxical considerations is only supposed to suggest that something similar is also happening in the case of pragmatic considerations to believe. Of course, an evidentialist can dig in his heels and maintain that normative explanatory reasons, in our sense, are not really normative reasons or, at any rate, that normative explanatory reasons of the pragmatic variety are not genuine normative reasons. But then this evidentialist owes us an independently warranted story about why it still appears that in certain situations specifically pragmatic considerations seem to speak in favour of specifically believing the relevant propositions (and not speaking in favour of merely desiring to believe, or trying to get oneself to believe, or undertaking an indirect strategy to get oneself to believe, and so on). Or one has to explain in a non-ad hoc manner why speaking in favour of believing that p is different from being a normative reason to believe that p. Again, I am not suggesting that there are no ways to come up with something like an appealing story of why this happens. The problem is that every possible way of doing it will involve complicating the overall picture by postulating distinctions and categories that don't need to be introduced on competing views. Indeed, the reasoning here, again, is based on an inference to the best explanation. The present proposal offers a simpler overall picture that doesn't need to appeal to error theories and look for independent motivation of further distinctions and categories (e.g. some non-normative category for pragmatic considerations that seem to speak in favour of believing some propositions). Of course, it is not a knock-down argument against strict evidentialists. But I think it puts pressure on the thought that pragmatic considerations can never be genuinely normative reasons, in a sense.

Another worry that one might raise against the present proposal is a version of a standard objection to any pluralist/contextualist account within the normative domain. This worry concerns the view's prospects for dealing with situations where the two reasons – that is, normative reasoning reasons and normative explanatory reasons – appear to conflict; that is, when they speak in favour of incompatible doxastic states. More specifically, the problem is not such tension per se but that the view should provide a credible story of how to combine the two reasons of different sorts – that is, of how to deal with the conflict. But on the face of it, the Erotetic view doesn't provide any instructions on how to combine reasons of these two distinct sorts. In other terms, if both of these reasons are genuinely of the same sort, one might expect that they have to be commensurable and should be available to be 'weighed' in some overall assessment, say, a sufficient overall reason to believe (or overall ought to believe) that depends on/is grounded in the combined sum of all the normative reasons that one has for and against believing in the relevant situation. However, it is not at all clear how one might combine normative explanatory and normative reasoning reasons. They are, to use Selim Berker's expression again, like 'oil and water'; they just don't combine. This worry is also parallel to the objection to moderate pragmatist accounts (refer to our earlier discussion). See Berker (2018) for a thorough and complete discussion of this problem for pragmatist accounts. So, applying this combinatory problem to the Erotetic view's treatment of the debate on the possibility of pragmatic reasons, one can ask: granted, that one will be practically/eudaimonically/and so forth better off if one believes that p (e.g., say, that one will survive) is a consideration that speaks in favour (in a sense) of believing that one will survive, and that one's evidence indicates that one will not survive speaks in favour (in a sense) of disbelieving that one will survive, but what *should* one believe at the end of the day? It still seems meaningful to ask: *what is the doxastic attitude that one has to have* tout court? It makes sense to think that there is a simple, plain question that we can ask about how one is supposed to decide the matter about believing or not that p. But, then, if this is the case, when one is trying to figure out this plain 'what should the subject believe at the end of the day?' question *sans phrase*, which considerations 'weigh' more, reasoning reasons or explanatory reasons, or do they perhaps have the same 'weight'? One might worry that the Erotetic view cannot explain how to measure these two sorts of reasons against each other and, indeed, how to manage situations of conflict between them in view of answering the plain *what should the agent believe* question *sans phrase*.

In reply to this worry, I would like to observe, first of all, that contexts in which one might reasonably ask 'what should the subject/I believe?' *sans phrase* are precisely the contexts where one *doesn't know* that one should/ ought to believe that p (or not-p, or suspend judgment, for that matter). These are (genuine) inquiry contexts, contexts where one seeks to learn what is the right doxastic attitude for one to have. The second thing to note is that, given the specifics of our distinction between reasoning and explanatory reasons, it should also be clear that in such (genuine) inquiry contexts, there can only be normative reasoning reasons for one to believe/ disbelieve/suspend judgment about p. For in such contexts, where it is not known (i.e. one doesn't know it) that one ought to believe/disbelieve/ suspend judgment about p, there cannot be explanatory reasons why one ought to believe/disbelieve/suspend judgment about p. The only consid-erations that can be part of an appropriate answer to the argument/ reasoning-requiring reading of 'Why believe/disbelieve/suspend judgment about p?' question can function as normative reasons in such contexts. Thus, the answer to the aforementioned worry is that, of course, it can be meaningful to ask the question 'What should the subject believe?' *sans phrase*, but only in contexts where it is not known that one ought to believe that p (or ought to disbelieve p or suspend judgment). But, one might object, how about the claim that the Erotetic view can vindicate pragmatist intuitions that in some cases pragmatic considerations seem to constitute normative reasons to believe (or disbelieve or suspend judg-ment)? If there are no normative explanatory reasons in contexts where it is reasonable for us to ask 'What should the subject believe?' *sans phrase*, and pragmatic considerations are identified with normative explanatory rea-sons, then how could the Erotetic view plausibly vindicate the pragmatist intuitions that pragmatic considerations (e.g. the survival case) can consti-tute genuine normative reasons in favour of believing in such cases? The key here is to note that observers of the case, say, we who discuss it, may well be in a context where it is known that the subject ought to believe that p (e.g. that she will survive) even if the observers also know that the subject's evidence speaks against p. We may well be in a context where there are normative explanatory reasons for the subject to believe that p. The pragmatist intuition is vindicated in this context. But, again, in these contexts, it doesn't make sense to ask the plain 'What should the subject believe?' question *sans phrase*. In these contexts, there are no normative reasoning reasons for the subject to believe that p since it is known what the subject ought to do. In sum, this line of reply to the worry endorses the claim that indeed normative reasoning and normative explanatory reasons are like 'oil and water'; they never mix, hence there is no genuine conflict. Crucially, this move is theoretically motivated by the existence of two mutually exclusive readings of 'Why F?' normative questions, the two readings that give rise to two distinct sorts of reasons – explanation providing and argument/input in reasoning providing sorts. But how about someone who does seem to experience the conflict in the relevant sort of case? The conflict may well appear real in such cases. Consider the agent in the survival case – she knows that believing that she will survive can boost her chances of survival a bit, but she also definitely knows (given her evidence) that even with such a boost her chances of survival are meagre. The agent in such a situation may well feel the inner conflict between the boost-in-chance considerations, speaking in favour of believing that she will survive and the evidential considerations speaking against believing that she will survive. Do we really want to say that she switches between inquiry/explanation contexts seamlessly and perhaps without noticing it as she changes the focus from one to the other of these two considerations? Surely, we sometimes do pass from the inquiry context to the explanation context and back, but arguably not in such a smooth and seamless way. I would like to suggest that the appearance of a conflict arises from elsewhere in such cases. Let's assume the context in which the subject of the survival is in the context of an inquiry. She really seeks to know what she should believe. Strictly speaking, there are for her only normative reasoning reasons (with respect to forming a doxastic state about whether she will survive). However, she is also aware that it *might* very well be the case that she ought to believe that she will survive. In other terms, she may realise that the possibility that she ought to believe that she will survive is a very real one. And realising this, she may also realise that the fact that believing that she will survive boosts somewhat the chances of her survival would in such a case explain why she ought to believe that she will survive. She is thus aware that this consideration is a potential explanation of the potential deontic fact that she ought to believe in her survival. But, arguably, she also realises that such a consideration is contrary to the reasons she presently has with respect to believing that *p*. The tentative suggestion here, then, is that the salient possibility for her that it might well be the case that she ought to believe in her survival *because* it would boost her chances of survival in the light of her still being in the context of inquiry, and thus having evidential considerations against believing in her survival, is what gives rise to the feeling of inner conflict in this case (and admittedly, in similar cases, *modulo* specifics of the situation). Indeed, not only is the Erotetic view compatible with the intuition of conflict; it seems it has a theoretical advantage over its rivals, since it provides a more substantial account – compared to, say, pragmatists – of why the conflict arises (and is able to vindicate the pragmatist pre-theoretical judgment that pragmatic considerations sometimes speak in favour, in a sense, of believing). The conflict arises on our proposal because of two fundamentally different activities one might undertake – the activity of inquiry and the activity of explanation. It is not some odd feature about belief or action that explains why there is an apparent conflict in the relevant cases. The appearance of the conflict is there because one is still in the context of an activity of inquiry whether to F, while realising that one option might be particularly salient as a reply to the explanation-requiring reading of the question of 'Why F?', since the very possibility that one ought to F becomes salient. Inquiry and explanation are pulling one in different 'directions', so to say; hence, the feeling of conflict.

The preceding discussion leads us naturally to the fifth and final worry. Given our response that there is really no genuine conflict between evidential (e.g. normative reasoning reasons) and pragmatic considerations (normative explanatory reasons), and hence that we should not expect that these can be combined, one might wonder in what sense then these two can still be things of the same sort. What's common to both reasons if they are not the same sort of thing? Why think that both are *normative reasons*? In other terms, what is the common 'normative' element in both? We know from what precedes that it's probably not rationality, it's not being grounds of deontic facts, but if so, what is it then?

To this I would like to reply that the common normative element is that both are sorts of appropriate answers to the normative question 'Why believe/disbelieve/suspend the judgment?'. The fundamental element here is the normative 'Why F?' question applied to doxastic states. In general, it's a key aspect of the Erotetic approach to normative reasons that the normative 'Why F?' question is more fundamental than normative reasons – normative reasons of all sorts are reduced to the sorts of answers to this normative question, and hence the unifying element among all sorts of normative reasons is that they are just the possible appropriate answers to that question in one or another of its readings. One might wonder, though, in what sense the 'Why F?' question is really normative. In general, in what sense can questions be normative? For one thing, as we have seen already, the 'Why F?' question can be translated as 'Why should/ought S to F?'. Thus, we see that on such an interpretation, 'Why F?' questions are about oughts and have in their content a normative element. But is this enough to make questions normative in the relevant sense? It is common to think that normative notions/properties/statuses exercise a certain force on us, a normative force. Typically, this is understood in the sense that they are capable of guiding us. Can the 'Why F?' questions have this sort of normative force to count as genuinely normative? As it happens, I think that they can. It seems to be a common idea that guidance comes in the form of commands or imperatives. On such an understanding, statements of reasons or oughts or values, or virtues, or indeed anything normative (if there are other normative things beyond reasons, values, oughts, and virtues), have to encode a command or an imperative (conditional, hypothetical, or categorical), probably by communicating an illocutionary force of commanding, permitting, prohibiting, suggesting, and so forth (cf. Potsdam and Edmiston 2015). In short, a common understanding of guidance seems to hide an implicit assumption that guidance is to be understood on the model of a command. But why should this be the case? That is, more precisely, why should we think that normative guidance is *always* in the form of a command (suggesting, permitting, prohibiting)? An alternative way of thinking would be to admit that sometimes guidance happens by questioning and not by a command. One might well guide someone in their quest by asking questions. The Socratic method, as it appears in Plato's dialogues, is one obvious example that would illustrate our point. Education is another, arguably less colourful, example. Sometimes the best way to ensure that my kids eat vegetables is by questioning them about it. In a situation where they don't want to eat vegetables and indeed ignore that they should eat them, a strategy that works (sometimes) is to ask whether they prefer to eat, say, broccoli or carrots, which might be understood, without too much of a stretch, as a question of the form 'Why eat carrots rather than broccoli?', which fits our general form of normative 'Why F?' questions. Similarly, to get them to better understand why they should eat vegetables in the case where they already know that they should, asking some questions helps. By asking questions, I can influence them in their quest for a better understanding through explanation. In short, it seems that genuinely normative guidance may happen through questioning and not only through command. But questioning happens through raising questions, and 'Why F?' is a question that can perfectly fit the bill on this account. This is, of course, only a sketch. But the point is that it is not obviously wrong to think that questions can be genuinely normative, even if normativity is tied to force and guidance. In sum, the common normative element in all sorts of normative reasons according to the present proposal is that they are all answers to the normative 'Why F?' question; the 'Why F?' question is genuinely normative, at least according to a common understanding of normativity that ties normative notions and properties to guidance, for normative 'Why F?' questions can genuinely guide one in one's quest to know what to do and to better understand and explain why one ought to do what one ought to do.

6.5 Concluding Remarks and Further Potential Applications

This concludes our exploration of the possibility of pragmatic reasons for belief. We observed that the present state of the debate about whether some pragmatic considerations may (sometimes) constitute genuine normative reasons to believe (or disbelieve, or suspend judgment for that matter) is in serious deadlock. On one side, we have evidentialists, who maintain that only truth-conducive considerations may be reasons to believe. On the other side, we have pragmatists who insist either that there are also pragmatic reasons to believe, or that all genuinely normative reasons are ultimately pragmatic. Both sides insist that their proposals perfectly fit our pre-theoretical judgments about some cases. We have seen that, surprisingly, they even maintain different interpretations of our pre-theoretical judgments about almost identical cases. In such a situation, it is very tempting to conclude that at least one side of the debate is wrong and, in particular, what they take to be pre-theoretical judgments in favour of their approach actually don't really support their view. An even more dramatic conclusion that one might be tempted to draw from such an entrenched disagreement is that no one is right here, and we should not look into pre-theoretical judgments when theorising about reasons for belief at all.

The dialectical line that was undertaken in the present chapter was to grant that actually both sides might be right, in a sense. Indeed, the suggestion was that our pre-theoretical judgments about certain cases do support the conclusion that nothing but truth-conducive considerations can count as normative reasons to believe, in a sense. And at the same time, our pre-theoretical judgments about some cases seem to support the conclusion that sometimes pragmatic considerations might be normative reasons for belief, in a sense. The key claim was admitting that this doesn't lead to a contradiction, if we accept the Erotetic view of reasons. Applying the Erotetic view of reasons to this debate leads to a conclusion that only truth-conducive considerations can be normative reasoning reasons to believe, the reasons that are relevant in the context of inquiry – that is, when one is seeking to reply to the argument/reasoning-requiring reading of the 'Why believe *p*?' question. And it also leads to a conclusion that some pragmatic considerations may constitute normative explanatory reasons for belief, the reasons that are relevant in the context of explaining why one ought to believe/disbelieve/suspend judgment – that is, in the context where it is taken for granted (including by the subject) that one ought to believe (etc.). In other terms, pragmatic considerations are relevant in the context where the 'Why believe?' question asks for an explanation-providing answer.

Applying the Erotetic view of reasons to the question of the possibility of pragmatic reasons to believe has a theoretical advantage of fitting with all the relevant pre-theoretical judgments about the cases (i.e. cases where we think that a consideration is a normative reason for a belief). That is, contrary to its rivals (i.e. evidentialists, pragmatists, and eliminitivism – that is, who would deny that there are normative reasons to believe at all), the proponents of the Erotetic view don't need to appeal to any error theory to 'explain away' the intuitions – to tell a story about why our pre-theoretical judgments about some cases should not be taken at face value. Thus, the main argument in this chapter is an inference to the best explanation, and as such it doesn't represent any ambition to 'knock out' alternative proposals. Yet, absent further counter-arguments, the present proposal presents itself as a viable option within the debate. Indeed, given its explanatory power (i.e. that it explains more with less, since we don't need any error theory on our proposal), I would like to suggest that it is a bit more than a viable option for overcoming the current theoretical deadlock concerning the possibility of pragmatic reasons for belief. We may well be warranted in thinking that it is to be preferred to existing alternatives of an evidentialist, pragmatist, or eliminitivist sort.

Now, the more general lesson that I would like to draw from this explanatory success is that it constitutes a further line of argument in favour of the Erotetic view of normative reasons. Chapter 5 contained a positive (also abductive) case in favour of the Erotetic view, from the considerations about the extensional adequacy of this view and its simplicity in explaining the dual life of normative 'Why F?' questions. We saw there that the Erotetic view seems to do better than its rivals on this account. The present chapter can be seen as an additional argument in that it contains a demonstration of a theoretically fruitful application of the Erotetic view to the problem of the possibility of pragmatic reasons for belief.

Interestingly, the application of the Erotetic view to the question of the possibility of pragmatic reasons to believe provides us with insights that might lead to further potentially fruitful applications of the view. One venue to explore would be the general issue of epistemic rationality (or justification). More specifically, the well-entrenched dispute between so-called internalists about rationality/justification, on one side, and externalists about rationality/justification, on the other side, might get a new treatment given the Erotetic view of reasons. Roughly, according to the internalists, rationality/justification of a doxastic state for one supervenes on how things appear from one's internal perspective (e.g. one's non-factive mental states); whereas according to the externalists, it (also) depends on external factors to the subject (e.g. the reliability of one's belief formation mechanisms, one's abilities and competence, or what one knows). The line that might prove to be fruitful to explore in this context would be to apply the distinction between normative reasoning and normative explanatory reasons to internal and external factors in internalist and externalist theories or rationality accordingly. Maybe we can see internal factors (as in internalist theories) as constituting normative reasoning reasons, and external factors (as in externalist theories) as constituting normative explanatory reasons. If this is on the right track, then the opposition between internalists and externalists can be overcome. However, the exact details of how this would work will be left for another occasion. Here we only register that paying attention to the double nature of normative reasons, as tied to reasoning and explanation, may provide still further insights and fruitful applications with respect to well-known problems in epistemology and meta-ethics.

References

Alvarez, Maria. *Kinds of Reasons: An Essay in the Philosophy of Action*. Oxford: Oxford University Press, 2010.

Reasons for Action: Rationale, Motivation, Explanation. In Edward N. Zalta (ed.), *The Stanford Encyclopedia of Philosophy* (Summer 2016 Edition), http://plato.stanford.edu/archives/sum2016/entries/reasons-just-vs-expl/.

Anscombe, Elizabeth. *Intention*. Cambridge, MA: Harvard University Press, 2000 [1957].

Arpaly, Nomy and Schroeder, Timothy. Deliberation and Acting for Reasons. *Philosophical Review* 121(2):209–239, 2012.

Asarnow, Samuel. Rational Internalism. *Ethics* 127(1):147–178, 2016.

The Reasoning View and Defeasible Practical Reasoning. *Philosophy and Phenomenological Research* 95(3):614–636, 2017.

Bader, Ralf. Conditions, Modifiers and Holism. In Errol Lord and Barry Maguire (eds.), *Weighing Reasons*. Oxford: Oxford University Press, pp. 27–55, 2016.

Basu, Rima. Can Beliefs Wrong? *Philosophical Topics* 46(1):1–17, 2018.

Benmakhlouf, Ali. *La force des raisons: Logique et médecine*. Paris: Fayard, 2018.

Berker, Selim. A Combinatorial Argument against Practical Reasons for Belief. *Analytic Philosophy* 59(4):427–470, 2018.

Boghossian, Paul A. The Normativity of Content. *Philosophical Issues* 13 (1):31–45, 2003.

Broome, John. Reasons. In R. Jay Wallace, Michael Smith, Samuel Scheffler, and Philip Pettit (eds.), *Reason and Value: Themes from the Moral Philosophy of Joseph Raz*. Oxford: Oxford University Press, pp. 28–55, 2004.

Reply to Southwood, Kearns and Star, and Cullity. *Ethics* 119(1):96–108, 2008.

Rationality through Reasoning. Oxford: Wiley-Blackwell, 2013.

Reason versus Ought. *Philosophical Issues* 25(1):80–97, 2015.

Reason Fundamentalism and What Is Wrong with It. In Daniel Star (ed.), *The Oxford Handbook of Reasons and Normativity*. Oxford: Oxford University Press, pp. 297–318, 2018.

Brown, Campbell. The Composition of Reasons. *Synthese* 191(5):779–800, 2014.

Brown, Jessica. Infallibilism, Evidence and Pragmatics. *Analysis* 73(4):626–635, 2013.

Brunero, John. Reasons and Evidence One Ought. *Ethics* 119(3):538–545, 2009.

Reasons as Explanations. *Philosophical Studies* 165(3):805–824, 2013.

Reasons, Evidence, and Explanations. In Daniel Star (ed.), *The Oxford Handbook of Reasons and Normativity*. Oxford: Oxford University Press, pp. 321–341, 2018.

Chappell, Richard. Fittingness: The Sole Normative Primitive. *Philosophical Quarterly* 62:684–704, 2012.

Crawford, Lindsay. Believing the Best: On Doxastic Partiality in Friendship. *Synthese* 196(4):1575–1593, 2019.

Crisp, Roger. Review of 'Value … and What Follows' by Joel Kupperman. *Philosophy* 3:452–462, 2000.

D'Arms, Justin and Jacobson, Daniel. The Moralistic Fallacy: On the 'Appropriateness' of Emotions. *Philosophy and Phenomenological Research* 61(1):65, 2000a.

Sentiment and Value. *Ethics* 110(4):722–748, 2000b.

Dancy, Jonathan. *Ethics without Principles*. Oxford: Oxford University Press, 2004.

Davidson, Donald. Actions, Reasons and Causes. *Journal of Philosophy* 60:685–700, 1963.

Actions et événements, translated by Pascal Engel, Paris: PUF, 1993.

Deonna, Julien A. and Teroni, Fabrice. *The Emotions: A Philosophical Introduction*. New York: Routledge, 2012.

Dietz, Christina. Are All Reasons Causes? *Philosophical Studies* 173 (5):1179–1190, 2016.

Drucker, Daniel. Policy Externalism. *Philosophy and Phenomenological Research* 98 (2):261–285, 2019.

Dutant, Julien and Littlejohn, Clayton. Defeaters as Indicators of Ignorance. In Mona Simion and Jessica Brown (eds.), *Reasons, Justification, and Defeat*. Oxford: Oxford University Press, pp. 233–246, 2021.

Echeverri, Santiago. Emotional Justification. *Philosophy and Phenomenological Research* 98(3):541–566, 2019.

Engel, Pascal. Présentation. In *Davidson 1993*, translated by P. Engel, Paris: PUF, pp. v–xxxi, 1993.

Truth and the Aim of Belief. In Donald Gillies (ed.), *Laws and Models in Science*. London: King's College Publications, pp. 77–97, 2004.

Belief and Normativity. *Disputatio*, II(3):153–177, November 2007.

In Defence of Normativism about the Aim of Belief. In Timothy Chan (ed.), *The Aim of Belief*. Oxford: Oxford University Press, pp. 32–63, 2013.

Interprétation, reasons et faits. *Critique* 2015, 6(817–818):502–517, 2015a

Retour à la raison. *Revue Philosophique de la France Et de l'Etranger* 140(3):359, 2015b.

Les vices du savoir. Marseille: Agone, 2019.

Le mauvais type de raison. In B. Langlet and J. M. Monnoyer (eds.), *Raisons, La question méta-éthique: autour de l'oeuvre de John Skorupski*. Aix-en-Provence: Presses Universitaires d'Aix-Marseille, pp. 145–165, 2020a.

Contre le neo-pragmatisme doxastique. *Klesis* 45:1–30, 2020b.

Epley, Kelly. Emotions, Attitudes, and Reasons. *Pacific Philosophical Quarterly* 100(1):256–282, 2018.

Faraci, David. We Have No Reason to Think There Are No Reasons for Affective Attitudes. *Mind* 129(513):225–234, 2020.

Fassio, Davide. The Aim of Belief. In *The Internet Encyclopedia of Philosophy*, 2015, https://iep.utm.edu/beli-aim/.

Finlay, Stephen. The Reasons That Matter. *Australasian Journal of Philosophy* 84 (1):1–20, 2006.

 Explaining Reasons. *Deutsches Jahrbuch Fuer Philosophie* 4:112–126, 2012.

 Confusion of Tongues: A Theory of Normative Language. New York: Oxford University Press, 2014.

 A 'Good' Explanation of Five Puzzles about Reasons. *Philosophical Perspectives*, 33:62–104, 2020.

Fletcher, Guy. A Millian Objection to Reasons as Evidence. *Utilitas* 25 (3):417–420, 2013.

Fogal, Daniel. Reasons, Reason, and Context. In Errol Lord and Barry Maguire (eds.), *Weighing Reasons*. Oxford: Oxford University Press, pp. 74–103, 2016.

Fogal, Daniel and Sylvan, Kurt. Contextualism about Epistemic Reasons. In Jonathan Jenkins Ichikawa (ed.), *The Routledge Handbook to Epistemic Contextualism*. London: Routledge, pp. 375–387, 2017.

Foley, Richard. *Working without a Net: A Study of Egocentric Epistemology.* New York: Oxford University Press, 1992.

Frege, Gottlob. *Posthumous Writings.* Edited by H. Hermes, F. Kambartel and F. Kaulbach and translated by P. Long and R. White. Oxford: Basil Blackwell, 1979.

Gendler, Tamar. On the Epistemic Costs of Implicit Bias. *Philosophical Studies* 156(1):33–63, 2011.

Gertken, Jan and Kiesewetter, Benjamin. The Right and the Wrong Kind of Reasons. *Philosophy Compass* 12(5):e12412, 2017.

Gibbard, Allan. *Wise Choices, Apt Feelings: A Theory of Normative Judgment.* Cambridge, MA: Harvard University Press, 1990.

Gibbons, John. *The Norm of Belief.* Oxford: Oxford University Press, 2013.

Goldie, Peter. Emotions, Feelings and Intentionality. *Phenomenology and the Cognitive Sciences* 1(3):235–254, 2002.

 Emotion, Feeling, and Knowledge of the World. In Robert C. Solomon (ed.), *Thinking about Feeling: Contemporary Philosophers on Emotions*. Oxford: Oxford University Press, pp. 91–104, 2004.

Goldman, Alvin. What Is Justified Belief. In George Pappas (ed.), *Justification and Knowledge*. Boston: D. Reidel, pp. 1–25, 1979.

 Internalism, Externalism, and the Architecture of Justification. *Journal of Philosophy* 106(6):309–338, 2009.

Gordon, Robert M. *The Structure of Emotions: Investigations in Cognitive Philosophy.* Cambridge: Cambridge University Press, 1987.

Greenspan, Patricia S. *Emotions and Reasons: An Enquiry into Emotional Justification.* New York: Routledge, 1988.

Gregory, Alex. Normative Reasons as Good Bases. *Philosophical Studies* 173 (9):2291–2310, 2016.

Grice, H. Paul. Logic and Conversation. In P. Cole and J. L. Morgan (eds.), *Syntax and Semantics, Volume 3: Speech Acts.* New York: Academic Press, pp. 41–58, 1975.

Aspects of Reason. Oxford: Oxford University Press, 2001.

Harman, Gilbert. *Change in View.* Cambridge, MA: MIT Press, 1986.

Hawthorne, John. Knowledge and Evidence. *Philosophy and Phenomenological Research* 70(2):452–458, 2005.

Hawthorne, John and Magidor, Ofra. Reflections on the Ideology of Reasons. In Daniel Star (ed.), *The Oxford Handbook of Reasons and Normativity.* Oxford: Oxford University Press, pp. 113–143, 2018.

Hempel, Carl. *Aspects of Scientific Explanation and Other Essays in the Philosophy of Science.* New York: Free Press, 1965.

Hempel, Carl and Oppenheim, Paul. Studies in the Logic of Explanation. *Philosophy of Science*, 15:135–175, 1948. Reprinted in Hempel, 245–290, 1965.

Heuer, Ulrike. Reasons and Impossibility. *Philosophical Studies* 147(2):235–246, 2010.

Hieronymi, Pamela. The Wrong Kind of Reason. *Journal of Philosophy* 102 (9):437–457, 2005.

The Use of Reasons in Thought (and the Use of Earmarks in Arguments). *Ethics* 124(1):114–127, 2013.

Horty, John F. *Reasons as Defaults.* Oxford: Oxford University Press, 2012.

Hughes, Nick. Luminosity Failure, Normative Guidance and the Principle 'Ought-Implies-Can'. *Utilitas* 30(4):439–457, 2018.

James, William. The Will to Believe. *The New World* 5:327–347, 1896.

Kaplan, Mark. Williamson's Casual Approach to Probabilism. In Duncan Pritchard and Patrick Greenough (eds.), *Williamson on Knowledge.* Oxford: Oxford University Press, pp. 122–139, 2009.

Kearns, Stephen and Star, Daniel. Reasons: Explanations or Evidence? *Ethics* 119 (1):31–56, 2008.

Reasons as Evidence. *Oxford Studies in Metaethics* 4:215–242, 2009.

Weighing Reasons. *Journal of Moral Philosophy* 10(1):70–86, 2013.

Weighing Explanations. In Iwao Hirose and Andrew Reisner (eds.), *Weighing and Reasoning: Themes from the Philosophy of John Broome*, Oxford: Oxford University Press, pp. 232–251, 2015.

Keller, Simon. Friendship and Belief. *Philosophical Papers* 33(3):329–351, 2004.

Kelly, Thomas. The Rationality of Belief and Other Propositional Attitudes. *Philosophical Studies* 110:163–196, 2002.

2003. Epistemic Rationality as Instrumental Rationality: A Critique. *Philosophy and Phenomenological Research* 66(3):612–640.

Evidence. In Edward N. Zalta (ed.), *The Stanford Encyclopedia of Philosophy* (Winter 2016 Edition), https://plato.stanford.edu/archives/win2016/entries/evidence/, 2016.

Kennedy, Christopher. *Projecting the Adjective: The Syntax and Semantics of Gradability and Comparison*. New York: Garland. [Santa Cruz: University of California, Santa Cruz dissertation, 1997.] 1999 .

Vagueness and Grammar: The Semantics of Relative and Absolute Gradable Adjectives. *Linguistics and Philosophy* 30(1):1–45, 2007.

Kennedy, Christopher and McNally, Louise. Scale Structure, Degree Modification, and the Semantics of Gradable Predicates. *Language* 81:345–381, 2005.

Kenny, Anthony J. Practical Inference. *Analysis* 26(3):65–75, 1966.

Kiesewetter, Benjamin. You Ought to φ Only if You May Believe that You Ought to φ. *Philosophical Quarterly* 66(265):760–782, 2016.

The Normativity of Rationality. Oxford: Oxford University Press, 2017.

How Reasons Are Sensitive to Available Evidence. In Conor McHugh, Jonathan Way and Daniel Whiting (eds.), *Normativity: Epistemic and Practical*. Oxford: Oxford University Press, pp. 90–114, 2018.

Kratzer, Angelika. The Notional Category of Modality. In Hans-Jürgen Eikmeyer and Hannes Rieser (eds.), *Words, Worlds, and Contexts: New Approaches in Word Semantics (Research in Text Theory 6)*. Berlin: de Gruyter, pp. 38–74, 1981.

Lasonen-Aarnio, Maria. Guidance, Epistemic Filters, and Non-accidental Ought-Doing. *Philosophical Issues* 29:172–183, 2019.

Lassiter, Daniel. *Graded Modality: Qualitative and Quantitative Perspectives*. Oxford: Oxford University Press, 2017.

Leary, Stephanie. In Defense of Practical Reasons for Belief. *Australasian Journal of Philosophy* 95(3):529–542, 2017.

Littlejohn, Clayton. Do Reasons and Evidence Share the Same Residence? *Philosophy and Phenomenological Research* 93(3):720–727, 2016.

Livet, Pierre. *Qu'est-ce qu'une action ?* Paris: Vrin, 2005.

Logins, Artūrs. Save the Children! *Analysis* 76(4):418–422, 2016a.

Necessary Truths, Evidence, and Knowledge. *Filosofia Unisinos* 17(3):302–307, 2016b.

Common Sense and Evidence: Some Neglected Arguments in Favour of E=K. *Theoria* 83(2): 120–137, 2017.

Two-State Solution to the Lottery Paradox. *Philosophical Studies* 177 (11):3465–3492, 2020a.

Is an Increase in Probability Always an Increase in Evidential Support? *Erkenntnis*, DOI:10.1007/s10670-020-00241-4, ahead-of-print: 1–25, 2020b.

How to Argue with a Pragmatist. *Inquiry*, DOI:10.1080/0020174X.2021.1919199, ahead-of-print: 1–16, 2021.

Lord, Errol. What You're Rationally Required to Do and What You Ought to Do. *Mind* 126(504):1109–1154, 2017.

Lord, Errol and Maguire, Barry. An Opinionated Guide to the Weight of Reasons. In Errol Lord and Barry Maguire (eds.), *Weighing Reasons*. Oxford: Oxford University Press, pp. 3–24, 2016.

Löschke, Jörg. Reasons to Act, Reasons to Require, and the Two-Level Theory of Moral Explanation. *Philosophical Studies* 178(1):169–185, 2021.

Maguire, Barry. The Value-Based Theory of Reasons. *Ergo: An Open Access Journal of Philosophy* 3:233–262, 2016.

There Are No Reasons for Affective Attitudes. *Mind* 127(507):779–805, 2018.

Maguire, Barry and Woods, Jack. The Game of Belief. *Philosophical Review* 129 (2):211–249, 2020.

Markovits, Julia. (2011a). Internal Reasons and the Motivating Intuition. In M. Brady (ed.), *New Waves in Metaethics*, pp. 141–165. London: Palgrave Macmillan.

(2011b). Why Be an Internalist about Reasons? In R. S. Landau (ed.), *Oxford Studies in Metaethics*, vol. 6, pp. 255–279. Oxford: Oxford University Press.

Marušić, Berislav. Promising against the Evidence. *Ethics* 123(2):292–317, 2013.

McBride, Mark. Kearns and Star on Reasons as Evidence. *Analytic Philosophy* 54 (2):229–236, 2013.

McCain, Kevin. Explanationist Evidentialism. *Episteme* 10(3):299–315, 2013.

Explanationist Evidentialism: A Defense. In McCain Kevin (ed.), *Believing in Accordance with the Evidence*. Cham: Springer, pp. 375–391, 2018.

McCormick, Miriam Schleifer. *Believing against the Evidence: Agency and the Ethics of Belief*. New York: Routledge, 2014.

Can Beliefs Be Based on Practical Reasons? In Pat Bondy and J. Adam Carter (eds.), *Well-Founded Belief: New Essays on the Epistemic Basing Relation*. New York: Routledge, pp. 215–234, 2019.

McHugh, Conor and Way, Jonathan. Fittingness First. *Ethics* 126(3):575–606, 2016.

McKeever, Sean and Ridge, Michael. Elusive Reasons. *Oxford Studies in Metaethics* 7:110–137, 2012.

McKeon, Matthew W. On the Rationale for Distinguishing Arguments from Explanations. *Argumentation* 27:283–303, 2013.

McNaughton, David and Rawling, Piers. The Making/Evidential Reason Distinction. *Analysis* 71(1):100–102, 2011.

Melden, Abraham Irving. *Free Action*. London: Routledge & Kegan Paul, 1961.

Mele, Alfred. Agents' Abilities. *Noûs* 37:447–470, 2002.

Meylan, Anne. Justification et rationalité des émotions. *Philosophiques* 45(2):477, 2018.

Millgram, Elijah. Williams' Argument against External Reasons. *Noûs* 30:197–220, 1996.

Mulligan, Kevin. From Appropriate Emotions to Values. *The Monist*, 81 (1):161–188, 1998.

Na'aman, Oded. The Rationality of Emotional Change: Toward a Process View. *Noûs* 55(2):245–269, 2021.

Nair, Shyam. Conflicting Reasons, Unconflicting Ought's. *Philosophical Studies* 173(3):629–663, 2016.

Nebel, Jacob M. Normative Reasons as Reasons Why We Ought. *Mind* 128 (510):459–484, 2019.

Ogien, Ruwen. *Les causes et les raisons*. Nîmes: éditions Jacqueline Chambon, 1995.

Paakkunainen, Hille. Can There Be Government House Reasons for Action? *Journal of Ethics and Social Philosophy* 12(1):56–93, 2017.

Internalism and Externalism about Reasons. In Daniel Star (ed.), *The Oxford Handbook of Reasons and Normativity*. Oxford: Oxford University Press, pp. 143–170, 2018.

Parfit, Derek. *On What Matters: Two-Volume Set*. Oxford: Oxford University Press, 2011.

Pascal, Blaise. *Pensées*. Translated and edited by A. Kreilsheimer. New York: Penguin, 1960/1995.

Pelser, Adam C. Emotion, Evaluative Perception, and Epistemic Justification. In Sabine Roeser and Cain Todd (eds.), *Emotion and Value*. Oxford: Oxford University Press, pp. 106–122, 2014.

Pickard, Hanna. Responsibility without Blame for Addiction. *Neuroethics* 10 (1):169–180, 2017.

Piller, Christian. Content-Related and Attitude-Related Reasons for Preferences. *Royal Institute of Philosophy Supplement* 59:155–182, 2006.

Pollock, John. *Contemporary Theories of Knowledge*. Savage, MD: Rowman & Littlefield, 1986.

Potsdam, Eric, and Edmiston, Daniel. Imperatives. In Mark Aronoff (ed.), *Oxford Bibliographies in Linguistics*. New York: Oxford University Press, 2015.

Preston-Roedder, Ryan. Faith in Humanity. *Philosophy and Phenomenological Research* 87(3):664–687, 2013.

Prior, Mary and Prior, Arthur. Erotetic Logic. *The Philosophical Review* 64 (1):43–59, 1955.

Pryor, James. The Skeptic and the Dogmatist. *Noûs* 34(4):517–549, 2000.

Rabinowicz, Wlodek and Rønnow-Rasmussen, Toni. The Strike of the Demon: On Fitting Pro-attitudes and Value. *Ethics* 114:391–423, 2004.

Raz, Joseph (ed.). *Practical Reasoning*. Oxford: Oxford University Press, 1978.

Raz, Joseph. *Practical Reason and Norms*, 2nd ed. Oxford: Oxford University Press, 1999.

Reisner, Andrew. Weighing Pragmatic and Evidential Reasons for Belief. *Philosophical Studies* 138(1):17–27, 2008.

The Possibility of Pragmatic Reasons for Belief and the Wrong Kind of Reasons Problem. *Philosophical Studies* 145(2):257–272, 2009.

Normative Conflicts and the Structure of Normativity. In Iwao Hirose and Andrew Reisner (eds.), *Weighing and Reasoning: Themes from the Work of John Broome*. Oxford: Oxford University Press, pp. 189–206, 2015.

Pragmatic Reasons for Belief. In Daniel Star (ed.), *The Oxford Handbook of Reasons and Normativity*. Oxford: Oxford University Press, pp. 705–728, 2018.

Rinard, Susanna. Against the New Evidentialists. *Philosophical Issues* 25 (1):208–223, 2015.

No Exception for Belief. *Philosophy and Phenomenological Research* 94 (1):121–143, 2017.

Believing for Practical Reasons. *Noûs* 53(4):763–784, 2018.

Equal Treatment for Belief. *Philosophical Studies* 176(7):1923–1950, 2019.

Ross, W. David. *The Right and the Good.* Oxford: Clarendon Press, 1930.

Rossi, Benjamin Cohen. Introducing a New Elusive Reason. *Ratio* 34 (3):227–235, 2021.

Rowland, Richard. *The Normative and the Evaluative: The Buck-Passing Account of Value.* Oxford: Oxford University Press, 2019.

Salmon, Wesley. Statistical Explanation. In W. Salmon (ed.), *Statistical Explanation and Statistical Relevance.* Pittsburgh: University of Pittsburgh Press, pp. 29–87, 1971.

vos Savant, M. *Ask Marilyn.* New York: St. Martin's, 1992.

Scanlon, Thomas M. *What We Owe to Each Other.* Cambridge, MA: Belknap Press of Harvard University Press, 1998.

Being Realistic about Reasons. Oxford: Oxford University Press, 2014.

Scarantino, Andrea and de Sousa, Ronald. Emotion. In Edward N. Zalta (ed.), *The Stanford Encyclopedia of Philosophy* (Winter 2018 Edition), https://plato .stanford.edu/archives/win2018/entries/emotion/, 2018.

Schmidt, Eva. New Trouble for 'Reasons as Evidence': Means That Don't Justify the Ends. *Ethics* 127(3):708–718, 2017.

Schroeder, Mark. *Slaves of the Passions.* Oxford: Oxford University Press, 2007.

Having Reasons. *Philosophical Studies* 139(1):57–71, 2008.

The Ubiquity of State-Given Reasons. *Ethics* 122(3):457–488, 2012.

State-Given Reasons: Prevalent, If Not Ubiquitous. *Ethics* 124(1):128–140, 2013.

Schroeter, Laura and Schroeter, François. Reasons as Right-Makers. *Philosophical Explorations* 12(3):279–296, 2009.

Setiya, Kieran. *Reasons without Rationalism.* Princeton, NJ: Princeton University Press, 2007.

Reply to Bratman and Smith. *Analysis* 69(3):531–540, 2009.

What Is a Reason to Act?. *Philosophical Studies* 167(2):221–235, 2014.

Shafer-Landau, Russ. *Moral Realism.* Oxford: Oxford University Press, 2003.

Shah, Nishi. How Truth Governs Belief. *Philosophical Review* 112(4):447–482, 2003.

A New Argument for Evidentialism. *Philosophical Quarterly* 56:481–498, 2006.

Shah, Nishi and Velleman, J. David. Doxastic Deliberation. *Philosophical Review* 114(4):497–534, 2005.

Sher, Itai. Comparative Value and the Weight of Reasons. *Economics and Philosophy* 35:103–158, 2019.

Silverstein, Matthew. Reducing Reasons. *Journal of Ethics and Social Philosophy* 10 (1):1–22, 2016.

Sinclair, Neil. Promotionalism, Motivationalism and Reasons to Perform Physically Impossible Actions. *Ethical Theory and Moral Practice* 15:647–659, 2012.

Singer, Peter. Famine, Affluence, and Morality. *Philosophy and Public Affairs* 1 (3):229–243, 1972.

Skorupski, John. *The Domain of Reasons.* Oxford: Oxford University Press, 2010.

Smith, Michael. *The Moral Problem.* Oxford: Blackwell, 1994.

  Internal Reasons. *Philosophy and Phenomenological Research* 55(1):109–131, 1995.

  Reasons with Rationalism after All. *Analysis Reviews* 69:521–530, 2009.

Smithies, Declan. Moore's Paradox and the Accessibility of Justification. *Philosophy and Phenomenological Research* 85(2):273–300, 2012.

  Reasons and Perception. In Daniel Star (ed.), *The Oxford Handbook of Reasons and Normativity.* Oxford: Oxford University Press, pp. 632–661, 2018.

Snedegar, Justin. *Contrastive Reasons.* Oxford: Oxford University Press, 2017.

Sobel, David. Explanation, Internalism, and Reasons for Action. *Social Philosophy and Policy* 18:218–235, 2001.

de Sousa, Ronald. *The Rationality of Emotion*, vol. 100. Cambridge, MA: MIT Press, 1987.

de Sousa, Ronald B. Emotional Truth: Ronald de Sousa. *Supplement to the Proceedings of the Aristotelian Society* 76(1):247–263, 2002.

Srinivasan, Amia. Normativity without Cartesian Privilege. *Philosophical Issues* 25 (1):273–299, 2015.

Star, Daniel. Reasoning with Reasons. In Jonathan Way, Conor McHugh and Daniel Whiting (eds.), *Normativity: Epistemic and Practical.* Oxford: Oxford University Press, pp. 241–259, 2018.

Steglich-Petersen, Asbjørn and Skipper, Mattias. An Instrumentalist Account of How to Weigh Epistemic and Practical Reasons for Belief. *Mind*, 129(516): 1071–1094, 2020.

Stroud, Sarah. Epistemic Partiality in Friendship. *Ethics* 116(3):498–524, 2006.

Streumer, Bart. Reasons and Impossibility. *Philosophical Studies* 136(3):351–384, 2007.

Sylvan, Kurt. Epistemic Reasons I: Normativity. *Philosophy Compass* 11 (7):364–376, 2016.

Timmerman, Travis. Sometimes There Is Nothing Wrong with Letting a Child Drown. *Analysis* 75(2):204–212, 2015.

Velleman, J. David. *Practical Reflection.* Princeton, NJ: Princeton University Press, online version, 1999 (originally 1989).

  On the Aim of Belief. Chapter 11 In J. David Velleman (ed.), *The Possibility of Practical Reason.* Oxford: Oxford University Press, pp. 244–281, 2000.

Way, Jonathan. Transmission and the Wrong Kind of Reason. *Ethics* 122 (3):489–515, 2012.

  Value and Reasons to Favour. *Oxford Studies in Metaethics* 8:27–49, 2013.

  Two Arguments for Evidentialism. *Philosophical Quarterly* 66(265):805–818, 2016.

Reasons as Premises of Good Reasoning. *Pacific Philosophical Quarterly* 98:251–270. DOI: 10.1111/papq.12135, 2017.

Reasons and Rationality. In Daniel Star (ed.), *The Oxford Handbook of Reasons and Normativity*. Oxford: Oxford University Press, pp. 485–503, 2018.

Way, Jonathan and Whiting, Daniel. Reasons and Guidance. *Analytic Philosophy* 57(3):214–235, 2016.

Wedgwood, Ralph. The Aim of Belief. *Philosophical Perspectives* 16:267–297, 2002.

The Right Thing to Believe. In Timothy Chan (ed.), *The Aim of Belief*. Oxford: Oxford University Press, pp. 123–139, 2013.

The Pitfalls of 'Reasons'. *Philosophical Issues* 25(1):123–143, 2015.

Whately, Richard. *Elements of Logic*. Delmar, NY: Scholars' Facsimiles & Reprints, 1827/1975.

Elements of Rhetoric, 7th ed. Carbondale, IL: Southern Illinois University Press, 1828/1846.

Whiting, Daniel. Right in Some Respects: Reasons as Evidence. *Philosophical Studies* 175(9):2191–2208, 2018.

Wiland, Eric. *Reasons*. London: Continuum, 2012.

Williams, Bernard. Deciding to Believe. In Bernard Williams (ed.), *Problems of the Self: Philosophical Papers 1956–1972*. Cambridge: Cambridge University Press, pp. 136–151, 1973.

Internal and External Reasons. In Ross Harrison (ed.), *Rational Action*. Cambridge: Cambridge University Press, pp. 101–113, 1979.

Moral Luck: Philosophical Papers 1973–1980. Cambridge: Cambridge University Press, 1981.

Internal Reasons and the Obscurity of Blame. In William J. Prior (ed.), *Reason and Moral Judgment, Logos*, vol. 10. Santa Clara, CA: Santa Clara University, 1989.

Postscript: Some Further Notes on Internal and External Reasons. In E. Millgram (ed.), *Varieties of Practical Reasoning*. Cambridge, MA: MIT Press, pp. 91–97, 2001.

Williamson, Timothy. *Knowledge and Its Limits*. Oxford: Oxford University Press, 2000.

Wittgenstein, Ludwig. *The Blue and Brown Books (BB)*. Oxford: Blackwell, 1958.

Wodak, Daniel. Redundant Reasons. *Australasian Journal of Philosophy* 98 (2):266–278, 2020.

Wright, Crispin. Warrant for Nothing (and Foundations for Free)? *Aristotelian Society Supplementary* 78(1):167–212, 2004.

Index

Ingram Content Group UK Ltd.
Milton Keynes UK
UKHW020651060723
424661UK00015B/406